The Ramblings of a
Great Eastern Engineman

by
Albert Grose

*Best wishes
Albert Grose*

Published in 1999
by
Albert Grose
'Meadow View'
Tan Lane
Little Clacton
Essex

Copyright © Albert Grose 1999

British Library Cataloguing-in- Publication Data

A catalogue record for this book is available from the British Library

ISBN 0 9537034 0 1

Printed in Great Britain by
Pentonlock Ltd.
21/27 Albion Road
Luton
LU2 0DS

Acknowledgements

This book could never have been completed without the assistance of a number of people who have helped me re-kindle my recollections of Hertford East in the final years of steam. Most of those people are men with whom I worked alongside on the footplate of numerous steam locomotives over 40 years ago.

An added pleasure for me during the writing of this book has been to renew old friendships with drivers and firemen after all those years. Lively meetings and long telephone conversations is ample evidence that the passage of time has done nothing to dampen our enthusiasm of the magic of steam.

Some of them have kindly loaned me photographs from their personal collections, and here I would make special reference to John Shelsher who, as a fireman at Hertford East and Kings Cross during the late 1950s, often carried a small 127 box camera that he acquired during his 2 years Army National Service days. With it he recorded some of the locomotives and colleagues during the course of their work.
The quality and presentation may fall some way short of the professional photographer, but the images he captured for posterity are priceless!
Many of John's photographs appear in this book, together with many more from various other sources, some of which I have been unable to trace the original photographers. For allowing me to reproduce these photographs my grateful thanks go to: John Shelsher, George Don, Stephen Ruff, R.C.Riley, A.Doyle, J.P.Mullett, T.B.Owen, C.J.Gammell, F.Hornby, Peter Childs, John Tarry, Paul Garratt, the Great Eastern Railway Society (GERS), the Historical Model Railway Society Photographic Service, Colour-Rail and to those others whose names I have been unable to trace.

In addition to the ex-colleagues who have given me the benefit of their recollections, several others have helped me enormously and enthusiastically during the compilation this book. Those I would especially like to thank are;
George Don, George Castle, John Tarry, Bob Smith, Eric Wrangles, David Dent, Paul Garratt, Stephen Ruff, Nigel Bowdidge and Lyn Brooks of the GERS and all those who telephoned me with their best wishes and encouragement.
My thanks also to Jerry Robinson of the Hertford Railway Circle for information and track plans and to Barrie Jackson of the GERS who kindly loaned me his copies of Train Working Timetables of the period.
Thanks also to my friends Les Tranter who painstakingly copied many of the old original photographs and to Cyril Hollingworth who carefully read and checked the final manuscript.

Finally, special thanks to my wife Jennifer whose encouragement and support has given me the confidence to complete this 'labour of love'.

Introduction

I have only had two employers during my entire working life. The first – from 1955 to 1961 – was British Railways (as it was called then). I then joined Unigate Dairies and, although I thoroughly enjoyed the next 35 years in the dairy industry, I have never been able to forget the thrill of working on the footplate of a steam locomotive.

Many years ago I began to record my memories of those few first years, but due to other commitments, that record never progressed beyond the first 6 pages. Having had to take an early retirement, I suddenly found that I had the time to make some small contribution to the memory of the Steam Age

I also realised that many of those dedicated railwaymen I knew so well have since passed on, with little or no record of their contribution to the history of the railway at Hertford East. I hope I have gone some way to ensure that the memory of some of them, at least, is perpetuated within these pages.

Maybe some day someone, who worked with them for much longer than I, will write a book telling us more about the lives of that dedicated band of enginemen.

I can honestly say that there was not a single man among the many I worked with that I disliked – certainly I had my favourites – but I got on well with every one of them.

They were all wonderful characters with whom I am proud to have shared a friendship.

In telling my story, I have tried to avoid going into complicated details and explanations. I prefer to leave technicalities to the railway historian whose knowledge in such matters is undoubtedly far superior to my own.

The history of the Hertford branch is told in '*150 Years of the Hertford & Ware Railway*' by David Dent and is a must for the bookshelves of all local railway enthusiasts.

Those who are fortunate enough to have lived in the age of steam will be able to relate to much of what is written, whilst for others, I have tried to be as descriptive as possible without losing sight of the main thread of the subject.

Upon reading of the unsociable hours and shocking conditions under which we worked, you may wonder why any of us tolerated the job. Many didn't and, toward the end of steam, the railway was always short of footplate staff at the bottom rung of the ladder. The job market was very buoyant in those days and much cleaner work, with regular hours, was readily available – and usually better paid too!

In 1957 a Cleaner's basic wage at Hertford for a 44-hour week was £3-42p. A Fireman's wage started at £7-75p and a First-Year Driver received £9-42p. Higher rates of pay for nightwork, weekend working and occasional overtime opportunities helped to improve take-home pay but even so, the pay was pretty poor compared with the overall labour market.

However, there was something about the railway and steam locomotives that held us to the job, a fascination that still exists to this day, even amongst those who were not even born when the last steam locomotive disappeared from British Railways.

If further confirmation is needed, each time I meet with my old railway colleagues we end up talking for hours about the days of steam – even though some of them spent their final 30+ years before retirement driving diesel and electric locomotives!

I think one of them summed it up when I asked him why he thought so many men were so dedicated to the steam locomotive. *"It wasn't just a job, it was a unique way of life"* he replied.

A perhaps-unusual addition to this book is a chapter written by another ex-fireman, George Don, who invites you to join him on the footplate of 69693 as he describes a typical day in 1950 when working a 'double-trip' on the Buntingford Branch Line.

Readers unfamiliar with working with steam engines may find that not all of my descriptions of life on the footplate are particularly appealing. However, to those who have 'steam in the blood' will know that this was all part of the magnetism of the steam locomotive, which compelled men to devote their entire working life to it. I emphasise men, because in those far-off days, the footplate of a steam locomotive was strictly a man's world. I honestly don't think any woman could have met the physical demands working on the footplate, or indeed would have tolerated the sometimes-atrocious conditions under which they worked.

Certainly there are female train drivers on today's railways now that the physical aspects have improved, and there are also ladies on the footplate of steam locomotives on some preserved railways. However, working conditions, locomotives, hours of work and servicing facilities are far better in preservation than they ever were in the old days.

Throughout this book, the events are true as far as I can remember, so too are all the people that have been mentioned.

During the final four-and-a-half years of my railway service I kept pocket diaries in which I recorded brief details on a daily basis, so I am fortunately able to be factual in many of my tales as regards to dates, engine numbers and drivers.

My descriptions of the men I knew and worked with are purely as I remember them after all these years and I apologise to any of them or their families if my impressions differ from how they prefer to be remembered.

This is the story of my life as a young Cleaner/Fireman for those brief few years with some glimpses of social activities outside my working hours. I hope you enjoy reading it as much as I have enjoyed recalling those happy times.

Finally, any errors or omissions are entirely my responsibility for which I beg the reader's understanding and forgiveness.

Albert Grose
Little Clacton
October 1999

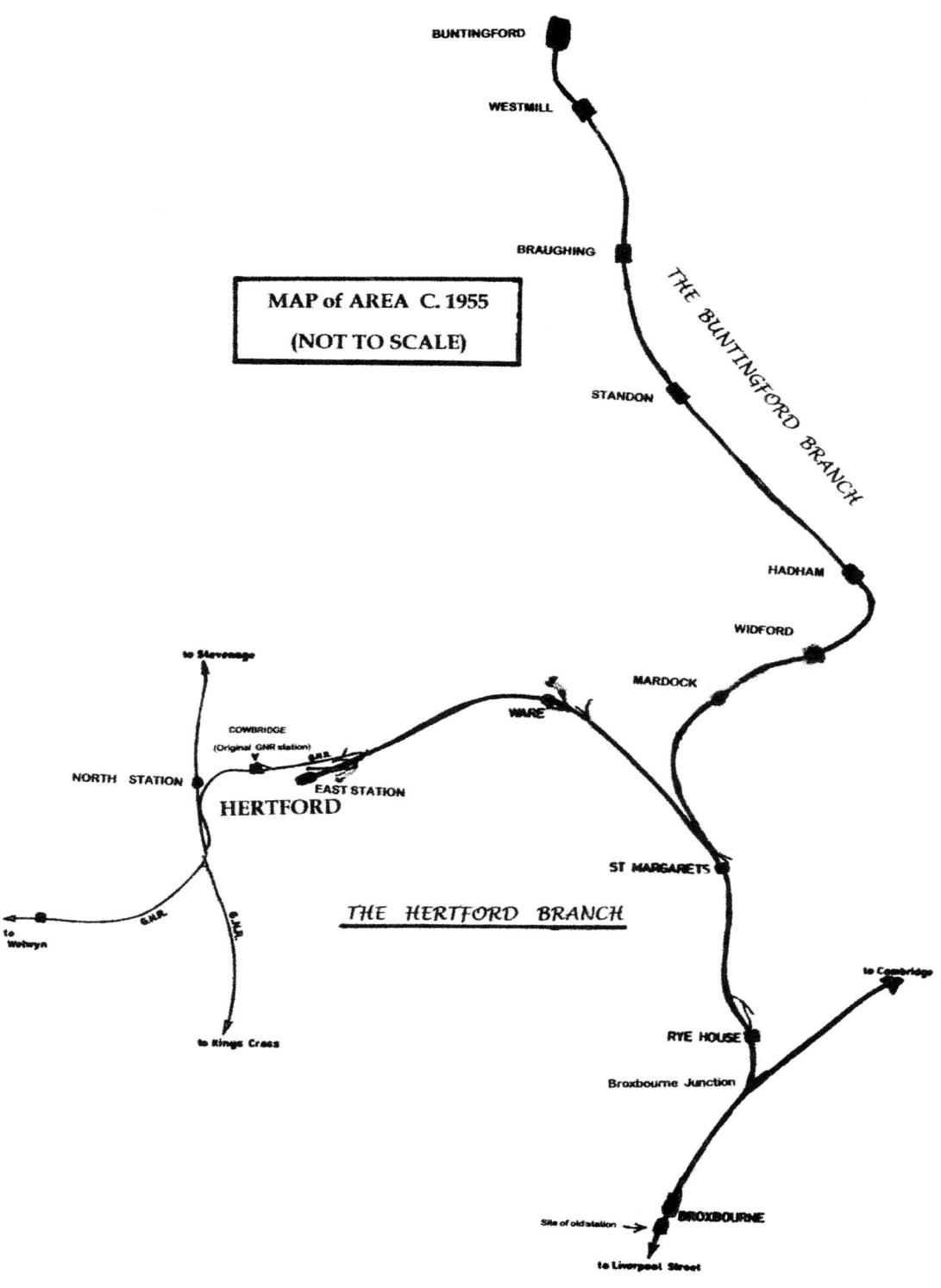

CONTENTS

Acknowledgements		3
Introduction		4
Railway Map of Area		6
Glossary of Terms		8
Chapter One	Engine Cleaner	9
Chapter Two	First-Year Fireman	47
Chapter Three	The Buntingford Branch	61
Chapter Four	A Day's Work on the Buntingford Branch - told by George Don	69
Chapter Five	Gaining Experience	101
Chapter Six	1957	119
Chapter Seven	1958 – A Very Chilly Start	127
Chapter Eight	1959 – From N7s to L1s!	154
Chapter Nine	1960 – Final Year of Hertford Steam	185
Chapter Ten	Final months at Hornsey	210
Appendices :	Steam Tank Locomotives	243
	Steam Tender Locomotives	244
	Diesel/Electric Locomotives	245
	Extracts from a 1960 Train Timetable	246
	Index to Sub-Headings	247

Front Cover Photographs
Top.　　　　　The Crest of the Great Eastern Railway. (*GERS*)
Middle left.　　Class L1 2-6-4 Tank No. 67715 at Norwich MPD in 1961.
　　　　　　　　　　　　　　　(A. Doyle/Colour-Rail/BRE302)
Middle right.　Class N7 0-6-2 Tank no. 69685 leaving St. Margarets for Hertford
　　　　　　　　East in June 1958. *(T.B. Owen/Colour-Rail/BRE432)*
Bottom.　　　Hertford East station in 1960.

Glossary

For readers unfamiliar with railway terminology, the following will help them understand the meanings of the more commonly used terms in this book.

Shed, Loco or **MPD** (Motive Power Depot) - an engine shed, engine yard and it's associated facilities.

Road – the railway lines or tracks.

Running Line – the main line as opposed to sidings and yards.

Branch – an offshoot from the main line with it's own terminus station at the end.

Spur - a short length of track that eventually comes to a 'dead end', e.g. a service line into a private yard.

Loop – a length of track that connects one set of lines to others that are some distance apart.

0-6-2 / 2-6-4 etc. – universally, a locomotive's wheel arrangements is recognised to be in the following sequence: Bogie (or leading) wheels at the front – Driving (coupled) wheels in the centre, and Pony (or trailing) wheels at the rear. So, a 0-6-2 has no Bogie wheels, 6 (3 pairs of) Driving wheels (or 'Drivers') and 2 (one pair) of Pony wheels.

A 2-6-4 has one pair of leading Bogie wheels, 6 'Drivers' and 2 pairs of Pony wheels.

Tender Engine – a locomotive that has a separate unit (the tender) permanently attached behind it containing supplies of coal and water.

Tank Engine – this is a locomotive that carries it's own supplies of coal and water on the same frame. The tank locomotives referred to in this book contained water tanks along each side of the boiler.

Bunker – the rear end of a Tank engine containing coal.

Regulator – this is a lever that controls the flow of steam from the boiler to the cylinders – in simple terms it can be compared to the throttle of a car.

Reverser – a large 'worm-drive' device by which means the driver controls the direction and gearing of the locomotive. It has a pointer that moves along in a calibrated slot, the nearer toward the centre the pointer is wound, the higher the gear will be. On a few locomotives, a large ratchet-lever was used instead of the worm-drive wheel.

Injector – a steam-operated device that injects fresh supplies of water into the boiler.

Bag – the long, flexible leather hose-pipe attached to the cast-iron water column, used for replenishing the engine's tank.

Ground Signal or Dodd – a miniature signal located at ground level that authorises short, (usually) reversing movements e.g. reversing from the main line into a siding.

Fitter – a locomotive 'mechanic.'

Turn or Shift – an allocated day's work or a turn of duty.

Up & Down Lines – in railway terms, London is always in the Up direction

Train – the carriages, coaches or wagons hauled by the locomotive

CHAPTER ONE

The First Year – Engine Cleaner

Applying for an Engine Cleaner's job

Back in the Age of Steam the dream of many a schoolboy was to become an Engine Driver but, for most of us, by the time we left school, the dream had vanished. However, in my case the dream persisted so, in the spring of 1955, several weeks before my 15th birthday, I applied to Stratford Motive Power Depot for the position of Engine Cleaner. The location I had asked for was Hertford East, which I knew to be the nearest Engine Shed to where I lived.
At that time the family home was at Wormley – a small village alongside the old Great Eastern mainline running along the Lea Valley. The nearest railway station was Broxbourne.

The Interview

I eventually received from Stratford a special rail ticket on which was hand-written my name and authorisation to travel from Broxbourne to Liverpool Street and back on a certain day – I cannot recall the actual date. Accompanying the ticket was an instruction to attend British Railways offices at number 222, Marylebone Road for an interview and a medical examination.

I duly arrived at the appointed time and met up with several other lads from various parts of the country. I cannot remember exactly the sequence of events but very early on I was handed a hank of grubby woollen threads and asked to pick out certain colours. Then I was shown a number of small cards and asked to identify the numbers hidden among hundreds of different coloured dots. This was followed by the usual eyesight tests – the railway placed great emphasis on ensuring perfect vision of their footplate staff – knowing the difference between red and green is understandably quite important on the railway, so someone who is colour-blind is automatically rejected.

There followed a thorough physical examination and questions on my medical history and general state of my health to date. I was then asked to complete a simple maths test and answer a few questions on history and geography – purely to assess my general intelligence – after which I was told that I would be notified of the result by letter.

Not so important!

Inwardly I felt I the day had gone very well for me and I had a spring in my step as I walked back to Liverpool Street for the train home. As I walked down the platform to board my train I really felt important enough to ride in a First Class

compartment home and jumped into the first one I found empty. I had just settled down when the guard opened the carriage door and asked to see my ticket.
As I showed it to him I explained where I had just been and that I would soon be joining the railway service.
He appeared singularly unimpressed as he ejected me from First Class luxury and into the austerity of a Third Class compartment!

Success!

Several days later I received a letter from British Railways informing me that my application had been successful and that I was to report to the Shedmaster at Hertford East Motive Power Depot at 8 am on Monday 27th June 1955. Incidentally, this was only a week or so after the resumption of normal services following a 17-day strike by the ASLEF Footplatemen's Union.

Introduction to Hertford East

I still remember how fine and sunny it was on that Monday morning in June 1955 when I cycled to Broxbourne station and presented the Ticket Inspector with my British Railways travel permit. He arranged for me to park my bicycle inside one of the sheds in the Down Goods Yard and I caught the 7.24 a.m. local, which would get me to Hertford East at a quarter to eight o'clock.

In addition to the sketch at the front of this book, for the benefit of readers unfamiliar with the area, I should explain where Hertford East fits into the railway map. It is at the end of a 7 miles branch-line off of the former Great Eastern Railway line out of the London terminus of Liverpool Street.
The Hertford branch leaves the main line just north of Broxbourne, which is 17 miles from London, Hertford East is 24 miles from Liverpool Street.
Approximately midway down the branch, at St. Margaret's Station, there was yet another branch (closed in 1965) that went across country to Buntingford. This single-line branch was almost 14 miles long.

There is also a Hertford North station about one-and-a-half miles across town, which is on a branch line of the old Great Northern Railway, that runs from Wood Green in the south, to Stevenage in the north, where it rejoins the East Coast main line. Towards the end of my railway career I would become quite familiar with this branch.

Connecting loop-line from North to East

During my time at Hertford there was a single-line loop a mile or so long that connected both North and East stations, which I traversed on just one occasion, it was during the night but I cannot recall the date or purpose of the trip.
This stretch of line was once part of a branch-line from Welwyn, which terminated at Cowbridge - the original Great Northern station in Hertford.

Although all Great Northern passenger trains terminated here, the line continued on and connected with the Great Eastern behind Hertford East MPD and was used for transferring Goods Traffic.

Cowbridge station closed to passenger traffic early in 1924 when the new line from Wood Green opened and Hertford North station was built.

A 1910 view of the approach to Hertford East station. Immediately to the right of the railwaymen's allotments, the Great Northern branch line can be seen curving away in the distance towards Cowbridge. The road over on the far right is Mead Lane.

Cowbridge Station

The old Cowbridge station, which was a mere few hundred yards from Hertford East, still existed more or less intact during the 1950/60s. It was sited at the back of McMullen's Brewery and in later years the Brewery purchased the entire site to expand their business.

Sadly, the Brewery demolished the station buildings and today no trace of it remains.

Latter-day traffic

Until the early 1950s, Hertford East engines used to work trains of grain hoppers via the Cole Green loop to the Welgar Shredded Wheat factory at Welwyn Garden City. They would then pick up a train of refuse hoppers at Hatfield and deliver them to the huge waste tip at Holwell on the return journey.

By the time I joined the railway, the grain traffic via the G.E. line had ceased and the remaining duties had been taken over by Great Northern engines from Hatfield and Hornsey, so Hertford men no longer used the loop. We would occasionally share a pot of tea with Hatfield men who used to come across on certain evenings to deliver empty tank wagons for the Tar Works on the other side of Mead Lane and take full ones back

One of the Hatfield crew I remember was Charlie Wrangles, brother of Eric who was a Passed Fireman at Hertford. Some time later, Charlie transferred to Hertford East as a Driver.

Towards the end the branch was rarely used more than a couple of times a week, by this time diesels had taken over. It was closed completely during the 1960's.

Early in 1962 a Paxman 800 Diesel/Electric locomotive is photographed coming out of the Tarworks at Hertford. A tanker lorry waits in Mead Lane for the train to cross. The spur leads to the old Great Northern branch, part of which can just be seen in the right-hand corner of the picture. The makeshift timber shed in the foreground was put there in the late 1950s to store oil, fuel and spares for Messrs Greenham's Ruston Bucyrus mechanical shovel that was used for coaling the locomotives at this spot.

Hertford East Motive Power Depot (MPD)

Returning now to the main part of my story, when I arrived at the station a Porter pointed me in the direction of the Locomotive Depot which was to the south of the station.

As I walked back down the end of the platform, on my left I noticed two ancient grounded coach bodies, which were the 'offices' of the female carriage cleaners.

The names of two of these cleaners were Gladys and Kath and, at the time of writing this book, I was pleased to learn that both of them are still with us.

The next building I passed was the Signalbox, beyond that was the turntable and then engine shed. Under the direction of one of the Shed Staff, I continued past the Shed and the small yard, finally arriving at the office door of the Shedmaster, Mr. Fred Hennessey a few minutes before 8 o'clock.

His office was at the station end of a modern, flat-roofed pre-fabricated building that also housed all the engine-men's facilities. This is where they signed on for duty, and included a locker room, washroom and toilets, a rest room containing a stove for heating and a small electric cooker for preparing food. It would be a while before I actually set foot inside this part of the building, as it was out-of-bounds to young, still 'wet-behind-the-ears' cleaners! The Cleaner's official rest room was the Enginemen's original old brick-built cabin against the side of the engine shed, next to the Lamp-room located beneath the water tank.

This building also housed the Coalmen - two men whose job it was to replenish the engine's bunkers from wagonloads of coal parked in the Coal Road.

This was a manual operation performed by muscle and shovel

In earlier years, a wooden coaling platform stood at the Engine Shed end of the Coal Road, but it had gone during my time. I learnt that this platform had caused the death of a driver some years earlier when he was accidentally trapped between a corner of the platform and an engine that was being moved.

By the date that I arrived, the Coalmen would stand in the wagon and throw lumps of coal into the bunker of the engine parked in the adjacent road. After he had worked his way to the floor of the wagon, a 'drop-down' side door would be opened onto a wooden trestle, allowing him to use this as a mini-platform to shovel the smaller coal into the bunker.

The coaling staff's working day would have been around 12 hours.

A third Coalman worked a night shift, although quite often, due to shortage of staff, the daytime pair took it in turns to cover the night turn which, in practice, was not particularly demanding and allowed plenty of time for some sleep. They did not take kindly to us rowdy lads sharing this small cabin while they were trying to enjoy a brief rest between duties, so we kept away from it for most of the time.

In those days, a steam engine shed was commonly referred to as a 'Loco' or a 'Motive Power Depot' – or MPD for short. I will refer to them as such many times in my story.

Road access to the MPD was via Mead Lane that followed the Great Northern line down from the station and terminated a few hundred yards past the Shed entrance at 'Hoppo's Crossing' - more of which I'll refer to later. The only building in the Enginemen's 'Car Park' was a bicycle shed. In those days cars were a rare possession – particularly for railwaymen – and it was not until near the end of steam that one or two appeared under the ownership of those firemen who had yet to take on the financial burden of wife and family!

I cannot recall seeing any driver bringing a car to work – if indeed any owned one – it was either a bicycle or 'Shanks' Pony', although I remember at least one driver, Alf Childs, who acquired a little Lambretta motor scooter sometime during 1957.

Above. A view of Hertford East MPD around 1911. Although some structural changes subsequently took place over the years, the track layout remained basically unchanged until the late 1950s.
Below. A 1910 view of Hertford East turntable and shed looking towards London. The photograph was taken from the Signalbox.

Above. This photograph, taken from Railway Street, shows Hertford East signalbox, while in the far distance can be seen the Engine Shed. The date is before 1957, as the alterations at the Turntable end of the Shed have not yet taken place. The Signalbox is still in use in 1999.

Below. Hertford East MPD looking towards the station in 1957. The enginemen's rest-room and Shedmaster's office are on the right. The white box contained the internal telephone used to advise the signalman when an engine was ready to leave the Shed. In the centre, the two engine roads are occupied and wagons can be seen in the Coal Road. The Up main line is immediately to the left of the point rodding running alongside the track. A Class J15 0-6-0 locomotive simmers in the Goods Yard.

Above. A view of the pre-fabricated building at Hertford East MPD. To the right of fireman Bob Brightwell is the entrance lobby where the men reported for duty by signing the Duty Book. Immediately behind him is the kitchen area. Left of him, with high-level windows at the rear, is the Enginemen's rest-room. The Shedmaster's office is on the far left. The building extended further right of the photograph, which housed the locker-room, toilets and washroom.
Below. A 1955 view, looking towards London, taken alongside the eng nemen's rest-room at Hertford MPD. The Northern branch line links up with the Great Eastern main line just beyond the signalpost. The enginemen's bicycle shed can be seen on the left. Out of sight on the extreme left is the spur that crosses Mead Lane to reach the Tarworks.

The Goods Yard

Directly opposite the MPD on the Down Side were the Goods Yards, the tracks of which ran back into an extensive covered-in area. At the time, I thought the covered area seemed quite luxurious for such a small branch-line station.
I later found out that these buildings were, in fact, part of the original terminus station which served Hertford from the line's opening in 1843 until replaced by the present station in 1888.
The regular Shunters were Bert Wicks and Ernie Jocylen – they were responsible for the carriage sidings as well. Ernie was reckoned to be the quicker of the two when shunting wagons in the Goods Yard. It seems he was a dab hand at avoiding some shunting moves by simply switching the labels on wagons that had similar loads! However, he did come unstuck on occasions, such as the time when a local Coal Merchant found that his wagon was loaded with ordinary household coal instead of the anthracite that he had ordered!

The Locomotives

In 1955 the entire fleet of engines allocated to Hertford MPD were Class N7 0-6-2 tanks, numbers 69680 to 69688 and 69693, plus another 2 (69633/34) which were allocated to the Buntingford Branch. I believe a couple of 0-6-0 Class J15 goods engines were also based there at one time – but they had gone by the time I arrived. Although not officially allocated to Hertford, there always seemed to be at least one other N7 of 697XX numbering in residence. I would guess one must have been allocated to us, as we would clean it on its washout day, something we would *not* have done had it been a Stratford engine!
Sometime during 1957 a little class J69 0-6-0 number 68500 was added to the fleet for exclusive use on station pilot duties. Toward the end of 1988, another member of the same class, numbered 68600 replaced the original engine.
The only obvious difference that I remember between the two was that the latter engine had slightly wider side-tanks.
I can still recall how I felt on the first few occasions that I climbed into the warm cab of an engine parked in the Shed Road waiting its next turn of duty. I had wondered beforehand if the feeling of immense pleasure of standing on the footplate would be as I had imagined it – I was not disappointed.

The Cleaner's job

The accompanying sketch showing the layout of the MPD and the immediately surrounding area will make it easier for the reader to make sense of my future ramblings as I describe the various locations during my daily routines.
The working hours for a cleaner were 8 till 5 with an hour's allowance for lunch, from Monday to Friday, and 8 till 12 on Saturdays, making a total working week of 44 hours. For this I was paid £3-4s-0d (320p) a week which, after various deductions, left me with a take-home wage of £2-17s-11d (290p). Out of this I handed my mother £1-10s-0d (150p) for my 'keep' and the remainder was all mine.

17

At that time my money was spent on things like gramophone records, going to the cinema and clothes.   Unfortunately I was also smoking at that early age – but so were most other people – so that too took some of my income. As a general rule, I was flat broke before my next wage packet was due!

Pay-day was Friday, when I would collect a little brass disc from the Shedmaster's office upon which was stamped my payroll number (0734). I then had to walk up to the station, go to the Ticket Office and hand the disc to the clerk who stood behind a metal grill.   He would then pass me a little tin (about 2 inches wide and 1 inch deep) which would contain my wages and payslip.   One simply emptied the tin and slid it back across to the clerk on the other side of the grill.

Hertford East MPD in August 1958, looking towards Mead Lane, showing the spur to the Tarworks.   Although everything else has long disappeared, the house to the right of 68500's bunker still exists, as does part of the track that is embedded in the road surface.

18

Hertford's station pilot -J69 0-6-0 68600 – shunts a van in the station area in 1960.
The semaphore signal in the foreground is soon to be replaced by an electric 'searchlight' type.

Every member of the Locomotive Department was paid in the same manner, so there was often a queue at the Ticket Office, occasionally joined by a member of the public wanting to purchase a train ticket.

Strange to relate, but for the life of me I cannot remember exactly how and when I was issued with my uniform, which comprised two sets of bib'n'brace overalls, two jackets and a grease-top cap. I think I must have drawn these from the Shed Stores on that first morning. Never mind, the fact was that here I was at last on the first rung of the ladder to Engine Driver!

On that first morning, I joined two other Cleaners who had just started, Norman (Slim) Whitehouse and Walter (Wally) Luck. Within a short time several other cleaners joined up and we became close friends in future years. A few of them that I readily recall are: Mick Chapman, Wally Coleman, Colin and Dennis Clarke, Lofty Chivers, John Girdlestone, Tiddler Deards, Tony Parrot – I am sure there are many other names that I have long forgotten.

The Shed Staff

After going through the preliminaries with the Shedmaster, he took us down to the far end of the engine shed, briefly introduced us to the shed staff and then left them to 'show us the ropes'.

Along the end wall was a heavy wooden bench to which were attached a couple of huge metal vices, while on the wall itself was hung an assortment of hefty spanners. Most of the nuts and bolts on a steam locomotive were giant-size, so it followed that all the tools were of similar proportions.

Several metal cupboards lined the wall on the left-hand side and set in the end wall on the left was a single door that faced the turntable.

Over to the right were a couple of wooden benches and steel lockers, which contained the Shed staff's personal effects.

I believe a temporary Locomotive Fitter was in charge at that time, soon to be replaced by a more permanent man by the name of Pete Jarman. Pete was a man of hefty build in his mid to late 30's. The Fitters Apprentice was George Don who was much younger and lived at Hoddesdon – I'll say a bit more about George later on.

The Fitters attended to all the day-to-day repairs reported by the Drivers on the locomotive Repair Cards. Sometimes this involved travelling out to a 'sick engine', which may have thrown a crankpin, developed a faulty injector or some other fault that prevented it from returning to the depot.

Boilerwasher George Phillips (left) and Apprentice Fitter George Don take in the air on Hertford East's turntable on a fine day in 1955.

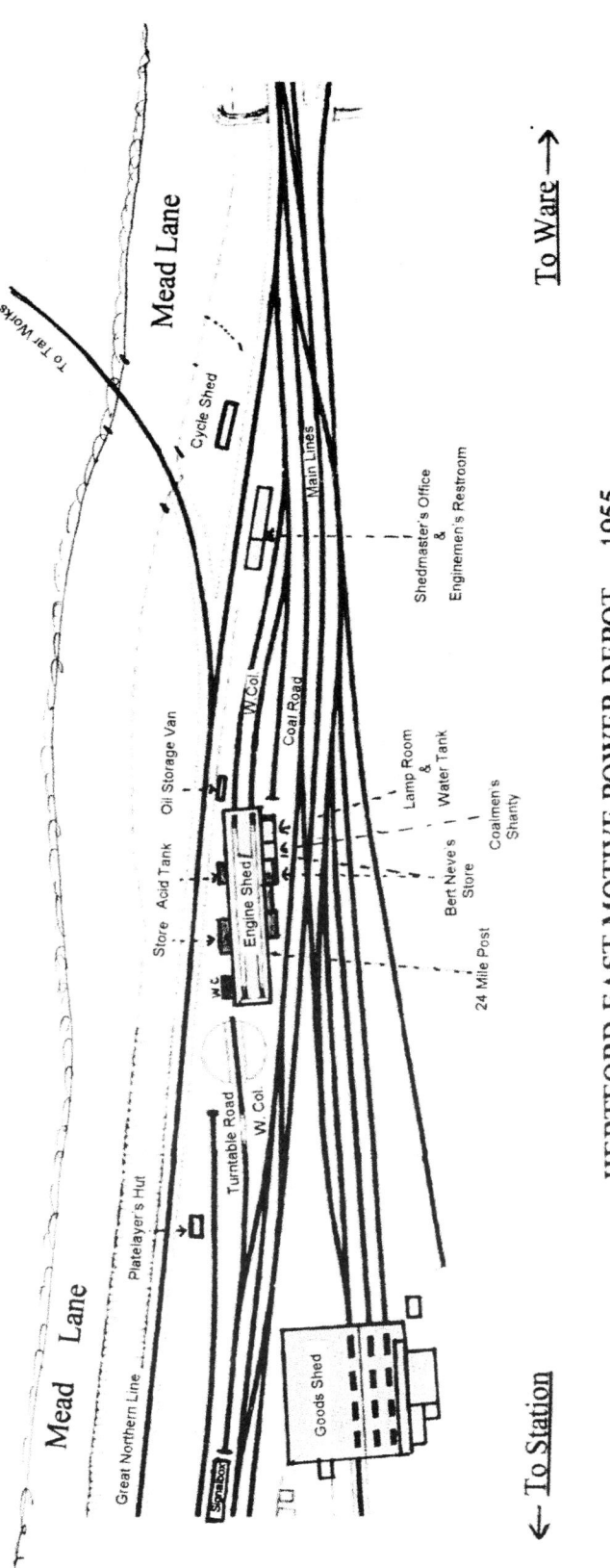

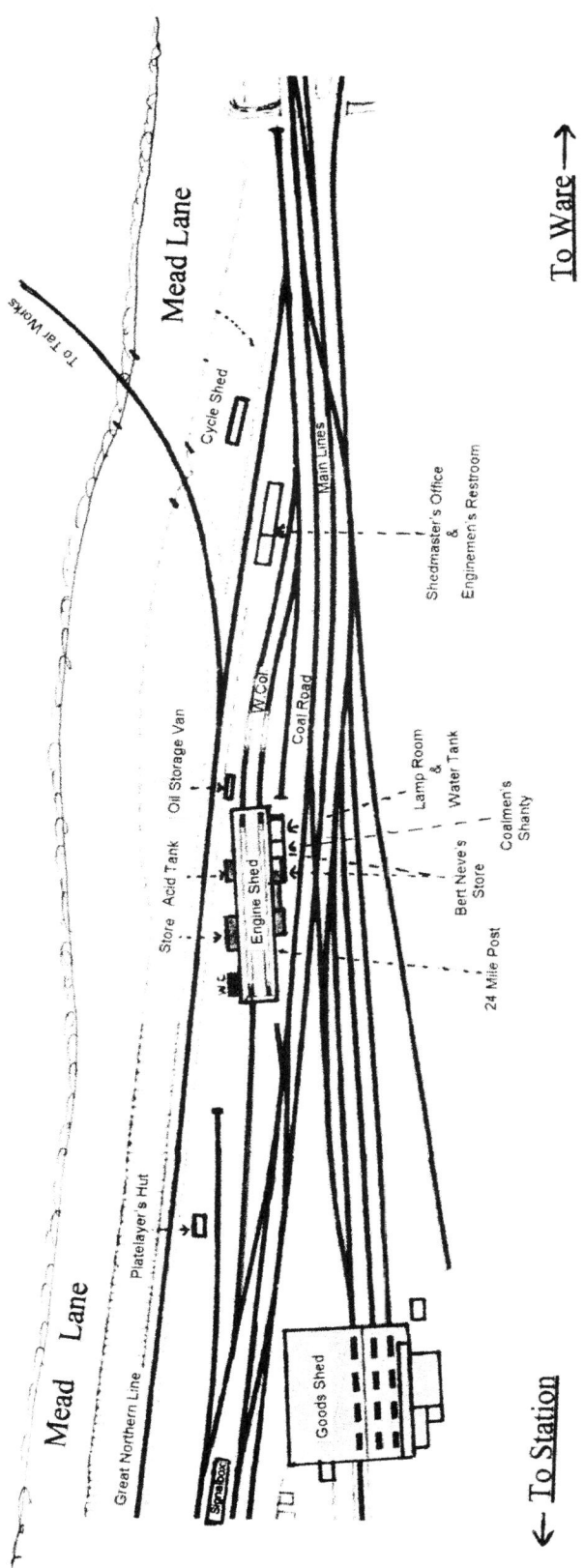

The resident Boilerwasher was George Philips, a real character who must have been the wrong side of 60 who retired at the same time that steam disappeared from Hertford in 1960. I believe George had been on the footplate in his earlier years as he used to tell us tales of the 'Gobblers' (Class F6 2-4-2 tank engines) on Brentwood Bank, which is a spot located about 14 miles north of Stratford on the main line to Ipswich. "Gah blimey cock", he would say, "they slipped so much they made grooves in the rails at the bottom of the Bank – they were B******'s!" Although George always looked a rough-and-ready individual, he owned a large house in one of the select areas of Hertford and was – as one might say – 'not short of a bob or two'!

Another lasting memory of George was his shaving habit. His first job when he arrived at work each morning on his rickety old cycle was to get out his shaving brush, soap and safety razor, and a mug of hot water – usually from the washout engine which would still contain hot water in the boiler. Having thoroughly lathered his face, he would proceed to drag the razor over the thick stubble, which sounded like coarse sandpaper rubbing over rusty metal! With skin like leather there was never any fear of George cutting himself, no matter how blunt the razor may have been.

It was George's proud boast that he got more shaves from a single razor blade than anyone, achieved by regularly honing it around the inside edge of a china cup!

What a great character old George was. It was George's responsibility to sweep out the boiler tubes (using a long steel rod on the end of which was affixed a piece of rag), remove the washout plugs from the boiler and wash out the accumulated lime-scale with a high-pressure hose. He also replaced firebars and the brick arch inside the firebox when necessary.

Another man, who I think was designated Assistant to the Boilerwasher, was Sid Machin, another 'oldie' who we used to call (when he was out of earshot) 'Dabfeet' on account of his peculiar 'Charlie Chaplin-like' shuffle when he walked!

Then there was the Boilermaker, George Tipton, he was based at Stratford and appeared at Hertford a couple of days a week. As he was not exactly 'one of the gang', he kept pretty much to himself, although I remember him as a decent enough chap. He was rather a tubby individual and we used to wonder how he managed to squeeze his portly figure through the small firebox door of an N7! His duties included caulking any leaky firetubes, tightening firebox rivets, servicing steam pressure safety valves and inspecting the condition of the boiler of each locomotive as it came in for it's periodic (fortnightly?) boiler washout and servicing.

Most of the aforementioned duties, apart from emergencies, were carried out when the engine was taken out of service for its fortnightly boiler washout and minor repairs. It was this engine that also demanded the attentions of we Engine Cleaners. Finally, there was the Yardman and ex-Fireman, Don Walls, who I would judge to have been in his early 20s, whose job included emptying the ash-pits and generally keeping the Locomotive Yard tidy.

Engine cleaning

Later during that first morning we were introduced to the Storeman, Bert Neve, who resided in a little store built against the wall of the Engine Shed next to the Coalmen's Shanty. Bert was an ex-Stratford mainline driver, who had to come off the footplate due to failing eyesight – which was a common problem among older enginemen.

A characteristic phrase of Bert's - when asking him for an extra hand cloth or maybe a new cap, - was a long drawn out *"Peeessss Orrrrrrff"*!

However, on this particular day, he issued each of us with a metal bucket, a steel scraper and a huge wad of cotton 'waste', which consisted of thousands of different coloured cotton threads which I guess really was 'waste' from the cotton product manufacturing industry.

Into the buckets went a mixture of paraffin and light oil, which had a dual purpose.

Firstly, it acted as a degreasant for loosening the layers of oil-soaked dirt, soot and coaldust from the various parts of the engine, which we then removed with our scrapers. Secondly, when applied over the boiler, tanks and cabside and rubbed dry with cotton waste, it would leave a pleasing shine on the black paintwork.

The worst job was going into the pit underneath and scraping the oily gunge off the inside cranks and rods – the black mess would run down your up-reaching arm and, if you were not careful, run down your neck.

Although the Shedmaster would occasionally inspect our work, and sometimes make us redo some part or other, the standards required were nothing like the old days when one hears of the foreman checking behind the wheels by wiping there with a white cloth!

Bill Bright's engine

The only engine I remember that we gave extra special treatment to whenever she came in for washout was 69683, whose regular driver was Bill Bright.

Bill was a quiet, friendly man who was the local Trade Union Representative of the Associated Society of Locomotive Engineers and Firemen (ASLEF). It wasn't because he was the Union man that his engine received special treatment, it was for the half-crown (12.5p) he often used to give us to do a good job on his engine!

The general arrangement at Hertford was that two sets of crew (i.e. driver & fireman) were allocated a particular 'regular' engine. The intention was that, during the whole of its working day, only the allocated crew would work with that engine. In practice however, circumstances often dictated otherwise and sometimes the crew would not work on their own engine for a whole week or more.

Some of the 'extras' we gave to 69683 was a real shiny boiler, including the dome on top. To achieve this we would get a lump of tallow (animal fat) from Bert Neve which, when spread over the warm boiler cladding, would melt into a shiny film. As the boiler got hotter, this film would form a hard, shiny skin that would last for several days, especially if it was given a quick rub over with an oily cloth every day.

From steam to electric. Storeman Bert Neve is photographed in far better working conditions and smarter attire than the old cloth cap and faded blue overalls he wore in steam days! When this picture was taken on 31st January 1964 he had been relocated in the Shedmaster's old office.

With a mixture of fine sand and paraffin we would scour the footplating along each side of the boiler, giving it a dull brownish/grey sheen.

We would also bring a silvery shine to the smokebox door outer ring by buffing it with emery paper. Some of the brass and copper piping around the Westinghouse air pump would be cleaned with red brick dust or fine sand mixed with oil. A final polish was achieved with another of Bert Neve's store items called 'Derby Paste'. I don't know what it was made up of except that it had a gritty, creamy-white texture and produced a good shine on brass and copper.

The internal cab fittings were kept sparkling clean by the engine crew and were not part of our responsibility. However, on this particular engine we did try to ensure that old cloths and newspapers covered as much of these fittings as possible to protect them from the thick sooty smoke which filled the cab when the fire was re-lit by the nightshift.

Although engine-cleaning was a filthy job, I personally derived a great deal of satisfaction in helping to transform a grimy workhorse into a gleaming piece of machinery, even if the cleanliness was only superficial and generally lasted no more than a few days.

Keeping myself clean

Looking back in later years, I didn't really appreciate the rotten job my mother had in keeping my overalls clean.   The amount of oil, grease, ash and coal-dust they would have absorbed by the end of the week must have been considerable. However, dear old mum always managed to boil them clean, although as the months passed their original dark blue colour gradually became paler until almost white and only half the weight!   But they did manage to survive the required 12 months after which new sets were issued.

Things were little different when I became a fireman – and it wasn't just the clothes that collected the dirt, believe me!

Coal dust and ash managed to find its way to every part of the body, irrespective as to how covered up you might be. I would jump into the bath every time I arrived home from work and the amount of black grime that washed out of my body was unbelievable.

Sister engines 69683 and 69684 at Hertford East MPD in the late 1950s. For some reason, on this occasion a special effort has been made with 69684, as she was not usually seen as immaculate as her sister.

Even then, it was impossible to remove every trace of grime from the hands, as some of it would actually penetrate the pores of the skin.

We did receive a weekly issue of 'Rozalex' antiseptic barrier cream from the stores that we were supposed to rub into our hands and arms before starting work.   This cream helped reduce the risk of contracting dermatitis.

The first wash of the day was great, as this cream prevented most of the dirt from getting into the skin and it washed of easily. However, our weekly allowance of Rozalex didn't stretch to more than one application per day so it only had limited benefit. Trying to get an extra issue out of Bert Neve was like trying to get blood out of a stone!

The most effective method of cleaning our hands was to soak them in a mixture of paraffin and oil and then dip into the engine's sandbox for a handful of fine sand.

After rubbing your hands together for a few minutes in this mixture, you would finish off with a liberal wash in hot, soapy water.

Although this treatment removed most of the grime, it did not do much to enhance the softness of one's skin, but looking on the positive side, there was never much risk of a pint glass slipping through one's fingers when washing the dust out of your throat later on in the 'local'!

Strange to relate, there were certain firemen and drivers who always seemed to be able to keep themselves scrupulously clean. I often used to wonder how they managed it – they did the same job as the rest of us – perhaps they were just that much more careful?

Towards the end of the 1950s I occasionally spotted a fireman wearing Industrial gloves, but I can't remember any of Hertford's men wearing them.

Personally, I thought the wearing of them increased the chance of getting blisters, as the skin became soft.   Apart from that, they were not standard issue so they would be an additional expense.

A product that I used to buy occasionally was a small tin of 'Swarfega' – a very effective hand-cleaner that is still available to this day. However, it never used to last long and, with the amount I used, I could not afford to buy it on a regular basis. Towards the end of steam at Hertford, a large drum of Swarfega could be seen in Bert Neve's store, but asking him for some would invariably result in him tilting his head back and drawling his usual "Peeeeessss Orrrffff".   I think he kept it in reserve for drivers and Shed staff.

Learning about the steam locomotive

With 3 or 4 cleaners all on the same engine, it did not take the whole of our day to do a reasonable job, so there was ample time for other things. Some of this time was spent getting to know the various parts of the locomotive, such as the functions of the numerous wheels and levers within the cab.

There was the steam pressure gauge, which had a red line on the 180 lbs. mark, which was the top working pressure of our Class N7 tank engines. The boiler water level gauges were situated at about chest height, one gauge either side of the cab front.   These gauges were in the form of vertical glass tubes protected by covers that were made of thick, toughened glass on three sides with a sprung steel flap at the back.   This flap had black-and-white enamel painted diagonal lines that highlighted the level of water shown in the glass. When viewed from the front, these diagonal lines would be reversed directly behind that part of the glass tube that contained water, whilst the empty area above the water level would show

Hertford East's station pilot, J69 68600 in the goods yard. Enjoying a spell on the footplate is Apprentice Fitter George Don with (I believe) a visiting colleague from Stratford. Just in the picture on the right can be seen the Water Tank and the small brick building which was Bert Neve's Stores.

the lines unaltered. The total water capacity of the boiler was barely an inch above and below the visible length of the glass, so if the glass showed empty then so too was the boiler!

We also learnt, from George Don, the names and functions of the cranks and rods which lay hidden between the driving wheels and beneath the engine's boiler.

George had started on the footplate in 1948 then, in the early 1950s, George had an ambition to emigrate to Australia to become an Engine Driver, but one of the essential requirements over there was that he would also need the qualifications of a Locomotive Maintenance Engineer. Apparently, due to the vast distances in Australia, an Engine Driver was also required to be a qualified Maintenance Engineer to deal with a breakdown miles from any other form of assistance. So, after graduating to Fireman in the Passenger Link, George had come off the footplate and taken up a Fitter's Apprenticeship.

As it eventually turned out, George ended up getting married so his plans to emigrate were abandoned!

The art of firing

After the servicing of the engine had been completed, we would take turns on the firing shovel by putting a few shovelsfull of coal into the firebox ready for the shed staff on the night shift who would do the lighting-up. George Phillips sometimes used to supervise our firing efforts to ensure we didn't do it the easy way with the firehole door wide open. Within the firehole door was a hinged flap that was held open by a ratchet, affording an opening resembling the bottom half of a slightly flattened circle. This opening was just high and wide enough to accept the blade of a level shovelfull of coal. The idea was to make a smooth swing from the coalhole and into the firebox below the open flap without spilling coal all over the cab floor.

Our initial efforts were pathetic. We would end up smashing into various parts of the firehole door, spraying coal all over the place and bending the leading edge of the shovel into a backward curl. By way of punishment, the tremendous jarring shock to arms and wrists served as reminders of our dismal failure for several hours afterwards!

Yardman (and ex-fireman) Don Walls demonstrates his firing technique on Hertford's station pilot 68600. *c.1959.*

Even after we had learnt to line up the shovel accurately, the coal still had to be guided to various parts of the firegrate by a deft flick of the wrist the moment the shovel entered the firebox. If any of us were to make it to the grade of Fireman,

29

these skills, and more, had to be mastered. Our efforts were on a stationary locomotive and without the necessity to maintain steam pressure – out on the main line, with the engine bucking around like a wild thing, firing would be much harder!

Believe me, firing efficiently on a steam locomotive was an art. To simply throw coal into the firebox willy-nilly would put you in trouble almost immediately because steam pressure would not be maintained. In simple terms, to put a 'round' in the firebox on an N7 meant one shovelful accurately placed in each of the front corners, followed by another in each of the back corners, one each side halfway down and one in the centre to finish. The aim was to maintain a level firebed with no 'holes' in it. Of course, different types of locomotives required different techniques, but my concern at this time was firing to an N7.

In real life this firing operation would need to be carried out swiftly on a locomotive at speed, which would often be rocking and jumping so violently that an inexperienced individual would find it nigh impossible to remain upright, let alone swing a shovel! However, true to the old adage, practise makes perfect and we improved as time went by.

Other Cleaner's duties

Another regular duty we had was to keep the ashpit at the turntable end of the shed clear of ashes and clinker. Don Walls usually attended to the two long pits in the Shed Roads, probably because there was much more activity down that end and required a great deal of care and alertness.

The Turntable Road ashpit and watering facilities were usually only used by Stratford and Bishop's Stortford engines that did not need to go into the Depot – they were not encouraged to use our coaling facilities!

Each morning a bucketful of brown-coloured briquettes, each about the size and shape of a small can of soup, had to be tipped into the water tank located high up on a brick structure at one corner of the shed. These briquettes softened the water as they dissolved and assisted in retarding the build-up of lime scale in the locomotive boilers. You had to climb a steel ladder attached to the side of the structure to reach the top of the tank. The bottom of this ladder was embedded in the ground about 4 feet out from the base of the tower. It was no mean feat climbing almost straight up carrying a heavy bucket in one hand and maintaining ones balance at the top whilst tipping the bucket's contents into the black, murky depths of the huge tank. Apparently, it was not unknown for a fireman to have a cooling dip in this tank in the height of summer – it was over ten feet deep - but it never appealed to me. The water was always a murky black colour and, despite the chemicals we regularly tipped into it, I do believe a family of eel-like creatures swam around in there!

Loading ash wagons

Another extra piece of work that was available was the loading of ashes into wagons, for which a bonus payment of £1.2s.6d (112.5p) per loaded wagon was paid. Strictly speaking this work was supposed to be performed outside working hours, but if there were an excessive build-up of ash and clinker the Shedmaster would allow a pair of us to do it during our normal working day.

We cleaners only handled ashes from the servicing pit in the Turntable Road. We had the daily task of keeping this pit clear by shovelling the ashes out of the pit and onto a growing pile of clinker alongside. There was a water column alongside the pit that we could utilise to dampen any hot ashes beforehand.

The growing pile of ash beside the pit was also made up of smokebox cinders and clinker that had been removed from the firebox during fire-cleaning operations.

Very often these ashes would continue to smoulder for days and remain red-hot below the surface. Before they could be shovelled into the wagon, they had to be thoroughly damped down, either with the Boiler-washer's hosepipe or by directing the leather bag of the water column over them.

An August 1958 scene of Hertford loco yard in all its workstained glory! Engines in view, from L to R are N7s nos. 69702, 69684 and J69 68500.

Although the water made the ashes very heavy, it was a better option than having hot, sulphurous ash blowing into your face as you threw each shovelfull up into the wagon.

There was one occasion when still-burning ash was loaded and during that night the wagon caught fire over in the Goods Yard, causing considerable damage to the wagon's side and bottom planks. Needless to say, the culprits did not receive payment for that load!

Hertford East MPD in 1937. Apart from the replacement of the Engine Shed roof, the scene was much the same during the author's time.

The wagons used for this purpose were of the smaller 12 ton (5-plank?) wooden bodied type. Even working as a pair, loading one was no mean feat, as the loading had to be completed in a single session - you were not permitted to leave a part-loaded wagon in the loco overnight.

Loading was comparatively easier for the first part when the side door was open, but once closed you had to swing each shovelfull over the top of the wagon from ground level this was punishing work on the arm muscles. It took about a week for the aches to disappear! To reduce the amount of shovelling work, we would occasionally throw one or two oil drums into the wagon and cover them up to create 'air pockets', but it was a risky 'dodge'. If you were found out, you didn't get paid at all!

'Fly' shunting

Getting the empty wagon from the yard in the first place was an interesting little operation. After picking up the empty wagon from the goods yard, the pilot engine would shunt the wagon from the main line into the turntable spur by giving it a sharp push across the points with the engine stopping short of the points to save it reversing out again. Depending on speed, the wagon would run up the spur toward the buffer stops below the Signalbox where one of us would be waiting to drop the brake handle to bring it to a stop.

Meanwhile, the Signalman would have re-set the points for the main line allowing the pilot engine to continue it's station duties.

The track was on a falling gradient to the turntable so we simply had to release the brake and allow the wagon to run down toward the turntable under it's own momentum. Of course, you had to walk beside it holding on to the brake lever in order to stop it at the desired spot.

Apparently, before my time, there was an occasion when a wagon was shunted from the main line particularly fast. It hit the buffer stops and catapulted back down the gradient before the cleaner could grab hold of the brake. The Signalman was quick enough to reset the points so the wagon hurtled down the spur, across the turntable, and off the short piece of track on the far side, which only had a wooden sleeper across the end to serve as a buffer stop. The wagon leapt across the few feet of ground and demolished the gent's toilet adjacent to the shed.

The new toilet in modern brick always looked out of place attached to the mellowed-brick wall of the main shed.

Acid, oil and sand

Along the wall on the same side as the toilet was another wooden lock-up, which I think contained some of the Fitter's equipment.

A little further on was a pink-coloured, bath-shaped tank, possibly lined with lead. The top of this tank was covered over with a sheet of mild steel. Being inquisitive, a couple of us slid the plate to one side for a closer look at the contents.

We had already been warned that it contained acid, but it looked for all the world like a few inches of water that lay there.

I remember shuddering at the thought of putting one's hand in there and we quickly slid the plate back into place. I never looked in there again.

This acid was used by the Fitters to burn off limescale build-up inside injector valves etc. It was also very effective in cleaning surface deposits from copper and brass fittings, simply by immersing them in this bath for a short time, then thoroughly hosing them down with cold water.

Walking on past the acid-bath, to the left of the path, was a grounded wooden van body in which were stored various pieces of equipment, including barrels of oil.

Nearby was a large steel hopper containing fine sand used for topping up the engine sandboxes.

The 'lean-to' buildings

Against the wall on the opposite side of the main Engine shed were the lean-to brick buildings of Bert Neve's storeroom and little office. Then came the Coalman/Cleaner's shanty, then the oil and paraffin issuing (Lamp) room, which was directly beneath the water tank, of which I made reference to earlier.

The Up main line passed within four or five feet of the corner of the shed building at the station end, so one had to be careful when walking along that side, especially if you were carrying anything that might foul a passing locomotive.

There was also a timber walkway most of the way down which covered the various signal wires and point-rodding which ran alongside the track. The access widened as the line of the shed angled away from the running lines toward the London end.

Lunchbreaks

I mentioned earlier that we usually kept clear of the shanty that we shared with the coaling staff and ate our lunchtime meal sitting with the shed staff or in a convenient railway carriage or a Guard's brake van across the yard.

During the warm weather, we would sit out on a grassy patch near the roadside fence opposite the turntable. Here we would eat our sandwiches and watch the different railway activities that went on continuously in front of us, both on the main line and in the Goods Yard on the far side.

There would also be the occasional Stratford engine that would come into the Turntable Road to take water and perhaps clean the fire. Sometimes an engine would come onto the turntable for turning and we would go and help the crew push the table round.

Mead Lane Café

Occasionally, if we could muster up a few coppers between us, we would go down the road to a dingy little café located on the corner of Mead Lane and Gashouse Lane. There we would have tea and toast and, if we were particularly wealthy, a sausage sandwich. On a nostalgic drive down Mead Lane early in 1998, I was absolutely amazed to see that this little café was still there! It wasn't open at that time for me to go inside, but I am sure it is vastly different from the greasy Formica-topped tables and rickety chairs from my railway days. Gone too, would be the genial old lady with the perpetual cigarette dangling from her mouth, irrespective as to whether she was cooking over the stove or serving at the tables. She did wear a white(ish) coat though!

These would be the only times we would get a cup of tea, apart from the occasional generous offer of sharing a brew-up with the shed-staff.

Man with a motorbike

It was during one of our lunch-breaks beside the lane that a chap came riding up on a scruffy old (ex-Army?) motorcycle that was obviously well past it's prime and asked if any of us were interested in purchasing it for £5. Well, that was a good fortnight's wages to us, so we had not the slightest intention to take up his offer, but we didn't let him know that.

Instead we said we wanted to try it out first, to which he agreed.

Now, apart from not having a licence and being under the age of 16 (minor points I thought at the time), I had never ridden a motorbike in my life. We had no proper riding gear or 'skidlid' (as a crash helmet was generally referred to in those days).

However, being young and carefree, and after a brief explanation of how to operate the throttle, gears and brakes, I roared off up the lane like a 'bat out of hell'.

I still remember the thrill of having all this power at my fingertips and tore back down the lane past my mates with the throttle wide open! The bike must have had a prang at one time which slightly twisted the frame as I felt the back wheel trying to overtake the front and me having to turn the handlebars left in order to maintain a straight line.

Anyway, we all took turns until the thing ran out of petrol, we then told the chap we couldn't buy it, as we didn't have any money. After a few mutterings, he trudged off dejectedly pushing his now-useless machine alongside. That was a smashing half-hour of fun – we never saw him again!

Learning the tricks

As I got into the daily routine of things, I was able to take a few liberties. For example, although my starting time was 8 a.m., I was not required to clock-in, so to speak, so provided I evaded the watchful eye of the Shedmaster, I could get away with a late arrival if I missed the 7.23 from Broxbourne. There was a 7.39 and, if I really overslept, a 7.54 which got me into Hertford at 8.15.

At the other end of the day, Slim Whitehouse and I often sloped off on the 4.24 p.m. train, ducking below the carriage window to escape Fred Hennessey's ever watchful eyes as the train passed his office.

Then there were the occasional footplate 'trips' which we would 'earn' by doing small favours for the engine crew. These favours would take many forms e.g. filling sandboxes, raking out the ashpan or smokebox or even cleaning the fire. All of these tasks I will describe in some detail later. The 'trips' we earned were strictly unofficial so again, care had to be taken to ensure the Shedmaster didn't find out. He would have been extremely annoyed if he discovered that his cleaners were out enjoying themselves during working hours, although most occasions were in our own time on the evening trains. Of course, such activities were rare and, in order to avoid detection, only one of us at a time could be absent during work periods.

My first footplate trip

I will always remember my very first footplate ride although it was for less than 2 miles on that occasion. It was with fireman Herbie Howard and driver Roy (Buck) Storey. It was completely unplanned and took place not many weeks after I started work.

I had got off the train at Broxbourne having finished for the day and crossed at the end of the platform to get my cycle from the Goods shed. In the cattle dock at the north end of the Down platform were Buck and Herbie with an N7 0-6-2 Tank engine. Although I was fairly new, I already knew Herbie as he was always asking us cleaners to do favours so he could nip across to the pub for a quick pint.

"Hullo Albert" called Herbie, "where are you going?". "Home to Wormley." I replied. "Hang on for a bit then, we're going that way later." Replied Herbie.

I explained about my cycle and was told to bring that up into the cab also! So up I went with my bike and very soon we were on our way, hauling a couple of wagons and a Guard's van. There was hardly room to move on the crowded footplate but Herbie had already made up the fire to provide sufficient steam for our short trip. We were 'chimney first' to London and I still remember the fascination of watching and feeling the rise and fall, side to side motion of the boiler as I looked ahead out of the cab window. Although in a short number of months such an experience would become commonplace to me, I will always remember the thrill of that first occasion.

The Level Crossing at Wormley, showing the Signalbox and a London-bound express hauled by an almost new 'Britannia' Pacific 4-6-2 - No. 70030 *William Wordsworth* – during the winter of 1953/4. This was one of the author's poor attempts at photography, using a 'Brownie 127' box camera.

Wormley Level Crossing

'Buck' stopped our train on Wormley level crossing, where I had spent so many hours as a youngster, and handed my cycle down to me. Signalman Len Syers came to the window of his box to see why we had stopped. As they continued their trip to Waltham Cross two stations up and I crossed the lines behind them, Len Syers waved to me from the Signalbox. I don't know if he recognised me then as one of the young 'trainspotters' he used to see sitting by his crossing gates. If I knew in advance of a planned footplate trip, I would tell my younger brothers and sisters the time our train would be passing Wormley crossing. They would be waiting and watching with anticipation as we approached and I would get quite a kick out of sounding the engine's whistle and giving them a wave as we sped past. So for a few months life followed a fairly routine pattern, sprinkled here and there with one-off incidents.

Two lovely ladies

As my morning train arrived at Broxbourne, 'Slim' Whitehouse – who had boarded at Waltham Cross - would look out for me from the carriage window so I could join him.
Sometime during early autumn we noticed among the passengers, 2 very attractive young ladies who boarded our train at St. Margaret's. After a few days of waving a 'good morning' to them as we pulled into the station, they actually joined us in our carriage. It turned out they were sisters and both worked in offices in Hertford. I remember the younger of the 2 had long jet-black hair and was named Anne, I cannot remember her sister's name.
Apart from regularly joining us for a friendly chat for the 10 minutes or so it took to travel to Hertford, they began to meet us at our lunchtime spot by the fence in Mead Lane.
However, whether it was because of the risk of sooty air-borne smuts on their immaculate clothing, or the fact that we never did get round to asking for a date, they stopped coming, so our meetings never amounted to anything serious.

During February 1956 my family moved home to Hertford Heath, which meant I no longer caught the morning train to work and instead had an easy 2 miles downhill cycle ride into Hertford which took me around 10 minutes.
The 'downside' was that I never saw the two girls anymore either!

A Stratford courier

I believe it was around this time that my weekly routine underwent an interesting change.
The 'internal mail' system between Hertford East Depot and Stratford comprised a large metal canister with brass fittings about the size of a small briefcase.
A reversible square brass plate was contained in a slotted compartment just below the hinged lid.   So, before closing the lid, our Shedmaster would reverse the plate to show 'Stratford MPD'. The act of closing the lid effectively locked the plate in place.   I never knew for certain what the box contained but I assume it was mainly Driver's Daily Time Sheets necessary for calculating the wages for themselves and their Firemen, so it was pretty important information.
I think the incoming mailbox would arrive on an early morning train and would be picked up from the station by the Shedmaster as he arrived for work.
As soon as he had emptied it of incoming mail and deposited the previous day's correspondence inside, it was ready to go back to Stratford.   This is where I came in.
I was given the regular job of taking this box to Stratford, at the same time collecting small sundry items of tools and equipment required by the Fitter to carry out small repairs and maintenance of our locomotive fleet.

Sometimes I would take a small item for repair, such as a length of copper pipe requiring a collar to be brazed on, or a brass clack valve needing refacing.
 I would be given an official order docket signed by the Shedmaster, which I would present to the Head Storekeeper at Stratford who would make up my order.
This particular individual was Charlie Lock who, wearing a cloth cap and glasses, with a cigarette permanently jammed between his lips, became one of Stratford's legendary figures.
I was always amazed that, among the thousands of components within this giant storehouse, this wiry little man knew exactly where each part was to be found!

The frequency of this journey varied, as I would only be sent on this errand if there were stores to be obtained.   On other days the canister was simply put on the first available train to Stratford. I was issued with a Travel Permit contained in a leather wallet and caught the first available Liverpool Street train, which would either be the 8.39 or, more often than not, the 9.25.   Neither of these trains went via Stratford, but if I caught the 8.39 and changed at Broxbourne, there was a connection from Bishops Stortford, which reached Stratford at 9.45.
However, as I had the whole day I was never in any hurry to get there and back.
It was much more pleasurable to 'ride the cushions' than to be cleaning engines!

When I arrived at Liverpool Street, I had the option of going across the footbridge to the far (East) side of the station and hop on one of the spacious Shenfield Electrics to Stratford, or go down below and catch an Underground train.
If I were carrying nothing but the mailbox I would catch the Central Line Tube. I would also treat myself to a box of Bassetts Liquorice Allsorts from the vending machine on the Underground platform, I believe they cost 6d (2.5p).   Anyway, all things being equal, I would arrive at Stratford at around 11 am.

Stratford Works

I would leave the station by the Main Entrance, turn left and enter the tunnel which ran under the station and the vast network of tracks, and come out near the first of the Work's buildings. It took a little getting used to the fact that I merited little more than a casual nod as I walked past the Gatekeeper, which was in total contrast to the reception I received when trying to get past the entrance as a young schoolboy!   I cannot clearly remember, but I think it was at this Gatehouse where I would deposit the mailbox.
Looking back in later years, it is with lasting regret that I didn't have the forethought to carry a camera during those trips, what a unique collection of photographs I could have built up!

Every visit produced something new, with locomotives nose-to-tail in numerous sidings for overhaul or the 'chop'. Some would be partly dismantled, being in the process of either rebuilding or scrapping.   Others may be already cut up and loaded into wagons, the severed smokebox still retaining it's numberplate on the door – those cast-iron plates could have been purchased for less than a pound at that time - what would their value be today?

Above. 'Britannia' Class 4-6-2 Pacific no. 70040 *Clive of India* on a Liverpool Street to Norwich 2-hour express. 1/6/57.
Below. A Class B1 4-6-0 no. 61254 on express duty in East Anglia on 1/6/57.

Then further over there would be locomotives newly out of the Paint Shops, freshly overhauled and looking like brand new machines. There was little to beat the beautiful sight of a B1 4-6-0 in gleaming Black Cherry with it's red/cream/grey lining and shining oily-steel motion, or one of the newer 'Britannia' Class 4-6-2 Pacifics looking absolutely magnificent in it's lined green livery. What majestic giants they were when viewed from ground level compared with the usual platform view.

There were many occasions when I would clamber up into the cabs of locomotives that were not 'in steam' just to admire the view from the driver's seat. Over the passage of time I climbed onto the footplate of most classes, including Britannia Pacifics, Sandringhams, Clauds, Holden's 1500s, to name but a few.

Of course, there were other classes equally as attractive, right down to the smaller passenger tank engines such as the 0-6-2 N7s we had at Hertford.

Apart from my visit to the main Stores, I would occasionally be directed to one of the Workshops if I required a special job to be done. I can recall going to one Shop to have some cold chisels sharpened by a huge man who operated a massive grindstone that was kept wet by the lower part of the stone running through a trough of water.

Another occasion was finding a Coppersmith in his tiny lean-to shed to braze a collar onto a length of piping. He was completely opposite in physical stature to the 'grindstone man' but equally as skilled in his chosen profession.

There was one time, when I needed repair to a complicated piece of brasswork, I was directed across the tracks to the Old Works on the East Side (nearest the station) to the Brass Foundry. This workshop was located on the upper floor of a huge building and the brightly-lit interior revealed rows of workbenches containing men, lathes and drills all working on numerous brass components. The parts they were manufacturing and the piles of brass waste trimmings and swarf scattered around glistened like gold, the whole place looked like King Midas' treasure house!

I used to have a large canvas and leather bag for carrying the smaller bits and pieces and, once I had completed the various duties, I would make my way back to Liverpool Street for the trip back to Hertford.

Lost property!

On one of these occasions I had the fright of my life because I thought I had got myself the sack! It came about like this:

One of my old schoolpals, Tony Trepte, worked for an advertising agency in Dashwood House, which was an elegant old multi-floored building, located at the top of the road just outside Liverpool Street station's main entrance. If I made it back from Stratford by around 12.30 I would give Tony a ring and he would pop down to join me for a coffee in the Station Buffet at the end of Platforms 1&2.

My train left at 1 p.m. from Platform One and called at all stations to Hertford, but when it got as far as Broxbourne it would draw into the siding and wait for the

Cambridge express to pass through before continuing it's journey to Hertford. This express left Liverpool Street at 1.24 p.m. and ran non-stop to Broxbourne, arriving at 1.52.

In order to spend an extra twenty five minutes with my pal, I would dump my bag of stores and any other bits and pieces in the Guard's Van of the 1 o'clock local, which was usually 'parked up' in Platform One from around 12.30 p.m. Having got rid of all my 'baggage' on the all-stations stopper, I would catch the 1.24 express, getting off at Broxbourne, where the 1 o'clock from Liverpool Street would be waiting to pick up any passengers for the Hertford Branch.

I then simply retrieved my bits and pieces from the Guard's Van when we arrived at Hertford at 2.19.

This arrangement went like clockwork until one day, when we arrived at Hertford, my bag and bundles of various piping were not there! Apparently, when the Guard arrived to take charge of the train at Liverpool Street and saw my pile of metal lying in the corner of his Van, with no destination labels attached, he promptly threw the lot out onto the Platform!

Well, blind panic set in, I dreaded the thought of going to the Shedmaster to tell him I had lost all the stores. That alone would have been bad enough, but what if the Fitter was waiting for one of those components vital for putting an engine back into service the following morning?

After the first wave of panic passed, and on the suggestion of the sympathetic Guard, I went down to the Station Inspector's office and told him of my predicament. He made a few phone calls after which, and to my great relief, he said the bits had been found exactly where the Guard left them and that they would arrive on the 2.48 out of London, reaching Hertford at 4.02.

I was still very apprehensive when I reported to Fred Hennessey but fortunately, he was quite calm about it as none of the stores were that urgent. He just told me to make sure I met the train at the Station and to pray that everything was all there before I went home that day.

After that episode, on future occasions I made a point of checking with the Guard of the 1 o'clock that all my gear was still on board before it departed.

Unfortunately, somehow word got around about my predicament and I was subjected to some friendly banter from several of the staff for quite a time afterwards. I remember driver Jimmy Pratt, who took great delight in greeting by mimicking my opening phrase to Fred Hennessey that day, by drawling *"I just went for a cup of cawwffee...."*.

Further education

Other diversions from the normal duties of an engine cleaner involved learning how to couple up the vacuum-brake and steam heating pipes between the engine and train. I also learnt the correct way of hooking up the screw coupling, ensuring it is screwed up tight enough to avoid oscillation between the locomotive and carriage, which could cause discomfort to the passengers.

We also learnt the art of using a shunting pole to hook up the heavy 3-link wagon couplings. There was a real knack to this as it was impossible to simply lift the coupling up on the end of the pole – it was far too heavy. The secret was to swing the coupling upwards in a small arc and - with a deft flick of the wrists - drop it over onto the hook of the next wagon, of which correct timing was essential. We sort of mastered it to a degree, but never to the level of the regular Shunters who made it look so ridiculously easy.

The Injector

At the outset, we were told that the very first thing to do when stepping on to the footplate of a locomotive was to check the boiler-water level.

To allow a boiler to run dry could end in very costly – and sometimes fatal – results, so we quickly learned the art of using the injector that was a device for injecting fresh water into the boiler.

First the water-cock had to be fully opened. This was situated fairly close to the ground beneath the cab and was operated by a long rod that projected into the cab.

Water running from the overflow pipe by the steps of the cab indicated that the cock was open. The steam valve was then opened, this was located at chest height in the cab alongside the firehole door.

Now the water running out of the overflow was boiling hot, so care had to be taken to avoid scalding anyone down below.

It was then a matter of gradually closing the water valve until the steam pressure was able to 'take up' the water flow and inject it into the boiler. At this point all emission from the overflow pipe ceased and a gratifying- and not unpleasant - whining sound told you that the injector was doing its job.

A duplicate injector was located on the driver's side but was usually only called upon in an emergency.

The Turntable

The ancient turntable was always a source of interest due to its temperamental nature. I do not know how old this table was, but it was operated manually by way of heavy wooden poles slotted into brackets at each end of the central platform upon which the engine stood. After releasing the locking catches via a long iron lever attached to the side of the platform, the engine crew would take opposite ends of the platform and lean on each pole to push the table round.

The release lever was attached to a locking mechanism controlled by the Signalman. If train movements were imminent, or actually in progress on the Up Main line, he would not allow the table to be operated for reason of safety, as the poles and the operators would come dangerously close to the Main line.

Wooden slats were fixed into the ground round the table to prevent the operator's feet from slipping.

The turntable itself consisted of a huge circular brick-and-concrete pit about 4 feet deep, round the bottom of which ran a circle of steel rail a foot or so from the inner wall. The actual table platform was made up of a pair steel girders placed side-by-side across the width of the pit and affixed to a centre pivot. At the end of each girder was attached a small guide-wheel that ran on the circle of rail at the bottom of the pit. Above the girders was a wooden platform about 10 feet wide upon which was placed the tracks flanked by a narrow walk-way on either side protected by iron railings.

Above. A rather faded – but rare – photograph of an engine on the turntable at Hertford East in 1955. There must have been some difficulty that day because the combined muscle-power of 3 men is employed in the task of turning class J15 0-6-0 no. 65545, whereas 2 would normally be sufficient.
Below. Hertford East - N7 69682 is seen passing the old Turntable Road water column with a London-bound train in the autumn of 1958

When an engine came onto the table it had to be stopped in exactly the right place otherwise it was not physically possible to make the turn. The idea was to inch the engine slowly forward until the table rocked on its centre pivot. Unlike a car, which can be stopped on a 'knife-edge' so-to-speak, the peculiarities of a steam locomotive makes such an operation very tricky due to the time lags between: a) applying power and obtaining movement, and b) applying the brake and coming to a halt.

Unless a perfect balance was achieved, the table would become jammed during the turn and we cleaners would be called upon to add some extra muscle.

Even then, there were occasions when the table would refuse to budge any further.

The only alternative then would be to move the engine a fraction in order to obtain a new balance. As the table was only part-way round, the engine had only the length of track on which it stood, allowing maximum movement of no more than a couple of feet either way – sometime less, depending on the class, and length, of locomotive. Therefor it required a great deal of nerve, as well as skill, to attempt this short manoeuvre, as even a slight misjudgement could end in total disaster.

There were no mishaps that I witnessed, although there was an earlier occasion when one attempt resulted in an 0-6-0 goods engine shooting off the table half-way round and ending up straddled across the Northern branch track beside Mead Lane. It was fortunate it was not in the reverse direction, as it would have fouled the main running lines.

I was told of another occasion when one of Stratford's Class L1 2-6-4 tank engines ended up nose-first into the turntable pit. For this to happen it must have meant the table had not been locked in position and had been partially turned and the L1 had run off the track directly approaching the turntable. I cannot understand how this could have occurred - always assuming the incident did actually occur.

My experiences with the turntable were very short as it was removed sometime (I think) during late 1956/57 when the Loco yard layout was re-designed.

At that time, a hole was knocked into the end of the shed and the Turntable Road re-aligned to run straight through the shed and into the depot beyond.

In normal circumstances there was a one-way system in operation, with engines entering the depot via the Turntable Road and leaving via the nearest section of the Great Northern branch.

Access to the GN branch was gained via a set of points at the London end of the depot and travelling up towards the station, where another set of points allowed traffic out on to the mainline behind the Signalbox.

A 'mushroom-type' water tank was installed at the station end of the branch for the benefit of engines (usually from Stratford or Bishops Stortford) that had no need to come in to the Loco for coaling or fire cleaning.

The old Turntable Road water column remained in situ but I believe the ashpit became obsolete due to re-alignment of the track. During quiet periods, visiting locomotives were still allowed to carry out fire and water servicing here and to go back to the station the same way rather than having to go via the 'one-way system' through the Shed.

Above. Soon after the Shed roof was replaced, further alterations were made when the turntable was removed and the track realigned to pass straight through the end of the Engine Shed.
The first photograph shows the work under way, and …………
Below. …..here is the final, ugly result. The work was completed early in 1958.

Above. Smartly turned-out N7 69678 up against the buffer stops in the carriage road that ran parallel to the Turntable Road. Locomotives did not usually use this siding, so the photograph must have been taken during the short period when the turntable was being removed during 1956/7.
Below. An L1 2-6-4 locomotive is seen coming off shed via the Great Northern branch in 1960. The neat, brick building in the foreground is the Platelayers shanty.

CHAPTER TWO

First-Year Fireman

Moving up the ladder

I was now approaching my 16th birthday in May, which meant I would be eligible to perform the duties of a fireman provided I passed the examination.

During the period that I had started my career with the railway, several cleaners had come and gone but Slim Whitehouse and Wally Luck were still with me along with a few others who were to become close pals over the next few years.

The Firing Examination

Sometime during May 1956 I was instructed to attend a course at Stratford to learn the basic responsibilities of a fireman. Passing this examination elevated you initially to the grade of 'Passed Cleaner', which meant you were still officially a cleaner but was proficient to assume the duties of fireman when required.

On arriving at Stratford I was directed to a classroom equipped with various components, drawings and photographs and, for the entire length of one wall, a miniature track layout complete with signals and levers.

I was one of about a dozen cleaners who had come from various Depots across the Great Eastern system.

An Inspector lectured us on the functions of the various types of signals, how a steam locomotive operates and the most effective and economical way of firing to them. Most of this I had already learnt from the Hertford footplatemen but what was new to me was the Rulebook. This was the railwayman's 'Bible' and contained hundreds of rules covering every eventuality.

Although not directly charged with learning every rule it was necessary for me to familiarise myself with them as it was one of the fireman's responsibilities to assist his driver in ensuring the safe operation of the locomotive and train at all times.

The examination course was on the Monday only and culminated in a firing trip on a class F6 0-4-4 tank on a passenger train from Stratford Low Level station to North Woolwich and back. It was easy stuff to me and, after asking me a few questions on the Rulebook, the Inspector shook my hand, told me I was now proficient for firing duties and to report to the Stratford Running Foreman before I went home.

I was puzzled about this last instruction but it transpired that, as Stratford was seriously short of firemen, it was policy for a few of the new recruits to spend the remainder of the week on simple firing duties within the Works complex.

My week on Departmental No. 33

I was assigned to the regular driver of the shunting pilot in the Old Works on the East Side, the same area that contained the Brass Shop that had fascinated me a few months earlier.

47

I cannot recall much about the old driver except that he was a kind, helpful chap.
Our engine was a little Class Y4 0-4-0 tank, Departmental Number 33 which had worked solely in the Old Works ever since it was built in 1921 (and continued to do so up to the Work's closure in 1963, when it was scrapped).   There was barely room to move in the tiny cab, though it did not really matter as there was very little for me to do.
The fire had to be freshly lit when we arrived at around 7.30 each morning, which was attended to by my driver.   He would appear with a shovelfull of blazing coals, presumably obtained from the Shunter's cabin, and place it in the tiny firebox. After adding a few pieces of firewood and some more coal, he would disappear again to make a can of tea.
By the time he returned the fire was going well and we soon started to raise steam.
As the boiler and its contents were still warm from the evening before, the engine was ready for work within an hour of our arrival.
The day was spent moving wagons around the different parts of the Works and I had little to do except pass on any Shunter's instructions if he happened to be on my side of the engine.   All in all it was real boring stuff for a young fireman who was itching to get out on to the 'open road'.

On the footplate of a B1

I hardly remember anything else of that week except for something which happened on the Friday morning.   When my driver came back from making the tea he said he had received a message that I was to go up to the station and relieve the fireman on an incoming Ipswich to London train. I duly positioned myself at the end of the designated platform and waited for the train to arrive.
I couldn't believe my eyes when an express came in sight and glided to a stop where I was standing.   I will always remember the picture of that immaculate black, class B1 4-6-0 numbered 61048 with a brilliant white 'express headcode' disc on each corner of her bufferbeam.
 I was sure I must have come to the wrong platform but no, the fireman was by the cab door with his coat on and bag slung over his shoulder ready to jump off.   As he hurried past me he said, "*She's all ok to London mate*", and he was gone.
I gingerly climbed aboard and nodded to the driver who confirmed that all I needed to do was to go and sit down in the leather padded bucket seat over on the fireman's side of the cab.   Everything in the cab was so clean, the fire was white-hot, the water level in the boiler near the top of the gauge-glass and the steam pressure needle just short of the red line, indicating a full head of steam.   The air was fully charged with that wonderful aroma of hot oil and steam, a smell unique to the steam engine.   There really was nothing at all for me to do.
I don't think Stratford was a scheduled stop because as soon as I was aboard the driver glanced back down the train, popped the whistle and promptly heaved the regulator open.   We seemed to accelerate up to express speed in no time at all and before I could take in the fact that I was acting fireman on an express train (albeit just there to make the number up) we were running into Liverpool Street.

As soon as we glided to a stop at the end of the platform, a relief crew climbed aboard to take over. My driver disappeared, leaving me to make my own way back to Stratford, which I did by crossing the footbridge and hopping on one of the Shenfield Electrics.

I never did find out the reason why a special stop had to be made at Stratford to let the fireman off, but I guess it must have been pretty serious. Anyway, although I was to work the main line on many hundreds of occasions, that was to be the one and only time I would act as fireman on an express passenger train.

Little more than an hour later I was back on the footplate of little old '33', what a contrast!

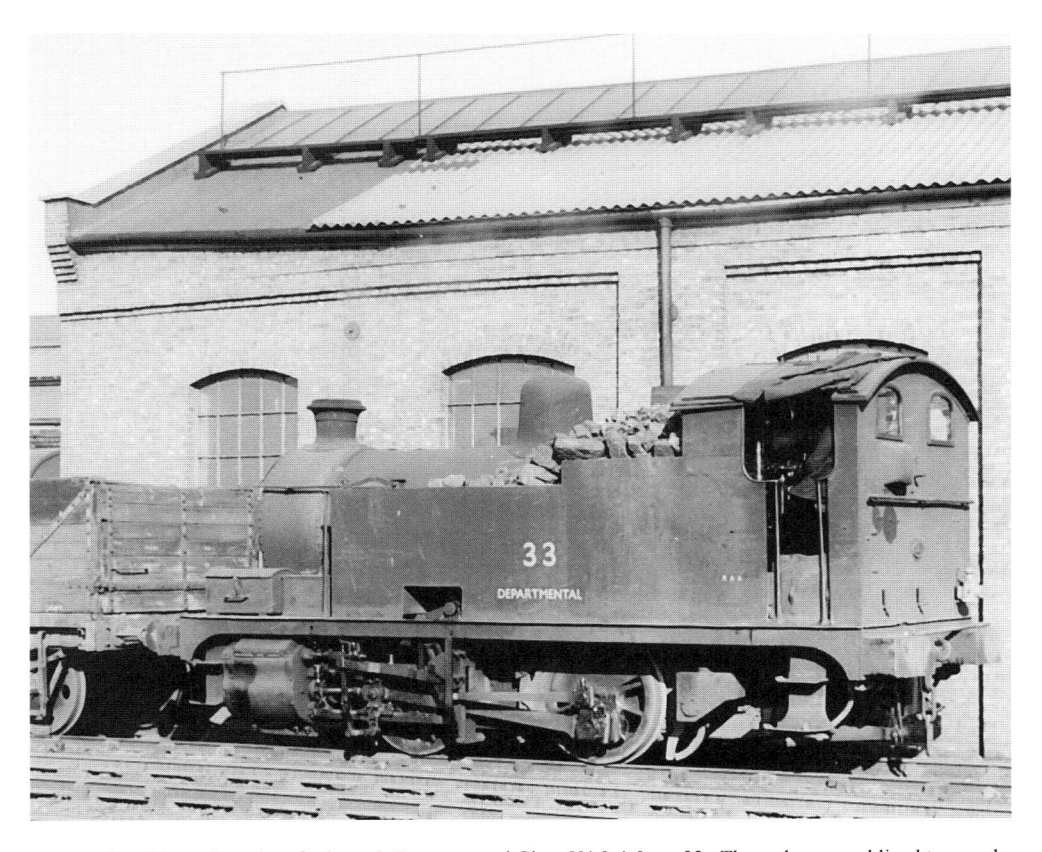

Outside the Old Works at Stratford stands Departmental Class Y4 0-4-0 no. 33. The author was obliged to spend his first week on this engine after being officially passed for Fireman's Duties. *(R.C.Riley)*

What a tale I had to tell everyone in our little group when I got back to Hertford the following week. Of course, I embellished my story a little bit so that my 10-minute trip stretched a little further up the main line to half an hour! But as this would have taken me up old George Phillips' beloved Brentwood Bank (and I could not describe it to him), I believe he easily saw through my romancing, but he played along so as not to embarrass me in front of my mates!

A Passed Cleaner

Although I, and some of my regular mates, was officially passed for fireman's duties, we continued to receive cleaner's rates of pay unless we actually performed the duties of a fireman – known as a Firing Turn. There were just two ways in which a cleaner could aspire to a regular fireman's wage:

This view of Class B1 4-6-0 no. 61135 is similar to the sight that greeted the author as he waited on the platform at Stratford to relieve the fireman of an Ipswich to London express during May 1956. This photograph was taken on 1/6/57.

The first was to accumulate a particular number of Firing Turns - 272 represented one Firing Year. Once you reached this total you were automatically paid as a First Year Fireman, even though you were still awaiting promotion to full fireman's status.

The second way was to be officially appointed as a fireman, which meant your name appeared on the Weekly Roster, which contained all the daily duties of footplate staff in the depot. Each shift was usually for the complete week and operated in a cycle covering several weeks. There were two Rosters – called Links – which covered goods and passenger train duties as well as duties within the Shed.

A newly appointed fireman usually started off in the Goods Link.

The payment system

A First-Year Fireman's basic pay was roughly twice that of a cleaner, so there was quite a difference. In addition to the basic pay, a fireman almost always received premium payments for shift-work and overtime. There was usually ample opportunity for working your Rest day, which also carried a premium payment.

Although the working week for footplate staff was 44 hours, made up of 8-hour shifts with no half-days, the work cycle was based on one day off a fortnight. Of course, Sundays were not counted as part of the normal working week but, as there was a requirement for staff, albeit much reduced, some Sunday working was obligatory. For this you were paid at the rate of time-and-three-quarters of the normal rate.

The Rest day cycle should have operated by a forward movement once a fortnight, i.e. Tuesday, Wednesday. Thursday etc., although in practice I found the system to be quite erratic. However, I also found the Shedmaster very accommodating on the rare occasions I particularly asked for time off. This may have been partly in appreciation of my willingness to work overtime and Rest days when requested.

It would be another 15 months before I gained promotion to the Goods Link as a regular fireman, until then I would be at everyone's beck-and-call for whatever job needed to be done. Mind you, I found the variety quite interesting and gained useful knowledge.

I was there to grab every opportunity to add to my tally of Firing Turns and looked forward to the day when I could kiss goodbye to cleaner's wages.

Until then I continued with cleaner's duties which, after my 16th birthday, underwent a change of working pattern which included night working.

Nightshift duties

In addition to the 8 till 5 day shift, I was frequently required to work nights, which was from 10pm to 6am. Of course, I was paid extra on these occasions, which was at time-and-a-quarter the normal rate.

I didn't do much cleaning on the night shift, I was more of an assistant to the duty fireman in checking fires and boiler water levels on the engines throughout the night, until each crew signed on in the morning and took charge of their allocated engine.

The thing I looked forward to most on this shift was the possibility of one of the early-morning firemen failing to report for work. In this event I would be called upon to take his place, which often led to some welcome overtime!

It didn't always work in my favour, because it often happened that the regular fireman had simply overslept and, as long as he arrived before our train left the platform, he would normally be allowed to take over. I was usually a bit peeved over this, as I had already done all the dirty work in preparing the engine. This meant gathering the necessary tools and cans of oil, trimming and filling the oil lamps, tidying up the cab, filling the water tank and sandboxes, making up the fire, filling the oil reservoirs on the mechanical lubricator and Westinghouse Air Pump etc. The driver and fireman each had their own checklist of components to be inspected and tested on the locomotive before taking it off the Shed. Roughly about 45 minutes was allowed in which to prepare an engine for the road. During the winter months an extra 15 minutes would be allowed to steam-heat the coaches of the train for the comfort of passengers.

Engine Preparation duties

One of the less pleasant workings was the 2.40 a.m. turn, when 2 engines had to be prepared ready for the road before working the first passenger train of the day which left at 4.24 a.m.

It could be quite a chore scrabbling around finding sufficient tools to equip each locomotive with the minimum requirements which, as far as I remember, were as follows:

1 metal bucket / 1 monkey wrench / 1 hammer / a set of 3 spanners / 1 flare-lamp / 1 gauge lamp / 3 headlamps (filled with kerosene and trimmed) / 1 coal pick / 1 firing shovel / 1 oilcan / a set of 3 fire-cleaning irons / 2 spare gauge glasses / 1 handbrush / 1 tin containing 12 warning detonators and 2 red flags.   Plus the usual issues of oil and paraffin.   If you were lucky, most of this equipment would already be on board, but if you were on a late-morning shift, you would invariably find that your engine had already been 'cannibalised'.

On locomotive types that had the rear-wheel sandboxes in the cab, almost always you would find a couple of gauge-glasses kept in one of them.

A padlock fitted to the toolbox gave some security to the smaller items, but it would not be long before it was broken into, often by the regular crew who had lost their key!

The preparation included filling the Westinghouse air-pump piston reservoir with oil, filling the mechanical lubricator with oil and ensuring that the drip-feeds were functioning properly.   Top up the sandboxes (horrible job) and check that the sanders were working, test injectors, air pump, water gauges and other instruments. Check coal supplies in the bunker, ensure smokebox door was closed tight and sweep off any ashes from around it. Make up the fire, ensure sufficient steam and water, top up water tanks, sweep the cab floor and tidy up in general.   During this time, the driver would have been round the engine, checking that she was roadworthy by clouting various nuts, bolts and cranks with a large hammer (making sure nothing had worked loose), filling various oilboxes and oiling numerous moving parts.

The worst day was Monday morning when, in addition to all the aforementioned, there would be the thick layer of oily soot to clean off the cabfront following the Sunday night 'lighting-up'.

Late once too often!

Generally speaking, oversleeping was an occupational hazard, as I myself would experience as time went by.   It was far more prevalent among firemen than drivers, probably because, being young and fancy free, they indulged in a lot more nightlife during their leisure time!

However, I remember one particular fireman who was notorious for turning up late after all the preparation had been completed by the night cleaner.   He would either turn up just before the engine left the Shed or be waiting on the platform as his engine was backing on to the train.   His first name was George.

On this particular morning Ted Osborne, his regular driver, was in a really bad mood, saying it was the third morning that week that George had overslept.
Anyway, we hooked up on to our train, which I believe was due to leave at 5.24 a.m. I cannot be sure of the time of year but it was not yet full daylight on this occasion. Departure time came with still no sign of George. Our N7 tank was bunker first to London, so I was on the platform side of the engine. The guard showed his green light and I called *"Right Away"* across the cab to Ted.

The filth and grime typical of depots at the end of steam is evident in this photograph of N7 69688 beside an equally dirty L1 no. 67715, at Hertford MPD in 1960.

Just as we were pulling out I glanced up the track and saw George hurrying up from the direction of the Shed, where he had obviously parked his bicycle.
As we were only travelling at walking-pace, he was fully expecting me to hop off and let him climb aboard. *"There's George up ahead"*. I shouted across to Ted. *"Do you want the overtime?"* he shouted back. *"Yes!"* I replied quick as a flash.
With that Ted wound the reversing screw into its lowest gear and heaved the regulator wide open. Almost immediately, what had been a walking-pace became a brisk gallop and poor old George's outstretched hand was unable to grab

53

the handrail in time and we left him standing by the side of the track!   *"Serves him b****** right!"* was all Ted had to say on the matter.

The outcome was that I gained a few hours overtime and another Firing Turn, and poor old George probably lost a day's pay.   I don't know if his timekeeping improved after that!

Locomotive Disposal duties

Another job I used to get on the night shift was occasionally 'disposing' of an engine, often so as the fireman could get a quick pint in the pub across the road before closing time.   Now, disposal could be a real messy job.

The main tasks were cleaning the fire, shovelling fine cinders out of the smokebox and raking out the ashpan underneath the engine.

The first of these jobs was to clean the fire.   This was done with the aid of a steel shovel (called a 'slice') with a long handle finished with an 'eyehook' at the end. For the N7s I guess it was about 6 feet long.   There were also a couple of other implements to assist in breaking up the clinker on the firegrate.   These were called a 'pricker' and a 'bent dart', the latter one of which was curved to enable clinker to be levered from underneath the firehole door at the back-end of the firebox.

Ideally, when the engine comes on Shed, the heat of the fire should have cooled to a dull red glow and have burned down to just a few shovelfulls of burning coals.

The technique was to use the long-handled slice to move the live fire to one side of the firebox and, with the aid of the tools mentioned, break up and shovel out the clinker from the opposite side.   Then the live fire is transferred across to the now clean firebars while the other half is cleaned.

Whilst the operation sounds fairly straightforward, there was quite an art to it.

Firstly, the steel shaft of the slice became very hot as soon as it entered the firebox through the firehole door.   Although it kept tolerably cool at the opposite end, it was essential to use a thick pad of waste cloth to protect the other hand that would be sliding up and down the shaft during the act of drawing it in and out of the firebox.

The blade of the slice would quickly become red hot and, if there were a large fire or you left it too long in the firebox, it would become white hot and start to bend like a lump of plastacine.   If that were allowed to happen it became very difficult to slide the blade beneath the clinker on the firegrate, it would just curl up like a wood shaving.   To rapidly cool the blade, you would dangle it below the cab steps where the injector overflow pipe was situated and turn on the cold water to run over it.

Another hazard was the high risk of scraping your knuckles on the back of the very confined cab when drawing the slice out of the firebox.   Many times I have skinned my knuckles between the metal ring at the end of the long handle and the protruding toolbox fixed to the back end of the cab.

A further danger to watch out for was the risk of injury to a colleague who may be walking by just as you are throwing out a shovelfull of red-hot clinker. Although it was general practice to shout out just before commencing operations, you didn't usually call out every time. However, whenever you walked by a locomotive, you automatically kept eyes and ears open for the unexpected, so accidents of this nature were quite rare.

Finally, the live fire is pushed forward against the tubeplate and a small amount of fresh coal is added

Having cleaned the fire, the next job was to empty the smokebox of sooty ash.

Before opening the smokebox door at the front, it was usual practice to make sure the steam-operated 'blower' was sufficiently open enough to prevent a backdraught of the fire filling the cab with smoke. The 'blower' was a steam-operated device that created a draw on the fire to ensure it burnt bright and kept the cab clear of smoke, fumes and flames.

The direction of the wind was also an important factor to take into account when shovelling out this fine ash. It was not very pleasant to have it blown back into your face and eyes. It was absolutely essential to check where your driver was before throwing this stuff around, you would be in deep trouble if he received a faceful of ash while he was making his inspection of the mechanical parts!

The normal wooden-handled firing shovel was used to empty out the smokebox. Having done that job and swept loose ash off the front of the engine and from around the asbestos sealing-ring of the smokebox rim, the door would be tightly closed again.

Finally, the ashpan underneath had to be raked out. This was ideally done while the engine was standing over an Inspection (ash) Pit, which was usually the case when on Shed. The ashpan 'dampers' (flaps) would be opened at both ends of the pan and cleaning involved using another long-handled iron (an 'ashpan rake') which had a half-circular flat piece welded at right-angles to the end. This was inserted in one end of the ashpan and the debris pushed out at the other end. It was important to ensure any wind was at your back to avoid getting smothered, but there were times when it was unpredictable and I have often climbed out of the pit smothered in fine, white ash and looking like a snowman!

After these jobs were finished, and the driver had finished his inspection, the engine would be moved round into the Coal Road to allow the coalman to replenish the coal-bunker ready for the following days work.

Having ensured the fire was sufficiently 'banked up' and the dampers closed, the boiler water level up near the full mark, cylinder drain cocks fully open and the handbrake screwed hard on, my job was finished. It was usually cup-of-tea time before making my way home.

Night-life on Shed

When on the night shift, the cleaner's duties included assisting the fireman in making regular checks on the fire, steam and boiler water levels on the engines. As the Shed was located in a residential area it was essential to keep noise levels to an absolute minimum. Of course, some noise was unavoidable and I guess the locals got used to that, but the deafening noise of an engine letting off steam at the safety valves was just too much, especially after midnight!

On night shift the cleaner was allowed to join the duty driver and fireman in their rest-room, which was brightly lit with fluorescent strip lighting and furnished with Formica topped, wipe-clean tables and tubular chairs with wooden seats and backrests.

After the Shed had been 'shunted', i.e. all the engines shuffled into the correct departure order for the following morning, a comparative silence settled over the shed for a few hours before the first morning crew signed on duty just after 2.30 a.m. Apart from the simmering of the locomotive fleet, the only other sound may be the coalman at work topping up the engine bunkers from the wagons parked in the Coal Road.

Coaling was done directly from these wagons, firstly by throwing the large lumps into the bunker by hand and then, when you had dug down to floor level, a wide-bladed coal shovel was used. Some of these lumps of coal were absolutely enormous and could weigh several stone, but the coalmen were muscular fellows and threw them across into the bunker with ease.

As a fireman out on the main line, I occasionally had reason to curse their strength. I would be putting a few shovelfulls round the firebox when suddenly a huge, solid lump of coal would slide into the coalhole, completely blocking it.

Then it was a case of bashing away at it with the coal pick until it finally started to break up into small enough pieces to be shovelled into the firebox.

This was a far from easy task as there was very little room in the cab of an N7 to swing a coal-hammer.   While this was going on, the fire might be dying down with the inevitable drop in steam pressure, then some extra effort would be called for to recover the situation.

A very frightened coalman

I remember one of the regular coalmen was a huge coloured chap by the name of Joe Macfarlane.   Joe was a very likeable chap and, because of his friendly nature, he was allowed into the Enginemen's rest-room during the night to cook his meal on the electric stove.

This all sounds ordinary, but Joe's meal comprised a tin of Kit-E-Kat cat meat and some rice all mixed up in a saucepan which gave off a very pungent 'fishy' smell!

Nonetheless, Joe always enjoyed it and his enormous strength was testimony enough that this diet did him no harm at all.

Normal practice was that when the coalman had finished loading the engine nearest the wagon, he would come over and knock on the window for one of the crew to move it away and bring the next one up.

 One night, old Joe had the fright of his life. This is how it happened:

While Joe was busy coaling the engine we had positioned for him, we were in the rest room with the lights out, having a quiet snooze.   Suddenly, we were awakened by an almighty crash.

On this particular occasion, instead of waking us up, Joe decided to move it himself.   After all, it looked easy enough, many times he had seen one of the engine crew wind the gear forward and open the regulator slightly, move the engine forward a few feet and stop, so what could be easier! So Joe got on to the engine and pulled the lever. What he hadn't realised was that, due to the time it takes for steam to reach the cylinders to create motion, the regulator had to be closed again well before the engine actually moved. He didn't know this and, because the engine failed to move straight away, he pulled the regulator open even wider! Suddenly, the engine shot forward and crashed into another engine parked a few yards farther on. Joe had leapt out of the cab just before impact.

When we ran outside we found the engine, still with steam on, trying to push the others along in front of it. At the far end of the shed, the leading engine's driving wheels were hard up against the upward curve of the rail-ends, and the overhanging bufferbeam had altered the shape somewhat of one of the Fitter's benches along the end wall. Apart from that, no real damage was done and peace was quickly restored.

We found poor old Joe huddled into a corner of his little cabin quivering like a jelly and muttering profound apologies. Once he had been assured that all was well, he slowly returned to normal and told us what had happened.

Needless to say, Joe never again tried to move an engine!

Gentleman Charlie

Another of the coaling staff I recall was Charlie, he too was coloured but, whereas Joe was tall, Charlie was a short, tubby man and an absolute gentleman. Like Joe, he was also as strong as an ox and had a lovely sense of humour. He laughed at everything, even if it wasn't particularly funny! Later on, Charlie was successful in obtaining a job as a Guard on goods trains and I remember waving to him on more than one occasion.

One day, sad news came through that Charlie had been killed in an accident in Silvertown Tunnel on the North Woolwich line. It was said that a coupling on his train broke and, during the operation of reconnecting the train in the darkness of the tunnel, he was trapped between the two portions.

As testimonial to his popularity, a huge number of mourners attended Charlie's funeral.

In relating this sad tale, I am reminded of a very close call in Broxbourne goods yard that almost brought my railway career to a premature end.

A near-fatal error

I had just finished my shift on the 7.08 am turn which was the Broxbourne shunting job in the Up Yard. Our relief had arrived and I just had time to nip across the tracks to catch a train back to Hertford, which I could see just arriving at the Down platform.

From where our engine was standing, there were several tracks to cross before reaching the Signalbox that was adjacent to the platform ends (this was the original station before it was resited further to the north). Without looking either way I dashed across the tracks and through the gaps between the wagons. I was completely oblivious to the fact that another engine was also involved in shunting in the same yard. Suddenly, a voice from somewhere (probably a Shunter) shouted a warning and I instinctively ducked and leapt clear of the track I was crossing. The steel buffers of the two wagons I had just ran between clanged together in the space where my head had been a fraction of a second earlier.

I was never that careless again, although I did get caught out in another way in the same yard a few months later, this time it was in a Guard's Van.

Hertford East based N7 no. 69682 runs past the Signalbox at Broxbourne station in 1957. On the left, preparations are under way for the construction of the new station.

A nutcracker in the Guard's van

On this occasion, were on the same turn and happened to be stationary at the bottom of the yard when the late-morning local freight train from the Hertford branch drew into the arrival loop. It stopped with the Guards brake van alongside us and, as we knew the Guard, my driver and I climbed into his van for a chat. Shortly after, the train started to move and, although I stood up ready to go, my mate and the Guard remained seated. The next thing I knew, I was flying through the air until my head came into contact with the iron pillar supporting the brake-wheel at the other end of the van.

It was my first experience of being in a Guards van of a loose-coupled train when it starts and stops suddenly. It's as though the van was at the end of a piece of elastic that stretched and then let go just like a catapult!

Both the Guard and my mate had a good laugh at my expense while I ended up with a lump on my forehead the size of a duck egg.

A grubby Class L1 no. 67732 waits hopefully by the coal wagons in Hertford Loco sometime during 1957. At this date 67732 would have been working out from Stratford so she is unlikely to be 'fed' from Hertford's coal supplies!

Broxbourne Goods Yard

During the 1950s Broxbourne was a pretty busy yard that handled traffic from all the way up the line as far as Cambridge, so shunting operations went on for 24 hours a day. In the normal run of things, shunting was traditionally the work of Tank Engines equipped with 'ratchet lever' type reversing gear but strangely, most of Broxbourne's shunting was performed with 0-6-0 Tender Engines, usually of classes J15, J17, and J19. Consequently, all forward and reversing movements had to be carried out by turning the screw-type-reversing wheel, this could place quite a strain on the arm muscles - particularly if the engine had just been overhauled when all the mechanism would be stiff.

In addition, at least one shift was used to 'run in' various locomotives that had undergone major overhaul in Stratford Works – a practice I was well aware of from my schoolday expeditions to Broxbourne station.

As we had no tender engines based at Hertford, all the locomotives used for shunting originated from Stratford and eventually returned there during the course of 24 hours, except for one, which worked the local goods to Hertford during the afternoon. This engine later worked the evening goods from Hertford to Temple Mills Yards at Stratford, which I will mention more of later.

The fireman's view from the footplate of Hertford's station pilot, Class J69 0-6-0 no.68600. She has just come off shed and is waiting for the signalman to change the points - seen directly in front of the smokebox – which will allow access along the Great Northern branch to resume station shunting duties.

CHAPTER THREE

Tales of the Buntingford Branch

The Buntingford Branch has been closed many years since, but it was a lovely little line and I hold many happy memories of my trips on it.
However, there was one grade of staff for whom some memories would be far from happy – the job of the poor old engine cleaner.

Buntingford – a Cleaner's nightmare!

During my months as a Passed Cleaner, I gained experience on most, if not all, the work covered by Hertford men, which included work on the Buntingford Branch, although there were two sets of crew based at Buntingford who worked solely on the Branch.   Although there were two N7's allocated to Buntingford, only one at a time was actually based there.   The other one, if not undergoing washout or repair, would operate as part of the Hertford stud.
Buntingford was a single line branch and was operated on a token-key system. There were passing loops at Hadham and Braughing.

One of the Passed Cleaner's jobs was a night turn at Buntingford Sub-shed.   He would be responsible for looking after the duty engine overnight, which was normally either 69633 or 69634, by maintaining the fire and boiler water level, as well as replenishing the engine's bunker and tanks with coal and water.
Both these locomotives were fitted with a special steam pump, which was used to pump water from a well up into the main water tank situated on a brick plinth next to the Signalbox.   This was also one of the duty cleaner's tasks.
With all this, I don't think the rate of pay was any higher than that of a normal cleaner, apart from the additional night-work rate.
As the minimum age for night-work was 16 years, and many of the jobs were allocated on a seniority basis – i.e. the shorter serving staff got the worse jobs! – I was never asked to cover this shift. I was not sorry to miss the experience as I used to hear tales of how eerie that place could be on a dark winter's night, particularly if the local lads were in a devilish mood!

I am reminded of one occasion when a fellow cleaner - 'Tiddler Deards' - was on duty when one of the firemen I have already mentioned, Herbie Howard, came out of the *Shah of India* pub at closing time.
Herbie crept down to the Cleaner's cabin in the darkness where Tiddler was sleeping, tiptoed through the open door, and put his hands around Tiddler's neck.
Well, poor old Tiddler went berserk and Herbie had to keep shouting *"It's alright Tiddler –it's Herbie!"*   He had to repeat this several times before the poor man calmed down.   I suspect the result of his foolish act must also have put one almighty scare into Herbie, too!   Unlike one cleaner I recall who packed the job in on account of his scary experiences on the Buntingford night shift, after steam

ended, Tiddler remained on the railway in the Track Maintenance Department right up to his recent retirement.

A rather fuzzy photograph taken from the top of the water tank at Buntingford showing the engine servicing road with the station in the distance. N7 69634's coalbunker is being replenished. Another N7 stands in front of 69634 which means one of them is probably working the daily Goods Train.

Finding time to sleep

When young firemen and cleaners were on night duty, it was not uncommon to go without sleep during the daytime if it interfered with our leisure activities!

We knew we would make it up some time later on. When that time came, even an earthquake wouldn't wake us. There was a period when I was on night duty when workmen were drilling the road up right outside our house.

Mother was concerned that it would interrupt my rest during the day. She needn't have worried, as soon as I got tucked between the sheets I went out like a light – road-drills notwithstanding!

Tiddler's 'lost day'

I think the record for sleeping went to Tiddler Deards one week when he was on the Buntingford late shift.

Late one afternoon I was riding passenger to Broxbourne to start my shift along with a young Passed Cleaner who was covering a Rest-day turn at Buntingford.

As we pulled into Ware station, the door swung open and in jumped Tiddler Deards in his overalls and carrying his lunchbag. The conversation between Tiddler and the Passed Cleaner (I can't recall his name) went something along these lines :

P.C. *"Hullo Tiddler, what are you doing today then?"*
Tiddler. *"Buntingford – what about you?"*
P.C. *"You can't be – it's your rest -day and I'm covering for you."*
Tiddler. *"Nah, you've got it wrong, my rest-day's tomorrow – Wednesday."*
P.C. *"Today is Wednesday – I had to cover for you yesterday 'cos you didn't turn up for work."*

It transpired that Tiddler had slept twice round the clock! He later found out that his mother – on seeing how tired he was – hadn't the heart to wake him the previous afternoon.

Buntingford drivers and their engines

There was 3 footplate staff that I can remember, they were Tom Gray, Tom Sydney and Arthur Sullivan. I think one of them may have been a fireman at the time, but I don't remember who the other fireman was.

The regular engines were 69633 and 69634. Of the two, 69633 was the most cared-for one, with 69634 just standing in on wash-out and repair days.

The crews kept 69633 in immaculate condition, including all the brass and copper pipework and fittings. Even the tools were kept in pristine condition, although the crew made sure they were not left on the engine when it was sent to Hertford for servicing. Instead, they were replaced with the roughest tools imaginable, which was often a nuisance when trying to clean out the firebox with a slice that was curled up at the blade end!

Hadham Bank

The only difficult section on the outward journey from St. Margaret's to Buntingford was the short, sharp climb up Hadham Bank, encountered immediately after leaving Hadham Station. It could (and often did) catch out the unprepared fireman who had failed to ensure he had a full head of steam and a bright fire at the start.

It was considered amateurish to have to stop for a 'blow-up' on Hadham Bank due to shortage of steam. Fortunately, I never got caught out.

Once over the top of the Bank, it was a gentle, 2-mile coast downhill into Standon Station.

On the return journey, the climb from Standon to the top of Hadham Bank was far less severe and I don't ever remember anyone being caught out through lack of steam in this direction. Once over the top of the Bank your train built up a tremendous speed under it's own momentum on the downhill dash of about a mile into Hadham Station.

I remember one particular morning in March 1959 when my mate was Pete Nolan, who was one of Hertford's senior firemen recently qualified for driving duties.

Pete lived in the Hadham area and that morning we did the usual dash down the bank and ran particularly fast into Hadham Station to impress Pete's fiancé who was one of the many passengers waiting on the platform.

We overshot the platform by the entire length of our 3-coach train and had to reverse back. Pete was rather embarrassed and his young lady was far from impressed! Pete's fiancé completely ignored him when she got off the train at St. Margaret's!

A fright at Westmill

On another occasion we took a late train into Buntingford and then, as usual on this particular turn, we returned engine-only to Hertford. With the knowledge that the quicker we got back to Hertford the sooner we would finish, we never hung about after we had unhooked our train at Buntingford. As soon as we got the signal, we were away pretty sharpish.

The next station up the line was Westmill, which had a level crossing. This crossing was rarely used by road traffic and the gates were usually left in favour of the railway, the station Porter controlled them.

A short distance out of Buntingford was a Distant signal operated by the Porter/Signalman at Westmill. If it was in the 'Off' position, we knew we had a clear run through the station. If however, it stood at 'Caution' then there was the possibility that the gates may not be open for us. That said, it was common practice for the Porter not to bother with the Distant signal – even though he had the gates open in our favour.

On this occasion a road vehicle had probably crossed the line since we had passed through with our train because the Distant signal was at 'Caution'. It wasn't until we gave the mandatory whistle on the approach to Westmill that the Porter remembered the gates and as we rounded the curve, we could see him frantically swinging the first of the 2 gates clear of the line. There was little chance of us stopping in time although my mate slammed the brakes on straight away. Fortunately, we slowed just enough to allow him to swing the second gate clear and we saw the mixed look of fear and relief on his face as we sped by in the growing darkness.

He (and we) were lucky that time, but I did hear of at least one occasion when Westmill's crossing gates ended up adorning the front of a light engine returning to Hertford, probably on a similar working!

Sheep at Widford

Then there was the time we ran into a flock of sheep just outside Widford Station.

It was another morning commuter train en-route for St. Margaret's and we were just getting into our stride after making a smart getaway from the station. As we passed under the road bridge and around the gentle curve, there was a flock of sheep in the cutting wandering all over the track.

My mate applied the brakes sharply and we stopped pretty quickly, but not before we had run into them. I had not realised until then just how stupid sheep could be. Although we had unfortunately killed some of them - at least one of which was mangled up in the cranks and rods beneath the boiler of our engine - the rest of the flock proceeded to wander between and under the coaches of our train. They were completely oblivious, or unconcerned, as to the fate that had befallen some of their flock!

Anyway, with the Guard's help, we ushered the living back behind our train toward the station, our efforts causing some amusement amongst the passengers leaning out of the windows. Eventually, we continued our journey to St. Margaret's.

The Station Porter meanwhile, had phoned for a vet and, presumably, the farmer.

There was a not unpleasant aroma of roasting lamb as we drew to a halt in the bay platform at St. Margaret's! Our engine was in such a state that we had to have a replacement despatched from Hertford while ours was taken back for cleaning underneath.

I was awfully glad I wasn't a duty cleaner on Shed that day!

A few years later a diesel railcar had a similar accident at the same spot, on that occasion 19 sheep were killed.

'Poaching' tales

Being a country branch line, it was inevitable that one would see a lot of wildlife alongside the line, we particularly looked out for rabbits and pheasants.

In my spare moments I used to be ready with a lump of coal to shy at any pheasants that our passage happened to disturb. I never did get any, even on the rare occasion that I did score a hit, it would perhaps stagger for a few feet, then fly off as if nothing had happened!

I have often wondered what geologists, centuries from now, will make of the large amounts of coal that they dig up in the fields that bordered the line?

There was one hot summer's day when a startled pheasant flew into our cab, unfortunately I had the firedoor open and it went straight in. It was reduced to cinders in the blink of an eye. It was not uncommon to arrive at the end of the line to find a dead pheasant lying on the front bufferbeam of your engine.

Personally, I never fancied eating one - even if my mother had been willing to prepare it – which I very much doubt she would!

Although the line had rabbits in abundance, the only way they could be caught was either by snares or shotgun.

The regular Buntingford-based drivers on the line were past masters at catching both rabbits and pheasants. I know at least one of them normally carried a shotgun in the cab and thought nothing of stopping his train, passenger or goods, in order to jump over the fence to retrieve a shot rabbit or pheasant.

To my knowledge nobody, passenger or landowner, ever complained of these activities. The crews were well-known figures in the community, in fact, the whole line seemed to have a marvellous 'family' atmosphere about it.

VIP treatment

One of the peculiarities of a country branch line was the special treatment afforded to regular travellers. Station staff got to know every one of their 'regulars' by name and should one of them be delayed in arriving at the station in time to catch his or her train, why, it would wait until he or she appeared!

However, even this practice could be stretched too far occasionally – retired driver John Tarry told the following tale to me when he was a fireman on one of the morning trains en-route to St. Margarets many years ago.

They were waiting at Hadham station for one of the local gentry to arrive to board the train – he was late that morning. The fireman's side of the engine was nearest the platform and after a while John's driver, Vic Finch, called across asking John what the delay was. *"Apparently, we're waiting for Mr. So-and-So."* John replied. Vic made it clear he was not going to wait all day, so John waved to the Guard asking for the 'Right Away'. *"You can't go yet!"* Protested Signalman/Porter Bert Turner, who was still glancing anxiously up the road for his missing VIP customer. After waiting a few more minutes, enough was enough and the Guard waved his flag and away they went, much to poor old Bert's consternation!

The following morning, on the same train, after they arrived at St. Margarets to meet the connection from Hertford to London, this particular Hadham gentleman walked up to the engine and said to John, *"I didn't catch this train yesterday"*. John replied *"No, you didn't – that's a fact – because I saw you walking up the road as we pulled out."* John then went on to explain that they had a time schedule to maintain and that if they waited at each station every time a passenger was late, it would be chaos.

To give him his due, this gentleman accepted the explanation in good grace and nothing more was said.

A very lucky dog

Yet another incident I can recall on the Buntingford line concerns an animal which, although we ran over it, had a miraculous escape.

We were at the head of a morning passenger train from Buntingford and on the last leg of the journey to St. Margaret's, having just left Mardock Station.

We were on a straight stretch of track and up ahead we could see a little black-and-white terrier dog standing defiantly in the middle of the track and barking at our fast-approaching train for all he was worth!   He obviously belonged to the farm whose house was just off to the right of us.

As we were chimney-first to St. Margaret's I opened the cylinder cocks, which instantly squirted loudly hissing jets of steam onto the track directly ahead of us.

But there was no frightening this little dog and we were sad to see him disappear under the front of our engine.   '' *He's had it*.'' I shouted across to my mate, who nodded in agreement.

I then happened to glance backward out of the cab and couldn't believe what I saw. This little fellow came tumbling out from beneath the first and second coaches of our train - we must have been travelling at least thirty miles an hour.   The momentum threw him down the shallow, grassy embankment and the last I saw was that he was up on his feet and still yapping away, this time at our rear end. Knowing the conglomeration of brake-rodding etc. that hangs beneath an engine, I am totally mystified to this day how that little dog escaped with his life!

The Oasis at Buntingford

I have some treasured memories of trips to Buntingford, like arriving on a hot summer's day, cleaning the fire and, with 15 minutes to spare before the return trip, diving into the '*Shah of India*' pub adjacent to the station.

Dripping with perspiration I could down two ice-cold pints of shandy in quick succession and still be back on the footplate with minutes to spare!

Days of fame

During the hundred or so years of its existence, this branch experienced the effects of severe snow blockages and wartime bombing, as well as hosting trials of Wickham & Co. railway rolling stock destined for export abroad.   It was also used during the making of at least two films – '*O'Leary Nights*' and '*Operation Bullshine*'.

Sadly, the Buntingford branch closed completely in 1965 and is now just a memory in itself.   Very little remains as evidence of the existence of this picturesque little country branch.

Braughing Station has been lovingly restored - including the original platforms - and is now a private residence.

Buntingford station still survives intact and is used as business premises, also still there is the '*Shah of India* ' pub, although it now has a new name.

Mardock Signalbox was carefully dismantled even before the line closed and was re-erected in the large garden of a private residence in the nearby village of Wareside, where it still stands in all its original glory to this day.   Although the original owner has since moved on, I am informed that the property deeds contain a clause demanding that this old signalbox be permanently maintained in good repair by future owners of the property. I do hope this is a true fact – it certainly appeared in immaculate condition when I drove by during late 1998.   When darkness falls,

the interior of the box is usually lit up, just as though the Signalman is there on duty ready to ensure a safe passage to a train that will never come…..
Several sections of the old trackbed are now public footpaths.
After he retired, driver Tom Gray and his wife ran the *'Fox & Duck'* public house in Buntingford for many years.

The entire history of this line is covered in Peter Paye's fascinating book *'The Buntingford Branch'*.

Earlier, I mentioned Apprentice Fitter George Don who, during his firing days, often worked on the line during the early 1950s. The next chapter of this book was actually written by George, which will give the reader some idea of a footplate crew's routine day at that time.It may be noticed that some of his descriptions of the layout at Hertford MPD differ in some small detail from my own recollections, due to changes that took place during the intervening years.

A steam scene at Buntingford in 1958. Class N7 69683 blows off steam as she waits impatiently to leave with a train for St. Margarets. Beyond the engine's bunker can be glimpsed the office of Moys, the local Coal Merchant.

CHAPTER FOUR

A DAY'S WORK ON THE BUNTINGFORD BRANCH IN 1950

By George Don

The following story is not a history of the Buntingford Branch-line, but simply a typical day's work by the men who operated it in the days of steam.
At the time of this story, the coaching stock was usually made up of 3 ex-GER wooden coaches with First and Third Class compartments, with a Ladies Only compartment next to the Guard's Brake Van.
The Branch was just over 13 miles in length, with eight stations, some of them little more than 'Halts'.
Travellers on the line could enjoy some of the most beautiful views, - particularly during the summer – when the fields would be a riot of colour, protected by hedgerows of Red and White Hawthorn and majestic, towering great trees of Oak, Elm and Birch.
Many pheasants, rabbits and squirrels could be seen, scampering off to hide as the passage of the train intruded on their privacy. You may spot a heron standing like a statue on the bank of a stream – maybe poised to catch a small fish or frog from the water – perhaps undecided whether to move or not. High above in the treetops, much noise is made by the rooks who look down from their lofty perches.
Maybe much of this is still there today, but sadly, unseen by any railway traveller. In 1965, after more than 100 years service to the community, the line was closed and the track torn up.
However, the memories of the line and the men who worked there will long be remembered, as will the steam locomotives like 69693 and many others before. The following chapter describes a day in my life as one of Hertford East's firemen as I recall a turn of duty on the Branch in the winter of 1950.

I apologise for some repetition with in my references to certain tasks, such as turning the injector on and off but, as that was part of the normal routine I felt I should tell it exactly the way it was.

"*Good morning Harry.*" I said to my regular mate, driver Harry Allan.
It was 3.30am on a dark and very cold, wet morning in November 1950. We both stood in the Signing-on Room putting our names on the Duty Sheet, having struggled to work on our bikes against a bitterly cold wind. We did not say much to each other – better that way with some drivers in the early morning!
The Signing-on Room was situated under the water tank at Hertford East Loco Shed which I remember very well. It was approximately 10 feet square with a door leading into the Pump room which housed an electric pump for drawing water from a well and up into the huge tank above. The underside of this tank looked down upon us, which actually formed the ceiling of the Signing-on Room.

There was one large electric light bulb hanging from one of the beams supporting the tank, which gave out a poor, yellowish light owing to the soot and grime on the bulb.

Harry lit a match for his fag and this helped to him to see where to put his name on the Duty Sheet, I then signed alongside his signature.

The engine allocated to us is Class N7 0-6-2 Tank number 69693 – it is our 'regular' engine. Along with the Duty Sheet there may be a report by the driver from the previous evening that, in itself, could be enough to put you off going to work.   The note may say "engine has a knock in the motion - to be dealt with on your return."   Harry would mutter "*Thank you very ****** much*"!

On the walls of the room were diagrams and more Duty Lists along with Permanent Way last-minute notices – temporary restrictions due to track repairs etc. - all to be read within the 15 minutes time that was allowed.

Up in one corner on the floor stood the cans containing measured quantities of the different types of oil we need, plus a small can of paraffin for the lamps.   As the Storeman did not start before 8am these cans would have been put out the previous afternoon for us early starters.

Harry remarks "*We had better get going – I see we have '93* " as we called her – why we referred to engines as 'HER' I don't know.

Harry Allan was a tall, lean man with a crop of silver hair, a thin, pleasant-looking face and a kind way about him.   For some reason, among his fellow drivers, he had the nickname 'Gubby', but I never referred to him by that name.

It was all systems go now as time was ticking away.   As we passed the Messroom (or Shanty as it was nicknamed) we stuck our heads in the doorway to wish the Night-staff a "*Good Morning*". Our words were totally ignored, as they were more or less asleep or maybe even dead going by the amount of smoke coming out of the coal-fired stove!

Cursing the weather, we made our way cautiously towards the Shed to find '93, splashing through puddles containing a mixture of water, oil and coal dust.

There she was in Number One Road standing by the water column.   As we were the first out, she was standing at the end of the row of engines.

There were three roads in the Loco of which two were half inside the Shed under cover with full-length inspection pits between the rails.   Outside, there was only a short pit alongside the water column.   The third road was the Coal Road used for coaling the engines from the wagons that were parked there.

The road could accommodate three wagons of which the side doors would be dropped onto props forming a floor from which the coalman would shovel the coal into the engine's bunkers – not a pleasant job.

Here we are, I put my foot on the bottom step to the cab and, holding on to the handrail with one hand, I swing the other hand containing the cans of oil up and deposit them on the cab floor above me.   Then I pull myself up and step into the dark cab, stumbling over lumps of coal that has spilt onto the floor.   I swing open the firehole door to let a bit of light into the cab and feel my way across to my side of the cab to release the handbrake.   This was always located on the fireman's side and, in the dull glow of the fire, I unwind it.

Then it was back over to the driver's side to check that the cylinder drain-cocks are open, this is a lever placed below the reversing gear.   Winding the engine into reverse, I look down to Harry who is still on the ground waiting to give me directions to 'set' the engine for oiling up.

This setting is very important, as to oil the inside Big-ends and Straps, they have all to be readily accessible when the driver crawls under the boiler to fill the little oil reservoirs incorporated in the top of each one. Setting the engine is done by slowly moving the engine and watching the movement of the side-rods and stopping when they are in a certain position.   From the side-rod position the other parts of the motion can be determined, enabling all the essential oiling points of the engine to be reached without the need for any further movements.

So, with a short warning 'pip' on the whistle, I open the regulator an inch or so then close it almost immediately.   A cloud of wet steam hisses out of the cylinder cocks, hiding my mate from view as we start to move slowly forward.   From below there comes a shout of "*HOLD IT, that'll do George, screw on the handbrake!*"

I dash over to the handbrake, stumbling again over the spilt coal on the floor, and bring the engine to a halt. Harry climbs up and hangs his lunch-bag on the hook on his side of the bunker and re-lights the remains of his roll-up, at the same time setting light to the wick of his flare-lamp.   I had already topped up this lamp with a drop of paraffin. The cans of oil I have placed in the tray above the firehole door so that the heat makes the oil flow easier – essential in the winter months when the cold makes this oil as thick as treacle.   I hand Harry his oil-can ready filled and he disappears off round the front of the engine to commence oiling.

Time for me to sort the fire out so, I turn on the blower – a device that sends a spurt of steam up the chimney – drawing the smoke from the firebox with it. I drag the long-handled shovel (called a Slice) through the front window, where it is stored on top of the water-tank on the fireman's side, and spread the fire evenly over the firebed.   This lights up the cab, making it a bit more cheerful and starts to warm things up a bit – including myself! I put some nice-size lumps of fresh coal round the back corners and a good bit down the sides, giving the firebox a good lining to get on with. The flames are now curling up around the firehole – a beautiful sight only experienced by Locomen.

I now check the boiler water level, clearing any muck out of the gauge-glasses by flicking the bottom stopcocks open and shut in one quick movement.   I see the glass shows the boiler is half full – not bad.

All this I have done while Harry has been oiling the side-rods and topping-up the oil-boxes along the footplate.   This is an example of essential teamwork, as I could not have done these jobs once Harry had gone into the pit underneath our engine.   He would have been *extremely* unhappy to be showered with hot cinders as I raked over the fire, or given a neckful of scalding steam as I blew down the water gauges!

On tank engines there is a steel shovelling plate screwed to the wooden floor and a coal chute with a sliding door to control the amount of coal entering the cab.

Above this, a steel cupboard is fixed to the bunker backplate in which the small tools are stored. These tools include spanners, hammer, a wrench and spare gauge glasses which are held in a small wooden rack riveted to the side of the cupboard.

Most importantly, there is a round tin containing ten detonators and two red flags as warning devices in the event of an accident. For instance, should we become derailed, fouling oncoming lines, the fireman has to run forward and place three detonators on the oncoming track as a warning to stop another train running into us. This action is to protect our train as required by one of the most important instructions in the Railwayman's Rulebook – Rule 55.

If it was dark, the fireman's task would be even more risky as he stumbles and trips over point rodding and signal wires that are lying in wait for him.

Back to the cab, the handle of the sliding door of the coal chute is conveniently wide enough for the blade of the firing shovel to slot into it when not in use. Another important item we have is a coal pick which is needed to cope with the breaking up of very large lumps of coal which block up the coal chute from time to time. This coal pick is stowed between the front damper and sanding levers on the fireman's side of the cab.

Beside the coal chute is kept a small handbrush used for sweeping up the cab floor. Each side of the cab at the bunker end are sandboxes for sanding the rail when necessary whilst travelling bunker first.

The seat on my side is a small, flat piece of wood attached to a metal hinge bolted on to the sandbox. Most times I find it easier to sit on top of the sandbox with one leg up on the small cupboard in front, even though it can be a cold perch in wintertime. The driver's seat is a bit better, being upholstered and about 12 inches square, placed on the boiler-side of the cab doorway next to the reversing lever. On this engine, the driving controls are on the left-hand side of the cab, but there are some engines of the same class that are driven from the right.

Along the full width of the back of the cab there is a shelf above the coal chute upon which we can store a few things. On the driver's side a couple of brackets are fixed to this shelf for holding the round Destination Discs. These flat, steel discs are about the size of a dinner plate and are enamelled white on one side, while on the reverse it has a mauve centre with about an inch wide white border. These discs are placed on brackets located on the front of the engine in a particular sequence, which informs the Signalmen of your destination.

During the hours of darkness, oil lamps would take their place. When running with no train, in addition to a white light at the front, a red lamp must be shown at the back. For this purpose, each engine must carry at least 3 lamps – one containing a purple shade and one a red shade.

Carried on water tank top on my side is a long-handled Slice, a Bent Dart and a Pricker. These are tools for cleaning the fire and to use out on the 'road' to rake through the fire if necessary. All these tools are reached by opening the front window, which swivels on a centre pivot. If the ringed handles of these tools are not dropped over the upright spike on the tank, they can become tangled. Then you have to climb alongside the tank to untangle them.

Standing in the pit beneath the engine, Harry has to squeeze himself between the Straps and Big ends to do the oiling, so we do not take water before he gets out, just in case it overflows. As soon as he has finished oiling underneath, Harry climbs up on the front framing and puts the water-bag in the tank and turns on the water. Seeing the bag in and the water running, I open the Level Indicator in the cab. This is a simple, vertical hollow rod with holes drilled about 3 inches apart all down its length. The top is bent like a walking stick and by giving it a quarter-turn the water runs out of the holes, gradually creeping higher as the water level rises in both tanks via the equalising pipe between the tanks. This may seem a crude indicator method, but it works very well.

During this time, steam pressure has built up so on goes the water injector on my side to top up the boiler. I give the driver's side injector a try just to make sure its working ok. Yes, it's all right so I turn it off again. It is most important to make sure both injectors are working properly before leaving the shed.

Opening the firehole door lights up the whole cab and I proceed to put a few more lumps in the firebox corners. I close the door and open the hinged flap set in the centre, at the same time I drop the front damper down a bit so as not to make steam too fast. I give the cab floor a sweep over and turn off the injector, seeing that the boiler is now ¾ full.

During this time I have also filled the Hydrostatic Lubricator with Black oil. This lubricator is located on top of the toolbox beside the boiler on my side of the cab, its purpose is to feed oil to the steam cylinders.

Picking up the wrench-spanner and the can of Black oil, I climb down and turn off the water just before it overflows. On to the front footplate, I ease out the water bag and close the filler lid. While I am up here, the Westinghouse air pump has to be oiled – this pump is bolted to the side of the smokebox. The oil reservoir is sited on top of the pump and has a drain cock near the base to drain off accumulated water. Having done this, I remove the screw top, fill up with fresh Black oil, replace the cap and tighten it up. The pump is commonly referred to as a Donkey and its purpose is to provide compressed air to operate the engine brakes and the brakes of the train if they are Westinghouse-braked stock. The normal required pressure is 95 lbs. psi.

This done, I check that the smokebox door is closed tight. If it happened to come open while on the move it would cause a 'blowback' of smoke and flames from the firebox into the cab which could cause serious injury to the crew.

Satisfied that everything is all right, I make my way back onto the footplate, squeezing between the water column and engine, wading through dirty black water and climbing over a heap of burning ashes lying alongside us. Up I climb into the cab – back to the warmth of the footplate – with a sigh of relief, as its damn cold out there.

Harry is putting the last of the axlebox trimmings into the brass oilbox pipe outlets. These are worsted wool trimmings that siphon the oil down the pipes to the axleboxes. On this engine, one large brass oilbox placed each side of the cab contains three outlet pipes.

Looking at his watch, Harry remarks *"Its time we weren't here"*.

Opening the Donkey pump steam valve, the pump roars into life, panting like mad at the start, then gradually slowing down as the air pressure begins to build.

A warning toot on the whistle and Harry opens the regulator just enough to move us down to the Shed Exit phone box. I jump down taking two lighted lamps with me, placing a white light on the front and a red one on the bunker bracket. The telephone is located in a wooden box fixed to a lamppost and is a direct line to the Signalman. This phone has probably been there from the year dot and to get the Signalman's attention, I have to crank a small handle and wait for him to answer. If it was raining you could get very wet waiting for him to answer your call. This system is common throughout the railway network, with telegraph lines carried on poles 60ft apart.

The Signalman picks up the phone and I wish him *"Good morning"* – possibly he has been having a doze since his last call – and inform him that we are ready to depart the Shed to pick up our train. After we collect our coaches we will run empty to St. Margarets Station to work the first passenger train of the day to Buntingford.

Not much speech from the Signalman, just the twang of a wire moving, followed by a couple of thumps from the ground signal as it shows a green light in our direction. The points out onto the mainline have already been set to allow the Shed Staff to move engines about in the Loco, sorting them in the correct order for their next turn of duty. Normally, if you passed this ground signal at red, you would drop off the end of the track through the open 'catch' points.

Returning to the engine, my mate just about has dried out from getting wet while oiling up.

Giving him the OK to move out as I climb back into the cab there is a hiss of air as the brake releases and Harry opens the regulator, moving us off into the darkness to the next ground signal. We stop as we pull out on to the Up Main and await a green line from the ground signal.

Incidentally, this type of signal is known as a 'DOD' – I don't know why!

The points change with a hefty thump and the Dod clunks from red to green. Harry puts the engine into fore gear – another hiss of air as he flicks the brake release valve – and opens the regulator. As we pass the Shed Staff Mess-room, Harry opens the cylinder cocks briefly, kicking up quite a noise just to annoy the dozing staff!

Having found our carriages in the siding, our shunter, Ernie Newton, calls us on with a 'half-white' light on his handlamp. We gently touch the buffers of the first carriage and Harry squeezes the engine right up to them as Ernie climbs between and couples up the train. A few minutes go by then out comes Ernie and climbs up onto the footplate with a cheery *"Good Morning"*. He heads straight for the fire to warm himself, saying how cold it is out there.

Well, we have to leave as our ground signal is giving us a green light, so off goes Ernie, dropping over the side clutching his handlamp as he goes.

Up comes the Guard moaning about the weather and everything else – and he hasn't even had to prepare an engine in the rain – that's the difference between them and us!

"*Got the 'vac', driver?*" he shouts.   "*Yes*" replies Harry. "*Right then, I will give you a light when I get into the Brake van*" the Guard says.   A vacuum ('vac') is created in the train pipe to release the carriage brakes, the amount of vacuum needed is 21 inches.

The Guard gives us the green light and Harry sets the train in motion with a jerk of the regulator handle. I had put the injector on a little earlier, so off with that, at the same time opening the ashpan dampers to allow air beneath the firebed.   The fire is doing well. With such a light load of 3 coaches, this fire will take us to St. Margarets just 4 miles down the road, and then I will give the firebox a good lining.

 I see Harry is trying to light up another fag against the wind blowing through the cab.   The trouble is, it is hand-rolled with not much tobacco and is so thin that his lighter burns most of it up before it takes a hold.

Out of the siding we go, passing the Signalbox on my side – as we are travelling bunker first – I give the Signalman a wave. We have a good head of steam so on goes the carriage steam-heating to cheer up our Guard and to warm the compartments for any passengers we might get.

The Hydrostatic Lubricator needs to be checked now to make sure it is oiling the cylinders now that things are warming up around the 'front end'.   The oil can be seen through a row of small, round sight glasses.   Small globules of oil passing up through the water inside these 'spy holes' tell me it is working okay.   This being all right, I take a glance outside as we approach Ware Outer Home signal. Passing over the open Meads between Hertford and Ware in winter is very cold – and with the wind blowing across the flood-water that seems to be there most of the time – it gets *bloody* cold.

 My mate is tucked up right in his corner out of the wind, buried somewhere under his coat!   Running bunker first to St. Margarets does not help either.

As we rumble over the small bridge which crosses the New River, the sound tells Harry exactly where we are and he sticks his head out of the cab to check the signal for the road gates at Ware Crossing.

A quick look tells him we have a green light so, without needing to check our speed, we rush through the Station.   The line through Ware until just beyond the road-bridge is single track, we know we have right of way but one always seems to look just in case something is coming the other way!

There is a Signalbox on the far end of the platform with a large Goods Shed next to it.   Giving the Signalman a wave as we pass, we head for St. Margarets Station. The safety valves begin to lift so I put on the injector to keep her quiet.   At the same time I turn off the carriage heating as I will be uncoupling at St. Margarets to run round our train ready for the first passenger train of the day to Buntingford.

As we approach St. Margarets Station, Harry closes the regulator and starts to apply the vacuum brake, bringing our train to a stand as we run into the Station platform. Looking back, we await the signal or a green light from the Signalman whose Box is on the Down side platform.   A green light is waved from the Box so

Harry reverses our train into the siding to enable us to 'run round' the train and then set back into the Bay platform.

I nip round to the front end of the engine to uncouple the train while Harry squeezes the buffers together, after first destroying the vacuum, which applies the brakes to the carriages. After I throw off the coupling, Harry eases off the buffers slightly, giving me a bit more room to uncouple the pipe-work.

First I disconnect the steam-heating pipes – after turning off the stop-cocks - and then uncouple the vac' pipes, clipping the ends onto their 'dollies' so as to maintain an airtight seal when I couple up at the other end. Next, I hang the heater pipes on to their chains to keep them tidy. I clamber up onto the front of the engine and hang an oil lamp on the bracket above the Smokebox, displaying a White light ready for the journey to Buntingford.

The ground signal is green, allowing us to run round to the other end of our train. On reaching the other end, Harry squeezes the engine onto the train once more and I dive between to carry out the coupling-up routine again. I connect the steam-heater pipes first, open the cocks, then I throw on the coupling and finally, connect up the vacuum pipes. The book says that you should always hang on the coupling first, but I do it this way as it suits me.

So it's now back into the warmth of the cab, Harry has taken off to make the tea ('a brew') in the Signalbox and to collect the brass Staff Ticket (or Token) which gives us right of way to pass over the single line as far as Hadham Station. This is the first Section of the line.

A free newspaper sometimes comes our way if we are lucky with the newsagent collecting his papers which arrive on the first train from London on the Down platform. Most newspapermen give us one as a bit of goodwill and everyone seemed to be happy in his or her jobs – except maybe the Guards!

Right, this is where the fireman is left in charge unofficially and experience and trust is earned. I 'blow off' the brakes on the engine and train by creating 21ins. of vacuum in the system, which releases them. I put the Westinghouse brake handle in the 'Running Position' and the engine air-brake reservoir discharges with a hiss. Checking that the reversing lever is in back gear, I open the regulator a bit and push our train into the Bay Platform, stopping alongside the distance marker painted on the edge of the platform.

Leaving the Westinghouse Donkey pump running, I apply the engine air brake and screw down the handbrake, that will hold the train sufficiently without the need to apply vacuum brake. The reversing lever I place in Mid-gear with the cylinder cocks open so as to avoid any possibility of the engine 'creeping' from a gradual build-up of steam in the cylinders.

Putting on the carriage steam heating again to keep them warm, I take a look at the fire and put a bit more coal round the box. Having built the fire up nicely with thick, grey smoke curling from the chimney, I close the dampers a shade so that the fire doesn't burn through too quickly. Otherwise the safety valves will lift, making one hell of a noise!

Time to give my hands a quick wash, so I fill the bucket with hot water, obtained from the live steam by-pass on the injector, swill some around the cab floor to lay the dust – sweep up and wait for Harry to return with the 'brew'.

Dawn is just breaking as Class N7 no. 69682 waits in the bay platform at St. Margarets with the first train of the day for Buntingford.

Through the escaping steam comes Harry with the can of tea and, yes, he has a paper under his arm!
A 'Brew' made in the 'Billy' or Tea can is quite something – it's a brew of its own and I've never had another like it since those far-off days.   The ingredients were made up of two spoonfuls of loose tea and two large spoons of the very thick type of sweetened condensed milk.   This is all put in the Billycan, filled up with boiling water and given a good stir. Usually, some of the tealeaves refused to sink, but it all went down very good just the same.
 Having a chat while we enjoy our cup of tea, he tells me about the Signalman's troubles that he has had to listen to while waiting for the kettle to boil.
Nearly time to leave, as the ex-London train is about to leave, heading for Hertford. Some boxes of fish being loaded into our train seems about the nearest things to passengers we have this morning.   Up comes the Guard to tell us how *******cold it is this morning, finishing with "*Well, Right Away then, driver.*"
 With that, Harry turns the lever into Fore-gear and releases the engine brake as I unwind the handbrake, he opens the regulator at the same time as I open the dampers and we are off at a nice trot.
Looking at his watch, Harry Allan notches up the engine, knowing that we have plenty of time.   So, into the 'wild unknown' we go - it's a dark trip in winter over

77

the Branch – not a light to be seen outside.

I sit back on the sandbox with one foot up on top of the cupboard ahead of me, all the front is lit up now by the white reflection of the fire through the firehole. Harry is curled up on his seat with his foot wedged under the reversing lever, sometimes I think he dozes off, or just closes his eyes listening to the change in noises of the track to let him know exactly where we are.

I turn on the injector as we run into Mardock Station, coming to a halt with a hiss of the air and vacuum brakes going on.

We drop off just a few newspapers and get a waved greeting from the Porter.

The Guard raises his hand signalling for us to leave and, with the train now just held by the engine's air brake, Harry puts '93 into full Fore gear and opens the regulator – releasing the brake at the same time. As we are on an uphill bend, this helps us get away smartly and he notches up the engine at the same time without the wheels slipping.

Turning the injector off, I settle back into my corner.   I notice that the carriage heating pressure has crept up rather high, so I close it down to 40lbs knowing that the carriages will be nice and warm by now. Glancing across the cab, Harry is having a go at lighting up yet another fag.

Its getting light outside now - making the weather look even more miserable. Quite a few leaves have blown down onto the rails, making them quite slippery, but '93 is a good engine for pulling away without slipping under such difficult conditions. It is not often that we have to use the sanders to help her 'keep her feet'. On the rare occasions that slipping does happen, I give the front sanders a few back-and-fore strokes of the lever beside the damper handle on the fireman's side and hope that they operate ok.

These sanders are gravity fed and more often than not, the sand gets damp in the boxes - located on the 'running plate' on either side of the Smokebox - and refuses to run out.

Time to put a bit more coal round the firebox – a dozen or so shovelsful will keep it built up. Most of the fresh coal in the bunker is now small stuff, so the few big lumps I found earlier must have been from the previous coaling.   No real worries – it just means I don't need to use the coal-hammer.   After giving the floor a quick sweep, I'm back on my perch again.

As we pass under the Road Bridge approaching Widford Station I turn the injector on.   This is the only station until Buntingford where the single platform is on my side of the engine. The platform is on a curve so this makes getting away a bit difficult.   Even before we stop, the Porter starts to wave us on - taking it for granted that there will not be any passengers – one of these days he will slip up and somebody will appear and will miss the train! This Porter must be the loneliest railwayman for miles around – not only is he the Porter, but Ticket Clerk, Parcels man and also Porter-Signalman if there are coal wagons to be put into the small Yard.

The quickness of the Guard giving us the Right Away catches Harry having a quick drink of tea, so he has to co-ordinate his moves very carefully, spinning the lever into Fore gear, releasing the brake and opening the regulator.   All this is done with one hand while he hangs on to his cup of tea with the other – not a drop is spilt – and off we go!

Turning the injector off, I step across to Harry's side to retrieve the now empty teacup – which is also the lid of the Billycan – and put it back on the can that stands on the shelf above the firehole. This is the same shelf that is used for warming the cans of oil.

Most of the signals on the Branch do not mean a lot because we have the Staff giving us right of way to Hadham, nonetheless, these signals must be observed. The approach into Hadham Station is uphill and here the track changes from single to double, acting as a passing-point for two trains to pass each other in opposite directions. The hard pull up to Hadham means the engine is working a bit and snorting at the chimney. This also means a pull on the fire, so a bit more coal round the box will keep the steam pressure gauge needle up on the red line.

Approaching the Station and checking that the signals are clear for us to run in, Harry starts to apply the vacuum brake and we come to a halt in the platform. Putting the engine into mid-gear, Harry applies the Westinghouse air brake on the engines so as not to roll backwards.

The Signalman greets us with a cheerful "*Good Morning*". His surname is also 'Allan' and he is an ex-Naval man with a Citation for bravery, someone told me a few years later.

After taking the Staff from us, he returns to his Signalbox to operate the Locking Frame and points so that we can leave. He then gives us a different Staff, which gives us the right of way from Hadham to Braughing.

The Guard has unloaded all the parcels – all two of them – with so much strain that he hardly has any wind left in him to blow his whistle through the steam and smoke. He struggles to wave his fat little arm to attract Harry's attention – you can guess that our relationship is not very good with this one!

Harry performs the usual – pulling away all very nice without any slipping – and turning the injector off, I put a bit more coal round the box. It's a bit of a climb now for a couple of miles, producing a healthy bark from the chimney along with plenty of smoke curling down my side of the cab, blocking out my view until we pass under a road bridge and reach the top of the bank. It's now a nice, downhill run into Standon Station.

Passing over the road crossing we run into the platform on Harry's side.

Nothing ever seems to happen here and we do not see any Porters to speak to as they are down at the other end. So, with a wave from the Guard, Harry releases the brake, gives the reversing lever a forward spin and opens the regulator.

We leave at a smart pace, passing the rarely-used Signalbox on our right – looking very sad and cold in the winter's morning light. It was once a very active box, controlling a fair sized Goods Yard. Standon was very busy back in the 1920s with corn and coal traffic – I am told that during the First World War wagonloads of hay were despatched from this yard for the Army horses in France.

The river follows – or should I say, we follow the path of the river – and we are now passing over a wooden bridge which causes a change in sound for a brief second before returning to the familiar clicketty-click. Putting a dozen shovelsful round the firebox to keep the steam pressure on line, I give the floor a quick sweep, check that the boiler level is well up and that the Hydro lub' is still working okay. Back to my seat for a while – this part of the track is surrounded by woodland so - with the daylight breaking, out come the pheasants and rabbits foraging for their breakfast. They always seem to find something along the trackbed so we do get a few casualties, these are picked up by the Platelayers who invariably sell them for a few bob to supplement their low pay.

As we coast down the hill towards Braughing the safety valves start to lift, so it's on with the injector again. As I stick my head out of the cab to check that the injector has picked up the water ok, I am reminded how cold it is out there.

I should mention that the injectors are bolted just below the cab steps on either side of the engine, with the water-valve control handle coming straight up through the floor. Each time the injector needs to be used, the water valve is opened prior to turning on the live-steam cock, which then picks up the water and carries it into the boiler. Sometimes the water and steam flow requires regulating before it will work properly, while this is happening water is running out of the waste pipe onto the track. If this is not controlled quickly, the water tanks could run dry which - in extreme cases – could mean the fire has to be thrown out, not a pleasant job if you happen to have a good fire in the box!

   As we enter Braughing Station, the track layout is similar to that at Hadham in that there are twin platforms and double tracks - the first train from Buntingford is standing in the other platform. They must wait to collect the Staff we are holding before they can move on. This train is worked by one of the two sets of footplate crew based at Buntingford. One of Buntingford's two regular engines – 69633 – is at the head of the train this morning.

Sister engine number 69634 acts as a replacement on the occasions that 69633 has to go to Hertford for repair or for its periodic boiler washout.

Not a lot happening here – "*Good Morning*" Walter the Signalman shouts to Harry – as the safety valves lift, letting out an ear-splitting roar. "*Sorry everyone*" I mutter to myself as I quickly put the injector on. This happens sometimes and catches you unawares, but it soon becomes quiet again. Taking his hands from his ears, Walter smiles and agrees it is not the best of mornings weather-wise.

Walter has been a Signalman at various stations throughout the Branch – a very pleasant chap around the 60s mark and had spent his entire working life on the Branch. Sometimes, if there is a long delay we spend a bit of time in the box with him and he tells us tales about his opposite-shift Signalman who is also his neighbour.

 Apparently, this chap was not easy to get on with and, although he was also a local Justice of the Peace, he didn't always practice what he preached!

So, as the tales were acted out, accompanied by much laughter and cups of fresh tea, we would leave there feeling great.

However, no delays on this occasion and the Guard is waving like mad, so we had better make haste. We have exchanged the Single Line Staff with Walter and the signal is off, so we say goodbye to Braughing. If we make a bit of a spurt now, it will add to our turn-round time at Buntingford.

So, off with the injector as Harry releases the brakes, tugs open the regulator and off we go, he winds the lever up a couple of turns as '93 starts to accelerate way. Having turned the injector off and checking that the boiler water level is now well up, I pick up the shovel and have a look round the fire – better put a bit more coal round the box to see us through to Buntingford.

We are going quite fast now, through the thickest wooded part of the trip, this shields us a bit from the wind and rain while passing through here. Not very much to do now as the fire is burning down nicely, we have a full head of steam and Westmill Station is in sight. There is just the one Porter here whose job it is to open the Level Crossing gates and anything else that's required of him.

Into the station we run and gently brake to a standstill.

Nothing and nobody to pick up or drop off so the Guard waves his Green flag at us and old '93 romps away as if she knows its almost time to rest for a while!

I had only put the injector on for a short while this time as half-a-glass is enough to last for the short hop to Buntingford.

I put a couple of shovels of coal down one side of the box only so as to have a bit of good fire to use when I clean it out at Buntingford ready for the return trip.

I close the firehole door flap to restrict the flow of secondary air and this will see us through.

The carriage heating is shut off so as to make sure the steam pipes cool down enough for me to safely disconnect them on arrival.

Up a slight incline toward Buntingford Station, we pass the Signalbox and Water Tower on our right and enter the single-platform terminus. My driver leans out of the cabside and, judging the speed and taking account of the wet rails, stops our train in exactly the right spot. This time he leaves the carriage vacuum brakes on and closes the vacuum ejector valve next to the brake handle.

So carefully timed were these actions that the train was brought smoothly to a standstill so as not to throw any passengers about that may have already stood up – not that it really mattered today, as we didn't have any!

We would normally run right up to the buffer stops and then set back after the passengers have got off, so as to 'run round' our train for the return journey. Knowing we were empty this morning, Harry has stopped short so as to save time. If the Stationmaster had been about we wouldn't be allowed to do it.

The Guard throws open the double-doors of the Brake Van ready for the unloading of a few pigeon baskets. After the Porter has freed the pigeons, the baskets are returned to the Guard's Van for the return journey while the pigeons fly off home for their breakfast.

While all this is going on I have got out of the cab and dropped down between the engine and carriages and wait for Harry to squeeze back on the buffers so that I can throw off the coupling. Then it's the usual routine, turn of the steam-heater cocks and then uncouple the vacuum hoses and the ends secured on their 'dollies'.

Finally, I uncouple the heater pipes and hook the ends on to their chains so that they swing clear of the track. I climb back up into the cab and Harry moves up clear of the set of points toward the buffer stops and past the ground signal.

The points change and the signal turns to green, which allows us to cross over onto the track running alongside our train and head for the loco to fill the tank and clean the fire. More importantly, it should give us some extra time to enjoy our breakfast.

As we approach the Signalbox, Signalman Matthews wave a red flag at us. As we stop alongside, he asks if we would shunt a wagon into the Goods shed, as it was a bit too hard for the Yardman to push in on his own. At one time, there were more men in the Goods Yard and they also had a horse for towing wagons in and out of the shed. But I guess the horse must have eaten too much and the costs were 'over the top', so the horse had to go!

After asking the Signalman to put the kettle on, we cross over into the Goods Yard and approach the offending truck. We give it a nice clout up the rear end - sending it in the direction of the Goods Shed entrance - with the Yardman in hot pursuit to get the brake on before it bounces back out again. After coming back out of the yard, the Signalman waves a green flag allowing us to enter the single track into the Engine Road. Only two engines can be accommodated on this short piece of track, alongside which is a small wooden coaling stage with a small office opposite, there is no Engine Shed as such.

This is the home of the engine allocated full-time to Buntingford and is kept in steam all the time until it returns to Hertford for repairs or a boiler washout. Beneath the water tank is a small room used by the spare fireman (usually one of Hertford's Passed Cleaners) who looks after the engine overnight. This room contains a small, coal-fired stove, a table, chair and a very nice black dirty kettle! So, after topping up the bunker with coal, filling the water tanks, making sure the boiler is full and banking up the fire so that it will last for a couple of hours, the Duty Fireman would retire to this hovel. There he would try to get the fire to burn bright enough to warm the place up a bit and boil the kettle for a brew, then he may put his feet up for a while and probably think to himself *"What the Hell am I doing here!"*

Well, now we have stopped in the Engine Road and, after screwing down the handbrake I have a look to see how much clinker there is in the firebox. Harry has gone up to see the Signalman.

Taking down the Long Slice from the top of the engine's tank, I start by moving the good fire over to one half of the box so I can get the Slice under the clinker left on the other side. I take a quick look over the side to make sure nobody is below before throwing out the first sliceful. Which side I throw it out of depends on the direction of the wind, I don't use the side that's going to blow all the ash back into my face!

I use the Bent Dart to push the clinker out from directly under the door and back corner and, after about half a dozen slicefuls, that half is done. Moving the fire across, I do the same thing on the other half of the box. I then spread the fire all over the clean firebars and make it up to a reasonable thickness with fresh coal, and leave it to burn through. Before it starts to make too much smoke, I will top up the water tanks by climbing up onto the boiler outside, throwing open the filler lid and putting in the leather pipe. I then pull on the chain that is dangling overhead which is attached to the water-valve and keep a steady pull on it to keep the valve open until the tank is full. As I am standing next to the chimney holding this chain, you can understand why this job needs to be done quickly before the fire starts to burn through.

It is no joke having to stand there choking in the black smoke that starts to roll out of the chimney!

Returning to the cab, I put the fire irons back onto the tank-top through the swivel cab window.   I use a cloth to handle them, as although these irons are over 6 feet long, they remain very hot for a long time after use, even in cold weather.

After sweeping up, I get some clean, hot water in the bucket wash my hands.

The weather is still miserable but the fire is burning through very nicely and I'm grateful for the heat it is giving out.

As it is now daylight, I collect the lamp from the front and place a white enamelled metal disc-board on the top bunker bracket ready for the return journey. I snuff out the lamp and return it to the Lamp cupboard on my side of the cab.

Harry returns with all the latest gossip on things that have happened of late, along with a fresh brew of tea. We make ourselves as comfortable as we can during the short time we have left and finish off our sandwiches.

The time soon passes - Harry checks his watch and remarks that we should get going.

On goes the Westinghouse Donkey pump and I take off the handbrake.

With a short pop on the whistle, Harry winds the reversing lever over and gives '93 a bit of steam, moving us slowly toward the Ground Signal.   Seeing that the signal is 'Off', we proceed out on to the main line where we wait for the Signalman to re-set the points and give us the signal to back on to our train.

As we pass the Signalbox we give Mr. Matthews a wave and continue down to the platform a few yards further on. As soon as we draw up to our train, I jump in between engine and coach while Harry squeezes up the buffers for me to throw on the coupling. Then on goes the heater and vacuum pipes and I open the heater cocks before returning to the cab.

Looking down the train, it seems the total number of passengers we have is nil, only the Guard in his 'kennel'.

By giving the fire a bit more up the front of the box and filling in the last of the bright spots, it makes sure that it is going to last all the way to St. Margarets – seeing that most of the run is downhill.

Turning round, I notice the Guard has appeared by the cab door – making his presence known by shouting "**Right away driver!**".   So, following this order, Harry releases the engine brake with a hiss and, opening the regulator we depart at a brisk trot down the platform, hoping to leave the Guard behind!

With a quick look back down the train I could see him grab the handrail of his Brake Van which happens to be at the rear of the train. Looking across to Harry, I could detect a slight grin when I nodded confirmation that our Guard had made it!

Better put the carriage heating on – setting the pressure at around 40lb psi – this should keep the carriages nice and warm should we pick up any passengers.

Having turned the Hydro Lubricator off when we arrived at Buntingford, I turn it on again and closely check the oil flow just in case any of the jets have become blocked.

We are now running bunker-first and Harry is getting all the cold wind through his side this way round.   To avoid this, he has to stand with his back to his seat looking out of the small, round window set in the rear of the cab - thus enabling him to see ahead of us – providing we have used enough coal to clear the view from this window.

For some strange reason, our engine seems to knock and clank a lot more when running this way round.   Also the Pony wheels beneath the cab are now leading the way which throws the engine about rather a lot, particularly when steam is shut off while coasting downhill.   The steam heater valve starts to blow - which means the carriages are warmed up - so I reduce the pressure a little.   The main boiler pressure is around 150lb psi now, with the regulator almost closed.

We are running slightly downhill through the woods at a fair pace towards Westmill Station.   The track turns quite a bit, throwing us about somewhat – but probably not as bad as in the carriages – and it doesn't help when it is wet and windy.

Now we are approaching Westmill so on goes the injector to stop the safety valves lifting, as steam pressure has now risen almost to blowing-off point.

The first sound of life from my driver's side comes with a roar from the first application of the vacuum brake, reducing our speed down to a crawl by the time we get to the start of the platform. A final check with the brake brings us to a stand at the end of the platform.   Here there are a set of road-crossing gates which are operated by the Porter. So great care always has to be taken when running into this small station to check that the gates are open to us – particularly as our approach is on a bad bit of track, which is on a downhill bend. If it happens to be a wet day, a fair amount of skill is required to stop in the right place.

Westmill has only a single platform on the driver's side, so I wander across to see how big the crowd of passengers is that are waiting to get on. Some hopes! – just the Guard and the Porter are the only people to be seen - "***Right!***" shouts the Guard and with this, Harry spins over the lever, opens the regulator, at the same time releasing the brake and off we go.

Crossing back to my side of the cab, I shut off the injector and take refuge in my corner – its warmer this side when running this way round.

I take a look at the fire through the trap, using the firing shovel as a shield against the intense heat and smoke – by turning the blade around, which concentrates the flow of secondary air - one can look all around the firebox. Everything is all right, the back corners are well-filled and the fire is burning through well.

Topping the bank, the regulator is eased back and the reversing lever wound up a bit as we run down towards Braughing.   We check the signal is giving us the 'all-clear' and run past the Signalbox and into the station. I put the injector on again as Harry brings our train to a halt.

This time there are a few passengers – 'city types' all going through to London judging by the way they are dressed – in pin-striped suits, bowler hats, brollies and, of course, the folded newspaper (probably The Times?) under the arm!

I reckon by the time they get to their offices it will be lunchtime.

Harry keeps the engine brake hard on to stop us creeping off – seeing as we are standing on a downhill slope. This being a double track and Staff/Ticket exchange station, we have given the Staff to Walter the Signalman.   We now have to wait for him to return to the Signalbox to operate the signals and issue us with the Staff for the next Section before we can proceed.

I've had a look at the fire and its doing well.   I shut off the injector and in rushes the train from St. Margarets pulled by 69633 – the Buntingford crew's engine. Having collected their Staff, the signal drops to clear and within a minute up comes Walter – out of breath but with a big smile – and hands me the new Staff.

"Thanks Walter" I say as the Guard waves his flag to get us under way again.

"Right Away, driver" I sing out and the engine brake is released, the lever wound over and the regulator opened – all these movements carried out with clockwork precision – and with a hiss of steam we draw out of the platform and away down the track. Through the wet and cold woods we head for Standon Station, the track twists and turns a bit and, as we are running bunker first, this makes old '93 roll about quite a bit.   We look out for the signal as we approach Standon, I turn on the injector just as the safety valves start to lift.

There is the usual sound from the brake valve as Harry checks our speed – applying the vacuum brake fully as we pass the Signalbox – and into the station we run.

Applying the engine's air-brake, we stop just short of the road-crossing at the end of the platform.   The platform is on Harry's side and I have a look out – not much going on – just a few more City Gents sorting out which compartment to get into and with who to travel with.   I expect it is important that you have to know your place when you work in London!

I waste no time getting back to my side where it's a bit warmer.   On the driver's side there is a large hinged metal shield between the driver and the firehole door. This is there to keep the firebox glare out of the driver's eyes, but it also stops the heat.

On hearing the Guard shout out *"**Right Away!**"* to Harry, I shut off the injector just as he releases the engine brake and heaves open the regulator – we are on our way again.

"Pass the tea George" Harry calls out as he moves himself over to the window at the back of the cab away from the cold wind.   I hand him the tea-can and he pours himself a lidfull, which puts a smile on his face, he hands the can back to me and I return it to the shelf above the firedoor.

 We are heading towards Hadham now – a steady climb for a mile or two to the highest point on the Branch – there's not a lot to see or do at the moment.

One thing that we never seem to notice is the tiredness we should feel owing to having got up halfway through the night.   Still, the way this job grows on you, it always seems worth the effort.   It seems strange that in the 1990's people are more than happy to pay a Preservation Society £80 or more for the opportunity to spend a few hours on the footplate of a steam engine learning the basics of firing and driving.

In my day the basic pay was less than £7 for a 48-hour week!

We are over the top of the bank now and running fast down towards Hadham station, Harry begins to apply the brake as we run under the road bridge halfway down the bank. Past the Signalbox and into the station, we come to a juddering halt due to the wet rails. There are a few more 'posh' passengers - on their way to London I expect – and they lose no time boarding the train after leaving the warmth of the Waiting Room. The staff at these stations always made sure there was a good fire going to warm the waiting passengers in those days – and those passengers in turn usually showed their appreciation to the staff at Christmas time. Changing Staffs again, we have a few cheery words with the Signalman while the Guard checks his timepiece. We get the wave – all proper this time with his Green Flag – so, dropping the lever and opening the regulator, at the same time releasing the brakes, we head off for Widford Station a bit further along the line.

Looking forward, I notice a tractor near one of the many farm crossings up ahead and give a long whistle just in case the driver is unaware of our approach.

Harry has taken the precaution of beginning to apply the vacuum brake just in case, but looking out it seems he has become aware of us – thank goodness.

On passing the tractor, the driver gives us a wave to say thanks – quite a few accidents have happened on these farm crossings over the years - so I'm told - not that any have happened to me.

We run into Widford Station and a few more passengers are waiting, one of them is Bert Wicks who is a Shunter at Hertford. Bert has his bicycle so into the Guard's Van he goes, giving us a wave as he does so.

"*Right!*" shouts the Guard and Harry goes through the usual routine and gets us under way again.

Now we are on a downhill run heading for Mardock Station – Harry gives the vacuum brake a small application to check our speed – we gather pace quickly along here.

Arriving at Mardock, there is nothing and nobody to pick up, so the Guard waves us to leave almost before we come to a stop. This helps the passengers as it gives them a bit more time at St. Margarets before catching the London connection. Some of them may want to get a paper from the Bookstand on the platform, run by W.H. Smiths of course – this Newsagent could be seen at almost every station at that time.

Round the curve we swing, running alongside the Hertford Mainline now, on goes the injector and, checking the signal as we approach the station, Harry applies the vacuum brake and brings our train to a smooth halt a few feet from the buffer-stops.

Already the passengers are standing up with the doors swinging open – no doubt all very keen to get to work!

Soon afterwards, the London train enters the platform in the hands of another Hertford crew and drawn by 69685 - an engine of the same class as ours – the fireman gives us a wave as they pass by.

The platform is suddenly hidden from view by a thick white cloud of a mixture of smoke and steam. This always smelt good – even if it was a bit dirty at times!

As the smoke clears, I can see that all our passengers have boarded the London train and the Porter is going along the platform slamming the doors shut.
The London Guard gives a whistle, waves his flag and away goes the train, making quite a noise as it gets to grips with its 8 coaches.
Suddenly it becomes very peaceful and quiet, just as though nothing has happened! There is just our Guard taking a few odds and ends out of his Van, and the gentle singing of the injector. It becomes even quieter as I turn that off, seeing that the boiler is now full and steam pressure is down to around 100lbs psi.   Taking a look in the firebox I see the fire has burnt down to a nice thin, even layer.
Bert Wicks comes by pushing his cycle and pauses to exchange a few words with us before going across to the other platform, where he will catch the next train to Hertford to start his day's work.
 We now wait for the Porter to finish closing all the doors on our train before setting back to run round ready for the return trip to Buntingford.
The ground signal is off and as soon as we get the tip from the Guard, Harry releases the brakes and gives '93 a bit of steam.   Before we start to move, he gives a short pip on the whistle just in case anyone happens to be in our way at the other end. We start to set back until we are clear of the crossover points, then, with a loud hiss the vacuum is destroyed.   Harry squeezes up on the buffers and applies the Westinghouse brake.   Climbing down, I proceed to the front end to uncouple the train.   As I am doing this, noises coming from the cab tells me that Harry is starting to fill the firebox ready for the return to Buntingford in about half-an-hour's time.
The signs are that Harry is going to let me take over on this trip while he has a rest and warm-up.
On climbing back into the cab I find I had guessed right, so I release the Westinghouse brake and wind the lever into back gear.   Harry gives me the nod that the signal is off and I give '93 a bit of steam and we back away from the train. After a few more shunts, we arrive at the other end of our train, after squeezing the engine up to the buffers and holding it with the air brake and drop down off the engine to couple up to our train. As soon as I have completed this task, I'm back pretty quick to the welcoming warmth of the cab. I turn on the vacuum brake and check that the needle climbs to the required 21 inches of vacuum and release the Westinghouse brake.
Harry shouts across "*Okay to set back*" so, turning the reverser into back gear, I open the regulator and slowly propel our train back into the bay platform.
We come to a gentle stop in the platform and, as we have a bit of time to wait, I shut off the vacuum ejector and the Donkey Pump so that we can enjoy a few moments of peace and quiet.
I jump out onto the platform and swap the White destination disc from the back of the engine to the front.
As I climb back into the cab, Harry says, "*She's all yours now*" – also, without him having to actually say it, those few words include "*So now keep your eyes open and keep your mind on the job!*"
Harry opens up the damper, kicks the firehole door shut and turns the Donkey

Pump on again and it races away until air pressure builds up – then it settles down to a steady *thump thump*.   He puts on the boiler injector to stop the safety valves lifting and wasting steam.

Settled in my corner, I apply the engine brake, which is a signal for Harry to release the hand brake that he had applied earlier when we stopped. I turn on the vacuum ejector and create 21 inches of vacuum in the train-pipe so - with the brakes of our train fully released – we are ready for the off.

Well, just a few minutes to go and up comes the Guard – a new chap this time. This Guard doesn't have a lot to say, apart from wishing us a "*Good morning*" and soon returns to his Van. There are no goods to be loaded or fare-paying passengers this morning – only a pair of Platelayers with the Permanent Way Inspector on his way to do a few checks on the line. This Inspector is a decent chap and will sometimes travel with us on the footplate but, as he is with the other 2 this morning, it's a 'seat job'.

The Hertford train has run in but there are still no passengers for us, so the Guard gives me the 'Right Away'.   Spinning the lever into forward gear and checking that the signal is off, I open the regulator, release the engine brake and off we trot, notching the lever up a bit once we get going. I settle down onto the driver's padded seat, which is much more comfortable than mine. Even so, the wind is just as cold on this side when I stick my head out!

Across the other side of the cab, Harry has perched himself on the sandbox and looks very relaxed and contented.

Although he appears indifferent to what's going on, I'm not forgetting that drivers have spent 15 years or more as firemen, so they know the ropes.   He can tell what's happening on my side just by the sound of the engine and he would straightaway be able to tell if anything was wrong.

We soon swing away from the main Hertford-London line that we had been running parallel with and start the gentle climb towards our first stop – Mardock. I let the lever out a little which is, in effect, dropping into a lower gear and the engine gives a sharper exhaust sound at the chimney – indicating that it is working harder as we are travelling uphill.

Nature is one thing you can observe on this branch, and there are plenty of rabbits jumping about this morning.

Looking ahead, Mardock is coming into sight so I close the regulator and coast into the station, applying the vacuum brake, we come to a gentle halt. I release the train brake and at the same time apply the engine brake to stop us rolling back down the slope. The platform is on my side - looking back I can see the Guard is having a good old shindig with the Porter about something or other – "***Right***!" he shouts at last so, doing all the usual things, off we go again.

The engine begins to slip a bit so I check that the brakes are fully released by pressing the Release Valve to clear any air that may be trapped in the brake system. As we get under way, I wind the reverser up a bit but leave the regulator on its first port.

The carriage heating valve starts to blow, so Harry turns the setting down to 40lbs psi, he is keeping the boiler steam and water levels well up and the fire is going well.

It is not as warm this side when the wind is blowing from the West, but I'm enjoying myself nonetheless.   I see Harry is having his usual problems trying to get another virtually tobacco-less roll-up going – why he doesn't buy a packet of real fags and have a decent smoke, I do not know – still, it keeps him busy I suppose!

We are getting near Widford Station now and are soon running under the road bridge and into the platform. I stop opposite a hut that is, in fact, the Waiting Room – there is always a cheerful fire going in here for the few passengers that come and go. This station boasts a small Signalbox, which is only used these days to let the Daily Goods train put a truck or two of coal in for the local merchant. Even this quiet station was to witness a serious accident a few years later in 1955 when a train ran into the Coal Merchant's lorry as it was crossing the line from the yard. The lorry was smashed up and the driver killed.   His mate – who was the Coal Merchant himself – was injured.

The Guard waves and we leave smartly – when getting the chance to drive, one tends to want a bit of speed – but Harry looks at his watch and tells me not to be in too much of a hurry or we will be too early. Our next stop is Hadham where the track is doubled to allow trains to pass.   We are still climbing hard through the trees on either side - everything is so wet this morning and nearly all the leaves are down – one has to be ever watchful of the engine suddenly slipping.

With the very cold wind taking all the boiler heat away from me, we press on, passing over a small road bridge which, incidentally, is still standing to this day – as if waiting for the next train to pass over.

Approaching Hadham Station, I can see the signal is off - giving us 'right of way' into the station – so straight in we run, stopping with the vacuum brake and holding on just the engine brake. Harry's got the boiler feed (injector) on to stop the safety valves lifting.

This station once boasted a footbridge and a large Waiting Room on the Up side, but sadly all this has gone in 1950.

In the distance we can see the smoke of the train from Buntingford heading our way on its return journey to St. Margarets.   The crew gives us a wave as they arrive at the Down platform. Around comes the Signalman to take our Staff to pass on to the other crew - shortly he returns with the one he has collected from them.   He will hand this one to us before we are allowed to leave.

We chat to the Signalman for a few minutes until we see our Guard appear at the far end of the platform.   He had been over to the other side for some reason or other – there are no toilets on these trains, so perhaps that's where he had been!

A Green flag from the Guard and I'm putting the engine into full Fore gear, releasing the engine brake and, with a hiss of steam, I open the regulator.

Although I had already checked that the signal is showing Green, I poke my head out of the window to have another look – just to let Harry know that I am concentrating on the job.

Harry does not interfere when I am driving – he just lets me get on with it – but I expect he checks in his own way without me noticing.

It's a sharp uphill pull until we reach the top of the bank so I give the engine a bit more 'stick' by winding the lever out to a lower gear – the increased pull of the exhaust lifts the fire a bit as well.   After topping the bank, I wind the lever back again to hold our speed as we run downhill all the way to Standon Station.

I wonder how my 'fireman' is getting on – he is very quiet and not making much use of the shovel – so perhaps I'm not working the engine hard enough!

Still, I'm enjoying myself very much on this side of the footplate.

Approaching Standon Station, the Distant signal is off which tells me that the Level Crossing gates are open for us so, as I am the driver, I give two long blasts on the whistle to warn of our approach.   Passing over the crossing of the A120, I see there are only a few vehicles waiting at the gates – this road was nowhere near as busy as it is today.

Into the platform we run and I apply the vacuum brake to bring the train slowly to a stop in exactly the right spot.   Almost before we have stopped, I push up the vacuum brake's Large Ejector to blow the brakes off the train, at the same time applying the Westinghouse brake to hold us still. Harry has the injector singing away and is busy checking the fire.

Although there are no goods on this trip, now and then a goat or a small calf - maybe bought by a Smallholder at the Market – would be taken home on the train, much to the dismay of the Guard. This is because of the smell these animals leave in his Van – they are supposed to have a sack tied under them to catch any '*you know what*', but this is not always so!

On getting "Right Away" from the Guard I release the brake and open the regulator. Taking a quick look back down the train as we start away – standard practice to check for open doors or last-minute passengers trying to scramble aboard – I immediately slam the regulator closed and apply the brakes, bringing us to an abrupt halt.

I have noticed one of the carriage doors is not properly closed.   The Guard pokes his head out of his window, probably wondering what's gone wrong.

Seeing the trouble, he has to climb down to track level – we have pulled clear of the platform – and walk back to give the door a good slam. The poor old Porter will get it in the neck on our return journey!   Climbing back into his Van, the Guard gives me a wave, I go through the usual routine to get us under way again to our next destination.

Harry had come over to my side during this delay and grunts his approval of my actions.

To get over all this excitement he goes through the motions of trying to light up another fag, after which he finishes off the rest of the tea so we can have a fresh brew at Buntingford.

 Next stop, Braughing Station.   Looking ahead, we can see the figures of two men who appear to be working on the track.   As they may not hear us approaching – due to them being well wrapped up against the bitter cold – I give a long blast on the whistle. An immediate wave from them is reassurance that our warning whistle has been taken notice of.

On passing, we both get a wave from the men, who turn out to be Platelayers checking the track, and perhaps picking up the odd pheasant or two that may have been knocked over during the morning.   This is one of their little perks of the job. During springtime they do a good trade in supplying bundles of peasticks to local gardeners, thus bringing in a small supplement to their income. These sticks are gathered during the course of their work in keeping the trackside clean and tidy, which involves cutting back the undergrowth to prevent lineside fires, which cause damage to farmer's fields and private properties alongside the line.

   The Platelayers have huts placed at intervals alongside the track in which to take shelter, store their tools and have a brew-up.   These huts are constructed from old railway sleepers with a brick-built end wall housing a fireplace and chimney. With an oil lamp for lighting, these little huts are very cosy places of refuge during bad weather. The Platelayers look to us enginemen to keep them supplied with coal, so we break the rules and lob off a lump or two as we pass by, throwing it out onto the lineside for them to collect later.

So, with Braughing approaching, I give a pull on the whistle to give warning of our approach.

The signal is showing Clear for us to enter the station and we draw to a standstill at the end of the platform.   As the rails are rather slippery, I make a gentle application of the brakes to avoid locking-up the wheels.   As usual, I apply the engine air brake and release the vacuum brakes on the train.

We are in plenty of time and - as his Van is next to the engine – the Guard strolls up for a chat.   Harry walks round to the front of the engine to check that all is well as regards oilboxes etc.   When he comes back, he turns off the carriage heating and takes a look at the fire, which must be all right, as he does nothing to it. He joins in a chat with the Guard while we wait for the Signalman to arrive.

Up he comes to exchange our Staff for the one he brings and he warns us that the 'Old Man' – Stationmaster – is going to travel with us to Buntingford.

He will have his Autocycle with him, which he will put in the Guard's Brake Van and, being a miserable 'Bugger', he will not arrive until the correct time of departure.   He tries to catch you leaving before time so that he can report you, this is why the Signalman has given us the tip.

Myself, I think he knows that the Signalman has told us, he likes to think he keeps us all on edge to show his authority.   Well, here he comes, together with his Cycle that he puts aboard with the gentle aid of the Guard.

Later on I'll tell you a little tale about this Stationmaster and his Autocycle.

"**Right Away!**" shouts the Guard and the signal is showing All Clear.

Releasing the engine brake, moving into full Fore-gear and giving the regulator an opening pull sees us away at a smart clip.

Heading now towards Westmill Station, I wind the reverser up a little, listening to the change of note in the exhaust blast coming from the chimney.   This sound tells me what is happening at the 'business end' and helps me to judge the right 'gear'.

Through the woods we run, the sky is now dark and heavy with rain.

Closing the regulator as we take the downhill run into Westmill, the safety valves start to lift, so Harry puts on the injector to reduce boiler pressure and to maintain boiler water level. It is obvious that Harry knows his stuff, as he has not needed to put any coal on the fire since leaving St. Margarets!
We run over the small road crossing and come to a gentle halt at the end of the platform. The Porter appears with a small packet and makes a great show of handing it to the Guard. No doubt this little play is for the benefit of the Stationmaster, whose presence on our train would have been relayed to the Porter via the 'Bush Telegraph', i.e. the internal phone!
Taking the package, the Guard waves his Green flag for us to leave.
Right, all aboard and of we go towards Buntingford with some haste.   I open up the regulator a bit wider and give a pull on the whistle to let them know we are on our way.   Winding the lever up just a bit, we maintain a good fast run.
Harry reminds me to be sure to run right up to the buffer-stops at Buntingford, so that the Stationmaster on board will have no cause to complain about anything.
Into Buntingford Station we run, stopping just short of the buffer-stops and I fully apply the vacuum brake.   I wind the reverser back in readiness for when the Porter calls us back to clear the points so that we can run round our train.
The Stationmaster has departed – along with his motorcycle – with no apparent hitches.
"*Right, ok to set back*" Harry calls across to me so, opening the regulator a little, we move the train back clear of the points.   Destroying the vacuum in the train pipe, I squeeze the engine up to the coach buffers and apply the engine's Westinghouse air brake to hold it while I jump down and nip 'in between' to uncouple.
As I climb back into the cab, Harry takes over his rightful place.   We draw forward toward the stops and as soon as we clear the points, they are switched over and the ground signal 'thumps' to green.   Back we run, over the points and past our train, stopping at Water Tank by the Signalbox. This time we don't go into the Engine Spur but stop at the water filler-pipe on the Running Line side of the Tank. Harry departs to make the tea while I apply the Handbrake and climb on top of our engine to fill up our tanks.   I unhook the chain, which keeps the leather pipe from dangling across the track when not in use, and drop the pipe into the filler-hole. I then have to stand there pulling on another long chain which opens the water valve – a very unpleasant job in this weather – but it fills very quickly thank goodness, so I'm soon down and back into the cab.
Taking the handbrake off, I put the engine into Fore-gear, apply a bit of steam and run back on to our train, once again squeezing up the buffers and applying the engine brake.   Then on with the handbrake once more, place the lever into Mid-gear and down I go to couple everything up again – making sure the steam-heating cocks are wide open.   Once again, I swap the destination disc round and then attend to the fire, which has now burned down pretty low.
The boiler water level is about halfway and steam pressure has dropped quite a bit, so I put a good few shovelsful round the firebox to get it started.   This is the main reason I moved away from water tank, as it is next to the Signalbox the

Signalman may not have appreciated being 'smoked out'. These are times when a fireman can't but help making a bit of smoke – after all, it is a *steam* engine!
As I am washing my hands, Harry returns with the can of freshly brewed tea, which he places on its usual shelf above the firehole door. He stares thoughtfully at his bag hanging on the hook and suddenly says, "*I think I still have a sandwich left.*"   A quick look confirms this to be true and he offers me half, knowing I have long-since eaten all mine. That's how good a chap Harry was so, giving him a grateful word of "*Thanks*", I pour myself a drop of fresh tea to wash it down.
Having finished our snack, I turn my attentions to the fire again, putting a good bit round the back corners and up the front of the box. The smoke from the chimney is a nice shade of grey and boiler pressure is rising rapidly, so on goes the injector to top up the boiler.
After applying the Westinghouse brake to keep us still, Harry opens the small valve on the vacuum brake to check that the train brake is functioning ok.   I release the handbrake, as it's no longer required.
My occasional glances down the platform tell me that, once again, there are no passengers travelling with us.   Still, I'd better put the carriage heating on, if only to keep the Guard warm!
All refreshed, we await the Guard's return.   The Porter is loading a few Pigeon Baskets into the Van.
The decline in traffic on the Branch is becoming obvious - I don't think we have even covered the cost of the coal today – but it's no use for us to worry about it.

Here comes the Guard ready for the return journey, he drops his bag into the Van and gives us the "*Right Away*". This seems a good thing to do, as it's bang-on departure time for our last run of our day's shift. I look ahead to check that the signal is showing 'All Clear' and call out "*Okay Harry, let's go*". Harry puts '93 into Back-gear and opens the regulator.
On a sudden thought, I look around to check – yes, the Single Line Staff is lying safely in the back tray – we must never leave without it.
Passing the Signalbox I give the Signalman a wave, at the same time saying "*See you tomorrow*" although I knew he would not hear me above the noise of the engine. I check the lubricator and carriage heating to make sure they are working all right, then I open the back damper fully to put some draught into the fire. Straightaway the smoke is starting to darken at the chimney, blanking out the carriages behind.

Looking out across the countryside, the view is quite bleak – the furrows in the ploughed fields look just like ribbons running across them – some of the early corn is beginning to show in green patches here and there.
Running downhill along the winding track towards Westmill, I give a pull on the whistle to warn of our approach so the Porter makes sure the crossing gates are open in our favour. Harry starts to 'get hold' of the train with a steady application of the vacuum brake and we come to a halt in the station platform.   It's only a brief

stop as there is nobody to pick up – the Guard waves his flag – so Harry goes through the usual routine of lever and regulator and off we go.

I have not put the injector on this time, as the boiler level is all right and steam pressure has not quite come right over yet, owing to the heavy fire that I have built up. All being well, the fire should last us right through to St. Margarets.

Harry is winding open the reverser a turn or two – in other words, changing gear – as we start to climb the slight rise towards Braughing Station.

As we are running bunker-first, I have made sure the coal chute in the bunker is closed tight to stop coal-dust blowing all over us, which happens when the bunker starts to get low on coal. There is a hose connected to the hot-water pipe of the injector that could be used to spray over the dust in the bunker but, as the chute is the only way out, the footplate becomes flooded with dirty black water. So, as I will not be opening the chute until we reach St. Margarets, it is better to brave the small amount of dust that blows in through the small gap at the bottom.

With a pull on the whistle as we approach Braughing, we run past the Signalbox and into the station, coming to a stop at the end of the platform.

The application of the Westinghouse brake just before we stop causes a slight judder, due to the wet rails. Harry releases the train brake but keeps the engine brake on to prevent us 'creeping' off.

Walter comes up to take the Staff and with a smile, jokes that *"It's not any warmer since you were here earlier!"* to which I reply, *"No, I'm sorry to say."*

We now have to wait for the train from St. Margarets to run in on the other platform – this will be crewed by the Buntingford men who we passed earlier.

A whistle from down the line signals their approach and the crew give us a wave as they run in. Steam pressure has now risen so I turn on the injector.

Once Walter collects their Staff he will be able to release the signal to give us 'right of way' before bringing the Staff round to us as our Pass to Hadham.

Off goes the Buntingford train giving us a farewell 'pip' on the whistle and up comes Walter with the Staff allowing us to proceed.

"By the way" says Walter, *"the 'Old Man' got there all right then?"* – meaning the Stationmaster and his Autocycle - *"Oh yes, no trouble."* Harry answers with a smile.

Because of an incident involving Driver Reg Butler some time ago, all the drivers are careful not to get on the wrong side of this particular Stationmaster.

It appears that Reg Butler was reported by the Stationmaster to Head Office over a particular incident that occurred on the Branch, so Reg bided his time and eventually got his own back. He was doing a relief turn of duty one day – which happened to be the very turn we are on – and round comes the SM with his Autocycle which goes into the Guard's Van as usual. The Guard waves his flag, giving the driver the "Right Away", but Reg took no notice and the train remained stationary in the platform. The Guard - thinking something has gone wrong with the engine – walks up to the cab and enquires as to what the trouble is.

Reg, I am told, was just sitting there looking across to his fireman and enjoying a fag. He turns to the Guard and asks *"Is it not right that Motorised Machinery travelling to a destination in the Brake van of a passenger train must not carry*

petrol in the tanks, as this is a Fire risk and against Company Rules?"
Well, Reg was quite right and this certainly 'put the cat among the pigeons' so to speak! The Stationmaster had to get out again as Reg refused to go any further while he remained on board with his Autocycle.
Ever since that day, the SM gets the Signalman to find out whom the driver is whenever he travels.

Anyway, back to the present and the Guard has given us the "Right Away' so Harry releases the brake and tugs open the regulator. As we move away, I shut off the injector and drop the flap in the firehole door to bring the boiler pressure up. Closing this flap restricts the air into the firebox and draws up the fire – just like holding a sheet of newspaper over the front of an open fire at home to make the fire 'draw'. As soon as the fire starts to brighten - and steam pressure starts to climb - the flap will be opened again.
*"**Pass the tea then George***!" Harry shouts across the cab, nodding toward the can. I pick it up and pass it over, knowing it will keep him happy. After a bit, he passes it back to me and I take a cupful myself before returning the can to the hotplate over the firehole.
We're getting near to Standon Station now and we look out to check that the signal is showing clear. Although we have the 'Right of Way' the crossing gates could be closed – maybe a vehicle has broken down across the tracks – one never knows what to expect. On this occasion, all is clear and Harry closes the regulator and starts to apply the brake as we pass over the river bridge just outside the station. As we approach the semi-redundant Signalbox, I put on the injector to keep the safety valves from lifting now that the boiler pressure is up.
After coming to a halt in the platform I cross to Harry's side to take a look at what's happening.
The Permanent Way Inspector and Platelayers who travelled with us earlier are boarding again to go inspecting somewhere else. After their very cold walk inspecting the track in the early morning, the warm carriage must be a welcoming relief. The Inspector always carries his Track Gauge with him, which is a polished length of wood with very highly polished brass adjustable slides on each end. These are adjusted for checking the width and certain camber of the track to ensure we all get a safe and smooth ride. The Inspector's Track Gauge is a symbol of his rank – a Badge of Office – as he carries it about in the course of his duties.
"***Right!***" the Guard shouts and with a sharp opening of the regulator and a few turns on the lever old '93 pulls away very smartly towards Hadham Station. Turning off the injector, I take a quick look around the firebox – it's all burning through very nicely.

Just as a matter of interest, alongside the track are short white posts with an arm on each side with black-painted numbers on them. These are Gradient Posts, giving the rate of climb or descent of that part of the track, and are a guide to the driver and to the Permanent Way Staff when relaying and maintaining the track.

Nearly fifty years later, the one we have just passed still stands in my garden as an ornament and permanent memory of the Buntingford Branch.

Under the road bridge we run on our way down the bank towards Hadham Station, entering the Passing Loop as we run into the platform. We come to a halt with the noise of the vacuum being destroyed, accompanied by the hiss of the engine's air brake which, as usual, is kept on to hold the train on this downhill slope.
 Up comes the Signalman to retrieve the Staff. Harry comes across and says to the Signalman "*Nearly done, then?*" "*Yes*" he replies, and hurries off to the Box to pull the signals off.
"*Did that young lady get in the train?*" asks Harry. "*Yes, she did.*" I answered, a bit surprised that Harry had even seen her among the other passengers waiting to board. But I learnt that Harry had a good eye for the ladies – never missed a thing! Having put the injector on to keep the safety valves quiet while standing here, I see the Guard has opened the door of the Ladies Compartment next to his Van and is chatting to the young lady in question. So perhaps we will get to know who she is and to where she is travelling.
The Signalman returns bringing the Staff allowing us through to St. Margarets, saying "*Bye, see you tomorrow.*" The Guard shouts "***Right!***" and, releasing the brake and opening the regulator, we move off at a steady trot. Harry quickly winds the lever up a few turns so as not to gather speed too quickly – its downhill now for a bit.
Turning the boiler feed off and taking a look up ahead, we are both horrified to see a farm tractor and trailer heading for the crossing and it does not look as if he's seen us. This is the second time this morning something like this has happened but – by pulling hard on the whistle - he seems to be slowing up, thank goodness. By this time, Harry has made a full application of the brakes and we are almost at a standstill. Fortunately, the wheels of our engine did not 'lock up' on the wet rail, which would have put us into a slide.
Having seen that everything seems to be all right now that the tractor has stopped in the nick of time, Harry releases the brakes. The Guard is looking out and is perhaps breathing a sigh of relief that he will not have to scrabble among the wreckage to pull out the tractor driver - who may be cut to pieces with blood all over the place - and asking him "*Are you all right mate?*"
After that he would have a long walk to summon help – there were no Mobile Phones in those days!
As we roll past the tractor, we don't know whether to shake our fists or just wave to the driver – still, the main thing is that everything is all right.
So on we go towards Widford Station and as we run in there is nobody to be seen, except for the one and only Porter who is already holding his arm out to let the Guard know we're not needed. The Guard waves us on so I call out "*Right Away*" to Harry even before we have stopped. Releasing the brake, we speed off under the road bridge and, still on a downhill gradient, away towards Mardock Station.
Harry winds the lever up a few turns, - which cuts off steam so as not to go too fast – and is soon closing the regulator as we are fast approaching Mardock, which is

little more than a mile from Widford.

On goes the brake and we pull up in the platform, I quickly put on the injector to stop the safety valves lifting and deafening everyone with the ear-splitting noise they make.

The Guard walks up as we are a bit early and remarks, *"That was a bit nasty back there, wasn't it?"* *"Yes"* replied Harry, *"a bit further and he wouldn't have made it."* The Guard looks at his watch and says, *"Right, let's be on our way."*

I shut off the injector at the same time as the usual loud 'hiss' signals the release of the brake. A turn of the lever and a slight opening of the regulator is all that is needed to move us off at a fair trot to St, Margarets – our final destination.

A couple of miles later, the line curves to our left and soon we are running alongside the Hertford East to Liverpool Street tracks to our right. We now start to get the very pleasant aroma of roasted malt and barley as we approach the Maltings just before reaching the station. Now we are passing the Maltings and the aroma is something 'out of this world' so to speak.

   Leaning out of the cab, Harry gets ready to bring the train to a halt in the station's Bay Platform. Care must be taken not to overrun, as there is a pair of bufferstops at the end of the tracks. In we run with the hollow 'whooshing' sound of the vacuum being destroyed in the brake pipe, bringing us to a halt.

On with the injector again, – there is already plenty of water in the boiler – only for a short while this time. I open the firehole door wide to give us a bit more heat while we await our next movement.

The Signalman comes across to collect the Staff, greeting us with *"How are you chaps?"* Harry starts chatting to him and is shortly joined by the Guard who relates the episode concerning the tractor earlier on this morning.

After they have both departed, I get the Slice down from the top of the tank and spread what's left of the fire evenly over the grate, then I add a bit more coal which should see us through to Hertford.

Harry has been watching the activity on the station and informs me that the young lady has gone across to catch the next Hertford train. This is the one we will follow to Hertford with our train – running as Empty Stock.

The Signalbox halfway down the platform on the Down Side – opposite where we are standing – is quite large for a country station but, because of the extensive yards, contains a fair number of Signal and Points levers.   It also houses a large Hand Wheel used to operate the Level Crossing gates. All this is operated by one Signalman, which keeps him very busy at times.

On our platform –the Up side – there is sited a large mirror facing the Signalbox at an angle to the Crossing.   This is used by the Signalman to observe the Crossing so that he can close the gates with safety.

Right, the signal for us is in the 'Off' position, so we can set back to run round our train. Blowing the brakes off and putting the engine in Fore-gear, Harry gives '93 a bit of steam and we shove the coaches back beyond the platform to the 'run round' position. Clearing the points, I climb down once again to uncouple.   This carried out, I come back out of the cold and give Harry the *"All Right"*, as the ground signal on my side clunks to 'Clear'. Back we run and eventually work our way round to the other end.

All coupled up, now we wait for the Guard to call us back into the platform ready to depart once we get the signal.

Harry picks up the tea can and asks, *"Shall I finish this up?"* *"Yes"*, I reply – and a good job too – as he pours out the contents of tea-leaves and stewed tea!

After he has finished this off, I wash up the can and return it to my bag ready for tomorrow's shift.

Just as Harry starts to light up another fag, there is the distant sound of a whistle. Yes, it's the Guard calling us back into the platform. Harry opens the regulator and releases the engine's brake, the Westinghouse pump starts up a rapid 'panting' as it tops up the air tank.

Back in the platform the Signalman gives us the "Right Away" to proceed on our way to Hertford, we thread our way over the crossover and onto the Hertford Down Main line. As we approach Ware level Crossing we see we have a clear signal, so we run under the Road Bridge, through the station and over the crossing without any delay. We give the Ware Signalman a wave as we pass as a 'thank you' for not stopping us.

I give the fire a bit more coal which should now be all right until we get finished, by which time it will have burned down just right for cleaning.

It's still very cold as we pass over Ware Meads as the wind whistles straight through our unprotected cab.

We're nearing Hertford now with all signals showing clear, so we will run straight into the station, 'run round' our train and shunt it under Passenger Shunter Bert Wick's instructions, then go off to the Shed to dispose of our engine.

The safety valves are about to lift as we draw to a halt in the station, so I put the injector on to give the boiler a top-up.

Bert is standing there ready to unhook us – having carried this out, he climbs into the cab to have a warm while we are running round the train.   *"It's bloody cold out there this morning!"* he says as he moves close to the firehole door.   These are the times when jobs such as Bert's are not very pleasant. He gives Harry his instructions: *"We'll pick these up and put them onto those in the Back Platform, then pull the lot out and set them back into Platform Two to form the 12.23 p.m. for London – **Right?**"* *"**Right**"*, Harry replies.

Bert climbs out and, after joining up with the other coaches in the Back Platform, he gets into the end carriage, giving me the signal to pull up *"Right Harry"*, I call across the cab. I am keeping my eye on the Shunter all the time, ready to relay his instructions to Harry, we draw forward until I shout *"**Stop**"*, followed by *"**Right, set back**"*.

 Now, having more coaches on takes a bit more effort to propel them along, causing '93 to slip a bit, so I give the front sanding lever a quick pull which soon cures the slipping.

*"**Keep going**"* I call to Harry as I watch the Shunter waving us back into the platform – then I shout – *"**Right, Stop**"* as Bert holds his arm out straight.

Bert comes up and gets between to throw off the coupling, while Harry squeezes

the buffers up to save unscrewing the coupling link.   Then round he comes and calls up *"Thanks, that's all for today."*
We now wait for the signal allowing us to run down the line toward the Loco. 'Off' it comes and with this, Harry pulls her over and opens the regulator, taking us up the main line and stops alongside the Loco ground signal. There is a 'clump' as the points switch over, followed by a 'clank' as the ground signal changes to Green.
Entering the Loco, I jump down and run forward to pull the Hand-points over to let us into Number Two Road. The ashpit in this road is vacant and has been cleared of ashes.   Arriving in the Loco at this time of the morning is usually the best time as the Yardman has cleaned everything up from the night before.   The ashpits are clear and all the spilt coal from the night's coaling activities has been cleared up. Stopping over the pit, I screw the Handbrake down and put on the injector to fill up the boiler, which knocks the steam pressure down to about 100 lbs. psi.   I then turn of the Hydro Lubricator and the Westinghouse Air Pump.
Now, while Harry is looking around the engine for any visible faults – other than those already reported – I will make a start on cleaning the fire.
Retrieving the Slice from the top of the tank, I proceed to turn all the 'clean' fire to one side of the box to expose the clinker underneath.   I use the Bent Dart to push the clinker out from the corner behind the door.   Then with careful use of the Slice, I will draw this lot through the firehole, through the cab doorway, and out into a heap on the ground.   This clinker is still quite hot to handle, so much care has to be taken.   When this side of the box has been cleared, I move the clean fire across onto the clean firebars and perform the same cleaning operation on the other side.
Finally, the clean fire is pushed to the front of the firebox - under the brick-arch - and fresh coal put on.
 The boiler is all right - the water gauge-glass is showing 'full'- safe to be left until the next crew arrives to carry out their spell of duty.
 The next task is to rake out the ashpan, which is not a pleasant job when the wind is blowing the wrong way!   The Rake that I will use is found lying in the pit as I climb in beneath the engine.   I have opened the ashpan dampers, so in goes the Rake to pull out the ash.   Of course, it's always the usual thing – wind is in the wrong direction and I end up with ashes and dust all over me – what a 'Bloody Mess'.
 Back in the cab again, I close the dampers now that that task has been completed, there's more fun to come when I go round to empty the ashes out of the Smokebox! Taking the firing shovel and handbrush, I climb onto the front of the engine and open up the Smokebox door – not too bad this time – I quickly shovel out what's in there and close the door up again.   After sweeping the ashes off the footplate, I go back into the cab to tidy things up – including myself – a fresh bucket of hot water is required to complete the disposal of the engine.
Harry has returned after putting in the Daily Timesheet and seeing the Fitter about the jobs that need to be carried out.
The last thing to be done is to take out all the Oil Trimmings in the large brass oil-

boxes in the cab and on the outside footplate. These are always removed from the oil-pipes and hooked just inside the boxes when the engine is not working.

As we are both washing our hands in the bucket of hot water, I say *"Well Harry, that's another day over."* *"Yes"* he replies, *"perhaps I can get on with some more house-building now!"* That was his 'hobby' – he was re-building two houses in Crib Street, Ware.

Taking our bags, we climb down and walk round by the Office, just in case the Shed Foreman – Mr. Hennessey – requires us for anything. Often it would be nothing more than a 'slanging match' with Harry, as this Foreman usually did with anybody that came near him. As luck would have it, he has gone up to the station for some reason, so we have a quick word with Bert Neve, the Storeman. We manage to acquire a couple of clean hand-cloths from Bert – sometimes an extra piece of soap would also come our way!

After that, we said our goodbyes and went our own separate ways.

One of Hertford East's N7s, no. 69685, leaving St. Margarets with a train for Hertford in June 1958. At this point, the Buntingford Branch line is running alongside the mainline tracks on the far side. Dominating the background is the huge Maltings from which used to emanate the beautiful aroma of roasting grain! Severely damaged by fire in 1986, the buildings have since been renovated and converted into residential dwellings.
(T.B. Owen/Colour-Rail/BRE432)

CHAPTER FIVE

Gaining Experience

The Temple Mills turn

Another turn that I got into quite early on was the Temple Mills Night Goods.
I liked this one because it meant plenty of overtime – both in number of hours on duty plus the fact that most of them were paid at premium rates between the hours of 10 p.m. and 6 a.m.
It was one of the only shifts that gave you a Saturday off as well as the Sunday.

At the beginning of the week I had to sign on at 3.25 a.m. on the Monday. After picking up a few wagons from the goods yard, we would amble up to Broxbourne where we would get relieved sometime after 7 o'clock. We would catch a train back to Hertford and sign off duty just after 8 a.m., which was quite a short turn of duty.
The timing was important as we were required to sign on again at 8.25 p.m. and the 12 hours off rule had to be obeyed.
We signed on at that time each evening including Friday. On Saturday morning when we signed off, that was it until Monday, as men working this shift were not usually required to work on the Sunday. It was effectively still a 6-day working week as the Monday counted as a double-shift.
Upon signing on at 8.25 p.m. we would cross the main lines from the Enginemen's Rest-room to where our engine would be waiting in the Goods Yard. The usual class of engine was an 0-6-0 Tender Type, usually of class J15 or J17, sometimes it would be one of the larger J39s.
There would be very little preparation needed, as this would have been seen to by the previous crew who brought her in during the afternoon.
Before the turntable was removed at Hertford the previous crew would have ensured that we would be facing chimney-first to London. After shedding our train in Temple mills Yard we would proceed to Stratford Engine Shed to turn our engine for the return journey. I have heard of some drivers during that time temporarily leaving their train at Northumberland Park and using the Tottenham Triangle to turn the engine, so avoiding the trip into Stratford Depot, which could sometimes prove to be a lengthy exercise.
After the table went late in 1956 we were nearly always tender-first to London, which could be extremely unpleasant on windy nights, when coal-dust would swirl into the cab from the tender and invade any exposed parts of our bodies – particularly the eyes, ears and mouth.
It was not too pleasant on wet nights either, although we usually had a cab-sheet which could be hooked between the tender and cab-roof to keep the worst of it at bay.
The duties involved on the 'Mills' turn commenced in the goods yard at Hertford where we would shunt a few wagons into a train and then head off up the line to Ware, somewhere around 9.30 p.m.

Ware had it's own little 25 ton Andrew Barclay 0-4-0 Diesel Shunter (No.11506) so all we usually needed to do was collect any wagons awaiting transit. This station had quite extensive yards for such a small town, which included the private sidings of Wickham & Co. who manufactured railway equipment and railcars. Most of their products went abroad after they had been tested on the Buntingford branch.

We would also shunt and collect at St. Margaret's and Rye House and then head for Broxbourne where we would be signalled into the Up Yard Reception Sidings.

Once we had picked up there it would be 'right away' as far as Northumberland Park yards. I can't recall us being involved in much activity in this yard, but I believe we usually had some more wagons added to our train. Then we would wait our turn to move on the final 4 miles to Temple Mills yards.

If we managed to make Northumberland Park before 10.30 p.m., I would sometimes drop off from our engine as we crawled over the level crossing at 'Park' station and run down Park Lane to an absolutely delicious Fish'n'Chip shop to get supper for me and my mate. We usually had time to finish our meal before we were given the road to Temple Mills.

After we had unhooked from our train at the 'Mills' we would be parked up somewhere whilst our train for the homeward journey was being made up.

This gave us time for perhaps a couple of hour's snooze before getting under way again somewhere around 2.45 a.m.

The level of comfort derived from this short nap depended on which type of locomotive you had. The worst ones were the little J15s that had a very sparse cab. It wasn't so bad during the summertime but in the winter, particularly in the wind and rain, it was nigh impossible to shelter yourself from the elements.

The fireman's side of the engine always seemed to bear the brunt of any bad weather!

Anyway, if we did manage to drift off, it seemed no time at before we were woken up by the shout of the Shunter calling us back onto our train. After hooking up, we would start to doze again, only to be disturbed by the distant voice of our regular Guard Harold Hills, calling " *Are you there matey?*" I would peer over the cabside and there would be Harold, in his heavy serge overcoat, standing by the bottom of the cab steps warning us that we were about ready to go. He would advise us of our load and that he would be aboard his van when we received the all-clear from the Signalman.

Unless we were put into a siding en route to make way for other traffic, our first stop was always Broxbourne.

After dropping off everything not destined for the Hertford branch, we would then trundle on towards Hertford, where our relief would be waiting. They would have signed on at 5 a.m.

We always seemed to have a far heavier train to bring back than on our journey out, and it was an uphill climb out of the Mills yard.

When we were about ready to leave my mate would slowly reverse our engine until we had pushed our train against the buffer stops at the end of the siding.

This enabled us to spring forward to get some momentum going before the full weight of our train took effect.   Remembering my experience at Broxbourne, I bet the Guard hung on real tight, ready for the terrific 'snatch' when the couplings snapped tight!

I mentioned earlier that the Guard came up to our engine prior to departure.

One of the details he gave was the number of wagons we had on, and what the weight was 'equal to'.   For example, he might say '' 30 on, equal to 45''.

I was never absolutely sure what *equal to* meant, I always assumed it meant – in this instance – 30 full wagons, equal to 45 empties, but I could be wrong.

A heavy burden for a 'little old lady'

I remember one occasion when we had '50 on, equal to 100' with a little 73 year-old J15 as our motive power.   My mate was considering asking for some to be taken off, which he had every right to do, but in the end we decided to 'give it a go'.

The trouble was, with the train being so long, we did not have so much distance to set back before making a run at the bank out of the yard.   It was on our third attempt that we managed to creep over the top of the hump.

As we negotiated Copper Mill Junction heading toward Tottenham I looked back and, in the early light of dawn, our train seemed to be never-ending!

We had a very slow crawl that morning, but the 'old girl' never let us down and we eventually made Broxbourne where a quite a few wagons were dropped off.

By the time we reached Hertford and got relieved, it could be anytime up to 7 a.m. that we finally signed off duty, so it was a fairly long shift although not, I must confess, particularly demanding.

We had a variety of locomotives on the various goods turns, all of them were the 0-6-0 tender types, the largest of which was normally one of the J39 Class, which weighed in at around 100 tons, including the tender. However, there was the occasional exception, when a Class 4-6-0 B1, B17 or even a WD 2-8-0 would put in an appearance although not, I would hasten to say, on the Temple Mills shift.

I read somewhere that towards the very end of steam, during the early 1960s, the only engine available for the Hertford goods on one occasion was a *'Britannia'* Pacific. I was not able to confirm whether it actually worked all the way down the branch, but if it did, what a sight that must have been, a *'Britannia'* at Hertford East!

The 6.3 p.m. Down 'Fast'

It was during 1956 that I had my first run with the 6.3 p.m. passenger train out of Liverpool Street.   This was Hertford's longest non-stop run, which was from Liverpool Street to Broxbourne, a run of about 17 miles to be covered in 29 minutes.   This was standard timing for an express train with a mainline locomotive, but with just an 0-6-0 N7 Tank and a very heavy train (it was always packed to standing room only). It was quite a demanding assignment.

Above. Class J15 0-6-0 goods locomotives were regularly used on the Hertford to Temple Mills goods. 65465 is photographed somewhere in rural Essex during the late 1950s.
Below. In much more presentable condition externally is sister engine no. 65475, probably photographed at her home shed – Cambridge - in the mid-1950s.

Above. Class J20 0-6-0 no. 64676, the most powerful of the different types of locomotives familiar to the author for working the Hertford to Temple Mills goods turns.
Below. A Class B1 4-6-0 was an extremely rare visitor to Hertford. Number 61249 is captured on camera in 1956. Passed Fireman Eric Wrangles leans out of the window whilst his driver – Ted Champ – does the same on the opposite side of the cab. The photographer – a Water Board employee who happened to be passing by - is standing by the roadside in Railway Place. Just look at that robust saddle on his cycle in the foreground!

It was not until after climbing the steep bank out of Liverpool Street to Bethnal Green that any semblance of speed could be achieved.

My opportunity came about due to the regular fireman being taken ill.

My driver that day was Arthur White and I remember he was none too happy having to take a 'green' fireman to work this particular train.   But no one else was available, so he had no choice.

We travelled up to Liverpool Street 'on the cushions' of the 4.24 p.m., arriving in London around 20 minutes to 6.   Arthur never much spoke to me on the journey up, but I don't think it was anything against me personally, he was a nice enough chap and we always got on very well on future trips.

On arrival in London we walked round to Platform One where our engine was already coupled up on to train and ready to go.   After taking charge from the Stratford crew it was a matter of having a quick check round before the off.

One of the things Arthur particularly told me to check was that the smokebox door was screwed tightly shut. Apparently there was one occasion when he had a terrible trip due to the smokebox door letting in air, resulting in extremely bad steaming.

On this occasion, all was well, with a good head of steam, the boiler water gauge-glass showing three quarters full and a healthy bright fire.

Soon we were under way and Arthur got our heavy train through the Bishopsgate Tunnels without the slightest hint of a slip and away we stormed up Bethnal Green Bank, slowing for the mandatory 15 mph speed restriction as we curved left toward Hackney downs.

We trotted smartly through Hackney Downs station, where on all other passenger trains would be our first stop, and down the gentle gradient into the tunnels toward Clapton.   By this time we were really getting into our stride as we sped through Clapton station, rounded the curve at Coppermill Junction and headed towards Tottenham.   I can still recall the thrill of rocking over the crossovers at speed as we approached Tottenham station.

Arthur needn't have worried about me, as the engine steamed perfectly with the minimum of effort on my part.   It was on that occasion that I realised that a non-stopper could be an easier job for the fireman than an all-stations train.   This was because there was less demand for coal and steam as there is when starting away after each stop.

When we arrived at St. Margaret's station, coaches were detached for Hertford, and we took the 3 remaining coaches through to Buntingford, which we reached – on time - 1 hour 23 minutes after leaving Liverpool Street 34 miles away. I believe this was the only 'through working' from Liverpool Street to Buntingford at that time, with similar a train going up in the morning.

Money thrown away?

 I previously mentioned the shunting turns we had at Broxbourne, one of which we signed on at 4p.m.and caught the 4.24 from Hertford to relieve a Stratford crew at Broxbourne.

This turn was often used to 'run in' engines that had been overhauled at Stratford Works, so one never knew what to expect.   It was usually nothing more than one of the standard 0-6-0's that had been overhauled, but sometimes it would be an express locomotive, such as a B1, B17 or one of the K Class 2-6-0s.

During the course of early evening on this job, we would take a string of wagons up to Waltham Cross goods yard and it was on one of these trips that a strange little incident occurred.

It was a bright summer's evening and we had just left Broxbourne with no more than half a dozen wagons and the Guard's van in tow.

I was leaning out of the cab taking in the summer air when, as we crossed the bridge over a small river (where I often used to watch trains from the footbridge as a lad), I happened to look down and spotted a £1 note lying beside the track.

You might think it would take some good eyes to identify such an object from the high perch of a moving train, but a one pound note in those days was quite large with conspicuous blue print, so spotting it was easy.

I shouted out to my driver, George Cousins *"Whoa George, there's money on the track!"* and he promptly applied the brake. We were only moving at a snail's pace so we stopped very quickly and I jumped down to retrieve my piece of good fortune.

As I picked it up I spotted another one fluttering in the grassy embankment, then another a little farther on, I couldn't believe my luck!

At the same time George had spotted yet another one in the 'four-foot' on his side adjacent to the Down main line. He also picked up a lady's handbag and various bits and pieces that were scattered around it.   It was now obvious from whence the cash had originated from.

As we were standing on the main line we quickly got under way again and proceeded to Waltham Cross. I have to admit that the thought did cross our minds to dispose of the handbag in the firebox and divide the money, which was worth quite a bit in those days, but honesty prevailed!

George went up to the Signalbox and contacted the Station Inspector at Broxbourne to report the find.   We handed everything to him upon our return to Broxbourne. We thought that was the end of the matter but, some weeks later, George had to attend an interview with, I think, a Railway Policeman who came to Hertford.

It transpired that the handbag had been thrown or dropped form a Cambridge-bound express and the lady who owned it claimed that there was considerably more cash in it than the £4 we had handed in – and where was the rest of it!

Poor old George said he was made to feel like a criminal instead of receiving thanks for doing the right thing.   Some people have a funny way of showing their gratitude!

Don't take the bait!

Talking of Railway Police, it was quite common that, when uncoupling the train upon arrival at Liverpool Street, small packages could be seen lying on the ground between the track and platform.

To all intents and purposes, it could have fallen off one of the station trolleys during loading or unloading but every driver forbade his fireman ever to touch them. It was generally believed that these objects had been 'planted' by the Railway Police to test the honesty of enginemen.

No time to waste at Liverpool Street

The intensity of the suburban passenger services in and out of Liverpool Street is legendary, I believe it was once recognised as the busiest in the world, and I fully believe it.

I think the Hertford East trains usually arrived and departed from platforms 4 and 5, with the occasional departure from platform 1.

Using myself as an example, the moment we drew to a stop at the Terminus I would jump down between engine and carriage to unhook the brake pipe and, in the wintertime, the steam heating pipe.

While still 'in between' my driver would reverse the engine and apply power to squeeze the buffers tight together enabling me to lift off the heavy screw coupling.

Having secured the brake pipes onto their respective airtight seats, I would climb up onto the side water tank, throw open the lid and feed in the long, leather bag attached to the water column which was located in the 'four-foot' between the tracks.

By this time, my mate would have climbed down ready to turn the wheel, which opened a valve to allow the water to flow. I would watch the level in the tank rise and call to my mate to close the valve as soon as the water came within an inch or so from the top. If he didn't happen to be about, it was possible to turn it off with your foot whilst hanging onto the side of the tank, with the other foot partly on the inch or so of footplating running along the bottom edge of the tank.

Having heaved the leather bag out of the tank filler and closed the lid, I would make my way back to the cab for a quick cup of tea before we were on the move again.

While all this was going on, particularly during the rush-hour period, our train had refilled with passengers, an engine had hooked on at the other end and away it would go. We would follow the last coach down to the end of the platform and wait for the points and signal to change to let us into the short bay adjacent to the running line.

No sooner had we stopped in the bay – sometimes less than a minute – than another train would arrive in the platform we had just vacated. Then we would be signalled back out of the bay and onto the train where I would again dive between engine and coach, this time to hook up the coupling and pipework.

Soon we would be away again. That is how things went on the Suburban Side of Liverpool Street, hour after hour.

The frequency of trains to and from Hertford East and Bishop's Stortford was nowhere near as intense as the Enfield Town, Wood Street and Chingford trains, which ran in and out of platforms 1, 2 and 3. They seemed to be in and out

non-stop, whereas there was the occasional lull between our arrivals and departures.
And the noise! There was the constant panting of the Westinghouse air pumps, tank lids clanging, steam hissing, whistles blowing, voices shouting, not to mention the Public Address system announcer trying to make him or herself heard above everything.

Enginemen's pride

There was one particular thing about the Enfield engines that I very much admired. It was the way the crew kept the brass and copper cab fittings polished, red paint was also applied to certain other parts, particularly the regulator handle.
I vowed to myself that when I graduated to the Passenger Link, my own regular engine would look as good – or better!

There was always a smoky haze hanging about Liverpool Street, which became quite heavy during wet weather, even though most of the station was under cover.
After the morning and evening rush-hour periods things became comparatively quieter, which must have been a very welcome respite for the full-time station staff who worked there.
We never envied the commuters who worked in London, what a dreadful place it must have been in those days.

A brush with the law!

During the early spring of 1956 I had my first run-in with the law. I was duty Cleaner on the 6 a.m. to 2 p.m. turn and was passing the Station on my bicycle at about 5.50 a.m. when the local bobby stepped out from the porchway of the Station Hotel opposite, flashed his lamp and ordered me to stop.
I knew why he was stopping me because, for the past half a mile, I had been riding with no lights on. At that time the lighting of my trusty cycle was by way of a Miller Dynamo Lighting Set (£1-2s-6d from Halfords) and worked by the dynamo unit running on the side of the tyre on my rear wheel.
For some reason, a few days earlier the side of my rear tyre had acquired a bulge, consequently, if I happened to go over a bump just as the dynamo wheel was passing the bulge, the dynamo ratchet would jump into the 'off' position.
That is what had happened that morning but, as visibility was pretty good, and no other traffic was about, I did not bother to stop and reset it.
This explanation held no sway with the policeman, who took my name and address before allowing me to continue on my way – with my lights on!
I was duly fined ten shillings (50p) for the offence, which was rather harsh considering that represented nearly a day's pay at Cleaner's rates.
Cyclists riding without lights are pretty commonplace nowadays - even riding on the pavement - but the law does not appear to take any notice. In all the years since, I have never known of anyone else ever being convicted for such an offence.

I often wondered if that bobby had a particular dislike for railwaymen for some reason?

The oil-drum accident

It was during one of these morning shed-duty turns that I received my first serious injury. I earlier mentioned the engine which was housed at Buntingford and, although it would return to Hertford for repairs and it's periodical washout, it still required oil on a daily basis.

So, once a week, supplies of the different types of oil were sent from Hertford depot by way of large containers roped on to the front running-plate of whichever engine was due on a Buntingford run.   The basic oils were treacly black oil, which was used to lubricate the main steam cylinders by way of the various types of Mechanical Lubricators, and the Westinhouse air pump reservoir.

Then there was a lighter grade of oil that was a general-purpose type used to lubricate the numerous bearings of all moving parts on the locomotive.

Lastly there was kerosene which was used to fill the headlamps, gauge-lamp and flare-lamp.

One of these containers was quite big, holding probably about 25 gallons of oil. It was of heavy gauge steel construction with a big brass screw cap at the peak of it's conical top. It had two handles, one riveted on each side of the topmost rim.

On an N7 locomotive the running-plate was about chest height from ground level and the combined muscle of 3 of us could comfortably lift this drum onto the plate. However, it was considered to be quite macho to perform the operation between just two of us by swinging it up from the ground, rather than a straight lift.

I had achieved this on previous occasions but this time something went wrong.

As we swung it upwards the bottom of the drum struck the edge of the plate and it crashed back down to the ground.   Unfortunately, I didn't jump back out of the way in time and the full weight of it landed on the big toe of my right foot!

Now this was before the days of steel toecapped boots.   The normal footwear was second-hand ex-army boots purchased from the local Army Surplus Stores for between 2s-6d and 5s-0d (12.5p and 25p) depending on condition.

My big toe swelled up to the size and colour of a black plum and was absolute agony.   After a couple of days I visited our family doctor who drilled a hole in the nail to relieve the pressure.   Fortunately, I had not broken any bones and it gradually returned to normal, except for the blackened nail, which eventually fell off as the new one grew.

Like most minor accidents in those days, I never bothered to report it, I'm not even sure if such a thing as an Accident Book existed then.

Even to this day I get the occasional twinge from that toe and cannot wear shoes that put any pressure on the top of it.   Such are the penalties of foolish youth!

Shiftwork - the effect at home

At home, my sleeping patterns were becoming a problem, both for my brothers and for me. Although we were a fairly large family, our Council house only had three bedrooms.

Mum and dad had one, my two sisters shared the smallest bedroom, and my two younger brothers and myself shared the other room. Then in July 1956 mother presented us with a baby brother.

My odd working hours - particularly the very early mornings - were disturbing the sleep of my brothers who were still attending school. Although I moved about as quietly as I could, I had to have a rather loud alarm clock, which also had the effect of waking everyone else within earshot – sometimes everyone except me!

So, soon after my baby brother was born, my parents decided on a reshuffle which went a long way to solving the problem.

My parent's sacrifice

My two sisters were given my parent's bedroom, I had their small bedroom, baby took my place with my other brothers and mum and dad took to a folding bed-settee downstairs. This was a huge sacrifice on their part as they not only lost a great deal of privacy, but they also had to contend with me stumbling past them in the dark on my way to and from work in the early hours.

I am sure they initially looked upon this as a temporary arrangement, but it was to exist for another 8 years until, first a sister then myself, married and flew the family nest.

But, as with most things, my parents never complained. They always put the welfare of we children first.

Looking back, I regret not showing more appreciation at the time, but I suppose most of us took far too much for granted when we were young and less wise.

However, there was one habit that I always practised without having to be asked, whenever I did any overtime, I made sure my mother had a share of it over and above the agreed normal amount I paid for my keep.

The Annual Holiday Rota

The 2 weeks Annual Holiday was, to me anyway, an unusual arrangement. There was no question of you seeing the Shedmaster to tell him the weeks you wanted off, oh no! A typewritten list would appear on the Notice Board showing every employee's name and the exact date of the 2-week's leave they were to have, and that was it.

Apparently, the dates were worked out on a rotational basis and it was only about once every 5 years that you could expect to be given any of the 'plum' weeks of July/August. The only way in which you could change to a different date was if you could get one of your colleagues to swap over with you.

Despite the aggravation it must have caused at home for some of the men with families - e.g. having to take a holiday before school term was up – the system seemed to work ok.   Knowing from personal experience in later years the headaches a manager can suffer trying to cater for everyone's holiday requirements, this system must have been quite a relief for the Shedmaster.

The Engineman's holdall

In common with all enginemen of the day, part of my standard equipment was an ex-Army khaki gas-mask satchel in which I carried my Rulebook, tea-can, soap, small towel and my sandwiches.   Later on, one of the drivers (Charlie Lee, I think) found a supplier of smart, leather satchels (also ex-Army), about the size and shape of one of those boxes used for storing 12" vinyl music discs. It was an ideal size for an engineman's needs and they were soon a familiar sight all over the railway system.   It had a strong leather shoulder strap and a generous flap with twin catches.   I believe mine cost me about 7/6d (37.5p) and, although in time I had to have some rotted stitching replaced, it lasted me for the remainder of my railway service.

Food arrangements and the all-important tea!

My favourite sandwiches were either banana (during the summer) or cheese (remember Kraft Cheese Slices?) and Pan-Yan Pickle, which I liked to toast whenever the opportunity arose.   Mother always added a Lyons Individual Fruit Pie, that is, until one hot summer's day when driver Ted Champ and I were having a snack between shunting duties at Broxbourne.
"*What's that you've got in the pie Albert?*" he enquired, nodding in the direction of the Lyons Fruit Pie that I had started to tuck into.   "*Apple and Blackberry.*" I replied, taking yet another generous mouthful.
"*Well*" says Ted, "*it looks a funny colour for apple and blackberry!*"
For the first time I actually looked at what I was eating and my stomach churned over in revulsion – inside the pie, between the layer of fruit and top of the pastry was a thick layer of furry, green mildew!
This was before the days of Sell By, or Eat By dates so, as with a lot of foodstuffs, there was no real way of knowing exactly how old the product was.
Needless to say, I went off fruit pies for a long, long time after that.
With the tea-can I had a small glass jar which contained a carefully measured mixture of tea and sugar, along with a small medicine bottle of fresh milk.   In those days, tea-making facilities was an essential part of a railwayman's daily life and woe betide you if you ever reported for work without the 'essentials'!
But how those 'essentials' could vary!   There were those who liked weak tea, others so strong that it coated your mouth.   Because of the problem of fresh milk going sour quickly, a lot of men used sweetened condensed or evaporated milk, but I thought that this destroyed the flavour of the tea.   There was only one driver I remember that used coffee – even that was 'Camp Chickory', which was (maybe still is) a black liquid in a square-shaped bottle.

The usual drill was that both crewmembers made a brew during the one shift, each sharing the other's.   There were the odd exceptions, I remember at least one driver who didn't take sugar, so he made and drank his own.

Then there was driver Harry Curtis, who brought his own tea from home ready-made, but without milk, in a Johnny Walker's whisky bottle, which he warmed up on the tray above the firehole door – which is where the tea-can resided.   For a

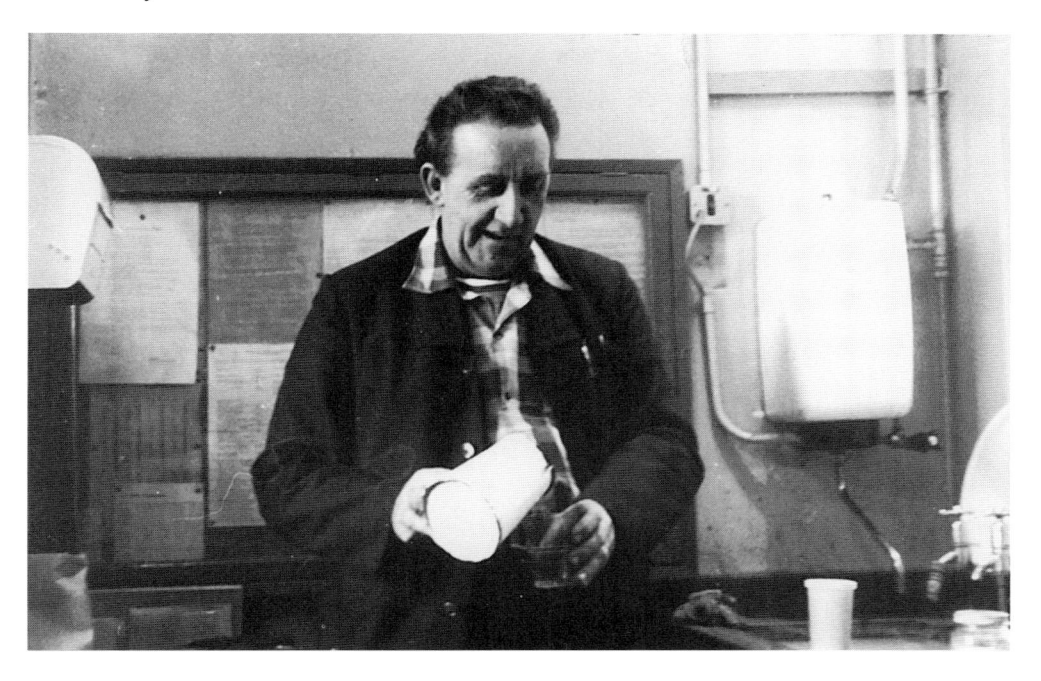

Old traditions die hard! Although this photograph was taken over 2 years after electrification had ousted steam at Hertford East, Driver John Tarry is preparing to make a 'brew' in the time-honoured tradition in the rest-room at Hertford. *c.* 1962

long time I wondered about Harry's tea-bottle, it looked for all the world like the bottle's original contents, but he let me have a swig of it on one occasion just to prove that he wasn't a secret alcoholic!   Incidentally, the fact that it was one of those square Johnny Walker bottles was no accident – its shape prevented it rolling around in the tray while the engine was in motion.

Mind you, during the wintertime some drivers would produce a miniature bottle of Scotch or rum which they would pour into the tea-can to 'spice it up'. Personally, although I used to drink it and feign enjoyment, I thought it tasted absolutely vile and ruined the tea.

Boiling water for tea could be readily found, in a black, iron kettle, on a gas-ring in every Porter's Cabin, Signalbox and Enginemen's rest room.   Apparently it was a standing Railway directive that boiling water should always be available in case it was needed in the event of an accident, how true that was I never did find out for certain.   I do know that you had to ensure that the kettle was topped up again with fresh water after you had used it.

Boiling water from the engines was *never* used, as it contained any number of chemicals to prevent lime-scale forming in the boiler.

During the course of a shift, the tea usually underwent a metamorphosis of sorts as it stood on the piping-hot tray above the firehole door. After several hours it became a stewed, thick brown 'soup', but rarely was any thrown away. If we were fortunate and had access to fresh water, we were able to dilute it a little (termed 'bashing'), otherwise we drank it as it was.

Johnny Shilston, the fireman on 69686, teases the photographer with a cup of tea out of the 'billy-can'. *c.* 1957

Unwelcome additives in the tea!

A common hazard during the hours of darkness was when kerosene from a leaky gauge-lamp dripped onto the lid of the tea-can and found it's way inside.

Then it usually was undrinkable and the fireman (who was always to blame!) incurred the wrath of his driver until fresh supplies became available.

Cooking on the shovel

Despite the romantic tales that are told of enginemen cooking eggs and bacon on the firing shovel, I never remember it being a very common practice. It did happen of course – I've done it myself – but it was an operation that required a little time and a stationary locomotive, so it was usually restricted to jobs that entailed shunting in the yard. There was never much ceremony attached to cleaning the shovel – maybe a splash of water and a wipe with a grubby cloth – the whole lot got sterilised in the firebox anyway!

What is true is that it always tasted absolutely marvellous – probably due to the secret ingredients of ash and coal-dust that managed to find its way in!

Hot food

A more common practise was to wedge an onion, potato or a meat pie between a steam pipe and the cab faceplate to heat up while running, to be enjoyed during the lunch-break, whenever that may be.

I remember that I bought a Walls Steak & Kidney individual pie on occasions and heated it up in the manner described. When it was hot enough it was simply a matter of peeling back the cellophane wrapping and getting your teeth round it. There were no niceties like plates or knives and forks on the footplate of a locomotive.

On one occasion, by way of a change, I bought a pork pie and heated up in the same way. It wasn't until I had scalding hot melted jelly running down my chin did I realise my mistake! After that little episode, I went off pork pies - even cold ones - for quite a long time.

Night-shift feasts and a game of cards

On night-time shed duties mother would often spoil me by packing a can of Heinz 'Pork Sausage and Beans' in my bag, which I would heat up on the electric stove in the restroom and enjoy along with a couple of thick slices of bread.

After the shed had been 'shunted' i.e. all the locomotives placed in their correct order for leaving the shed in the morning, all the boilers filled and fires banked, it was customary to play a game of cards. The usual game was Napoleon but sometimes, with the right group of players, we would play 3 or 9 card Brag.

We would often be joined by enginemen coming in on the late shifts, so it was not unusual for 7 or 8 players to take part. Quite often these card 'schools' would continue well after the first of the morning shift had signed on for duty, with just the occasional break for checking the engines and making fresh tea. There was also a sudden rush if the safety valves lifted on an engine – the Shedmaster did not take kindly to us if he received a complaint from irate residents of the houses opposite the shed.

Stakes were not usually more than the old threepenny piece for each deal but even so, if your luck was out, your losses could amount to several shillings during a session. Some Drivers would not allow these card schools on their shift, so those occasions were usually spent with the lights out and a couple of hours shut-eye.

An errant locomotive

There was another interesting event that took place one night when I was acting Night Cleaner.

After the Duty Driver had worked out on a piece of paper the order in which the engines were to be marshalled, he would ring the Signalman and ask for access out onto the Up main line. Having got this, all the engines would be shunted out nose-to-tail so that they could then be moved back into one of the two shed roads in the correct order, one of us holding the points over via the sprung lever.

It was never deemed necessary to couple-up the engines, simply to leave the handbrakes screwed on a little.

On this occasion, all the work had been completed and we were settling down to a pot of tea and a sandwich, when Cliff Warren, the signalman, rang up to ask if we were finished with the main line.

The duty driver, who I believe was Ted Govier, replied *''Yes Cliff, finished ages ago.''* To which Cliff replied "Are *you sure, my instruments tell me the line is still occupied*?" Ted stuck his head out of the messroom window and looked out to where the points led onto the main line. *'' No Cliff, nothing there old mate, we're all in''* he called back down the phone. But Cliff was persistent, maintaining there was something there, and caused the mystery to deepen when he added that his track-circuit lights showed that, whatever it was, it was moving in the direction of Ware!

So we all went out into the shed yard and checked as the driver called out each engine number from his piece of paper. Sure enough, one of our N7s was missing!

A familiar night-time scene in the rest-room at Hertford Loco - four enginemen in deep concentration over their game of cards! Clockwise from L to R they are ???, driver Bob Smith, ??? and Driver Ted Govier.

After a quick few words with Cliff, our driver and fireman dashed out of the depot with another engine. It was a distance of 2 miles to the level crossing at Ware station and they caught up with the 'runaway' about a mile-and-a-half from Hertford, still rolling slowly along all by itself. Apparently the cylinder cocks must have accidentally been knocked into the closed position and a small amount of steam had been leaking through the regulator valve and built up in the cylinders. Added to the fact that it was a very slight downhill gradient towards Ware, sufficient power was generated to keep up some momentum following the shunt out onto the main line.

Anyway, no harm was done and, as there was no other traffic for a few hours, there was no problem in both locomotives returning to the shed on the 'wrong road'.

The night an L1 'shrunk'

I'll have to jump forward several months for this one, but as it is still on the subject of the night-shift shunt operations, I will tell it now.

By the time this incident occurred, most of our 0-6-2 N7 fleet had been replaced with Class L1 2-6-4 tanks, which were quite a bit longer than the N7s.

As part of the alterations in the Loco early in 1956, the spur allowing us access out onto the mainline at the London end had been taken out.

Access to the Up main line from the Great Northern spur had been removed at the same time.

Instead, there was a short head-shunt that stopped a few feet before a small culvert that ran diagonally under the tracks and towards the road. It also became possible to gain access to the GN spur from this new stretch of track. No proper bufferstops were fitted at the end of this Headshunt, instead there was a wooden sleeper laid across the rails a couple of feet from the end, which I believe was loosely held in place by a length of chain.

From memory, I believe we could just get 4 L1s and an N7 clear of the switch points by squeezing them against the sleeper at the far end.

One night while we were doing our shuffling we noticed that we had managed to get 5 L1s clear of the points – a hitherto impossible combination! We scratched our heads and looked again down the string of locomotives to make there was not one of the shorter N7s among them, but no – there were definitely 5 L1s.

So we walked down the end of the line to the buffer-stops and what we discovered gave us quite a shock. We had pushed the wooden sleeper back off the end of the track and the trailing bogie-wheels of the last L1 had dropped off the end of the track! Or at least 2 of the set of four wheels had, the other pair was just hanging on to the very ends of the rails.

 We carefully moved three of the engines out of the way and coupled the other one onto the front of the last one. We gingerly pulled the stricken engine backwards until, fortunately, the derailed pair of wheels climbed back onto the track.

First in line for overtime

Returning now to the summer of 1956, I was constantly making it known that I was available for whatever extra firing turns came up. This wasn't purely for the extra money in the immediate instance, but was also aimed at amassing my 272 firing turns as quickly as possible in order to be classed as a First-year Fireman.

There was an important financial reason for this, it would mean that my minimum weekly wage would increase from something like £3-30p to over £7 for 44 hours!

I remember one occasion when, having finished on the Temple Mills turn early on a Saturday morning, with no booking for Sunday, I happened to mention to the Shed Duty Driver Alf Childs that I was available for overtime if needed.

My parents and family were away at that time visiting relatives in Somerset so, after cooking myself a late breakfast, I curled up on the sofa to read the morning paper. A little later I saw Alf Childs pull up outside my front door on his little Lambrettta motor scooter. He had come to ask if I would like to cover the 7.25 p.m. shift that evening.

Although I had arranged to go out with 3 of my pals that night, I needed the money so agreed to take the job.

I soon fell asleep on the sofa and the next thing I knew my mates were hammering on the front door. The time was well after 6.30 so it was one mad rush to get myself washed and shaved to go off to work again. My pals were none too pleased as one of them – Tony (the one I used to meet for coffee at Liverpool Street) - had got the use of his father's car for the evening.

When I next saw Tony, I learnt that he skidded on a bend and wrapped the car around a lamppost during that Saturday evening and, although he and my other two mates escaped with minor scratches - the car - an almost brand new Rover 90, was a write-off. I have often wondered if I would have got off as lightly had I not taken that extra shift?

Bank Holiday working

Unlike the present-day railway system, the Christmas period Bank Holidays were quite busy, it was surprising the number of people that used the trains on Christmas Day.

I was required to work on Christmas Day in 1956, but I didn't mind really. For any Bank Holiday working, pay was the same as that for a Sunday, i.e. time and three-quarters. In addition, you were entitled to a day off in lieu paid at normal rate.

I used to accumulate these 'lieu days' and take them as an additional week's holiday during the year although there was little chance of having this extra time off during the summer months.

You were not permitted to carry lieu days into the following year, at a certain point – when, I cannot clearly remember – you were automatically paid for any remaining days not taken.

CHAPTER SIX

1957

At the beginning of 1957 I had to my credit 131 Firing turns as a Passed Cleaner. Also at the start of this year I began to keep a diary containing brief details of each daily shift starting time, engine number, driver's name and any other items of significance. After the passage of so many years, leafing through the pages of these diaries has been like opening a picture book of my railway experiences. Without them, this book could not have been written.

A very sick L1

On January 11th I was on the 7.8 am shunting turn at Broxbourne with driver Ted Champ on 0-6-0 J39 no. 64807. We were parked up in the Cattle Dock at the Cambridge end of the Down platform when a local train for Hertford slowly gasped it's way to the end of the platform. It was the 11.30am out of Liverpool Street crewed by Stratford men with a 2-6-4 L1 tank engine number 67734.

At the same time the Station Inspector arrived to advise us that Control had issued instructions that we were to swap our engine for 67734, which was not steaming.

I quickly built up the fire while the engine movements were being carried out and handed over to the Stratford fireman as soon as we had backed onto his train.

The problem with the L1 was that it was short of steam and when I looked into the firebox I could see why. The firebed was one mass of dull red ash right up to the level of the firehole door!

Having crept back into the Cattle Dock I managed to raise sufficient steam to bring the boiler water up to a respectable level but was not able to do much about cleaning the fire given the location we were in. I would guess that the fire had not been cleaned the night before and whoever did the morning preparation had simply piled fresh coal over a very dirty firebed.

Fortunately for me, we were not required for any more shunting before the arrival of our relief who would work the engine on the local goods to Hertford later in the day. The fireman would then have to clean the fire in readiness for working the Temple Mills Goods later that evening, although I would guess another engine would have been found by then, as an L1 was not really suited to that sort of working.

Locomotive Inspector George Mason

A couple of weeks later, on the 4th of February, I was duty Passed Cleaner on the 10 till 6 night shift, when I had to cover for a sick fireman on the first train out at 4.24 a.m..

On the return journey, the 7 a.m. out of Liverpool Street, I had my first experience of an Inspector joining us on the footplate of our N7 no. 69688. The Inspector was the well-known George Mason and I took great care to keep smoke at a minimum to avoid getting into his bad books, George had a thing about making unnecessary smoke.

119

My driver that morning was Arthur White, the same driver with whom I was with on the 6.3pm 'fast' out of London several months earlier on one of my first passenger turns.

Our trip passed without incident with George and Arthur chatting away most of the trip, I received a cheerful nod from Inspector Mason as we parted company at Hertford.

An unidentified L1 2-6-4 leaves Hertford in 1957. Note the pair of old Great Eastern grounded coach bodies, which were used by the female carriage cleaners.

16 Tons of overtime!

Always in the market to earn some extra cash I teamed up with fireman John Shelsher, to unload a 16-ton wagon of coal on to a reserve stack over in the Goods Yard. This was during the last week of February and was done after we had finished our 10 p.m. to 6 a.m. turn on Shed Duties. I can't remember exactly how long it took us, but it really was backbreaking work shifting 8 tons apiece for a fixed payment of £2 each. Still, the extra money was useful.

Stranded in London – by flood?

Another occasion, which was a real money-spinner, came my way on the 2nd of April when I was on the afternoon (2 till 10) spare duty. A fireman didn't turn up for one of the late afternoon passenger workings to London and I was given the job.   I was paired up with driver Fred Sutton on 69699.   We got to Liverpool Street ok. but we didn't get away until around midnight.

Unfortunately my diary only says 'stuck in London until 12 midnight', but not the reason why!   I believe it was the night the whole station was flooded through torrential rain, as I clearly remember sitting one evening in the bay at the end of the platform and watching the rain come bucketing down non-stop for several hours. We could actually see the water on the ground rising higher and higher until it eventually covered the rails!

At that time all the points were electrically operated and the water put them out of action.   Consequently, the whole of Liverpool Street came to a standstill.

When we did finally get away, I remember running into Tottenham, which was the lowest ground level since leaving London, and finding the tracks well under water.

I had to close the dampers to prevent water being scooped up into the ashpan and dousing the fire.

I am sure this must have been that particular night that my diary refers to.

As a result of all that, I finally booked off duty at 3.30 a.m. - 13 and-a-half hours after signing on!

Off-duty trips to the Isle of Wight

During the early part of 1957 a couple of my mates and myself met some girls who were on holiday from the Isle of Wight.   The outcome was that in June of that year we undertook the first of several trips to the Island to see them.

The drill was that we would go over during a Saturday morning, sleep 'rough' somewhere overnight - on our own, I hasten to add! - and return home on Sunday.

We always went by train and I was the lucky one who could travel at a reduced rate by obtaining a Privilege Ticket (PT) from the Booking Office.   In order to get a ticket, I had to first obtain a special form from the Shedmaster giving the necessary authorisation.   The reduction was quite generous, resulting in my paying only about a quarter of the full fare.

However, there were occasions when I was on night shift prior to the weekend and forgot to arrange for a PT form to be left for me.   This did not present a problem as I discovered that, providing I wore my greasetop railwayman's cap, I could just walk through any Ticket Barrier exchanging nothing more than a brief nod to the Ticket Collector.   Afterwards, I just stowed my cap in my overnight bag until the return journey!

Free travel concessions

After a year's service I was entitled to 3 free travel tickets to anywhere on the Eastern Region, and one free ticket to anywhere on British Railways.   There was no limit to the number of reduced-rate Privilege Tickets I could have. making full use of my annual free ticket allocation.   I suppose that as I was single and didn't have 'away days' with the family at the seaside, I preferred a break from railways on my days off.

Apart from a couple of journeys to my relatives at Taunton in Somerset, I cannot remember

A very eventful week

The week commencing 29th of April 1957 was quite eventful one way and another. On the Monday I was on at 4.45 a.m. for a passenger turn and in the evening, I went with some of my pals to the Granada Theatre at Walthamstow to see a live appearance of one of my favourite Country singers, Slim Whitman.

We went up by bus and afterwards had a wander around the town. By the time we had caught a trolleybus back as far as Waltham Cross we were too late for a connection to get us home, so we had to walk. It wasn't too bad for my pals, who all lived in my old village of Wormley, but after I parted company with them I still had about another 4 miles to walk.

As I was walking down Hoddesdon High Street, the town clock struck the half-hour at 5.30 a.m.

I then remembered that my old mate, Norman (Slim) Whitehouse, was on the 6 o'clock turn that morning, so should be passing through at any moment on his motor scooter, so I was hopeful of a lift.

Sure enough, in the distance I could hear the buzz of a motorcycle coming from the direction of Waltham Cross. In anticipation of a ride home for the last couple of miles, I stepped out into the road and waved my arms for him to stop.

To my horror I heard the engine's revs scream even higher as he speeded up and headed straight for me, I just managed to jump clear at the last second. He shouted some unintelligible remark as he shot past and disappeared into the distance.

I finally reached home around 7 o'clock and, as I was on duty again at 9.03, I had very little chance of any sleep.

I saw Norman in the rest room when I signed on and asked him what his game was. Apparently he had no idea that it was me waving him down but thought it was some drunk just wandering about in the road! We had a god laugh about it afterwards.

Wednesday was my Rest Day but I worked a spare turn.

I must have been working out of my normal rota as I finished the last 3 days of that week doing an 8.05 p.m. shift, after starting the week at 4.45 a.m.!

Ice-cold milk

The afternoon of June 25th found me in the carriage sidings on the Up side of Bishops Stortford station on 69683 with driver Cyril Thompson. We had just brought in a train from Broxbourne and had some time to spare before the return journey. Cyril was an ex-Stortford fireman who had recently transferred to Hertford East to fill a driver's vacancy, so today we were back on his old stomping ground.

As we waited there I was alarmed to see Cyril pick up the tea can from the tray above the firebox and promptly throw the contents out onto the track.

"Hey, what's going on?" I protested. *"Be patient laddie"* said Cyril and washed the can out under the injector overflow water pipe at the bottom of the cab steps.

I say 'washed' rather than cleaned as the water in the engine tanks had been treated with all sorts of chemicals to prevent the boilers scaling up.

Still, in those days hygiene was a word mostly confined to the dictionary, so it never bothered us!

"Keep an eye on things Albert." he said and scrambled up the high, grassy embankment and over the wire fence into the Dairy situated directly above us.

Several minutes later he returned with a can full of ice-cold fresh milk – absolutely delicious on a hot afternoon!

The name **Bishops Stortford Dairy Farmers** was emblazoned along the sides of the buildings and little did I realise that, less than 20 years later, I would be based at that same Dairy as a District Manager with Unigate Dairies.

A Fireman at last

A milestone was reached on Bank Holiday Monday, August 5th when I gained promotion to a fully-fledged Fireman in the Goods Link.   Coincidentally, I was only 5 short of the required 272 firing turns that would have guaranteed me regular Fireman's rate anyway.

My regular driver was Ted Champ and I counted myself very fortunate to have been paired with such a good mate.   Ted was a very quiet, self-assured person with a dry sense of humour and a very tolerant nature, always willing to give the benefit of his experience in order to prepare me for a driver's role.

Another thing that always intrigued me about Ted was that he was always signed on duty well ahead of time, no matter how early our shift was.   He would be there all bright and chipper, with me rushing in at the last minute all bleary-eyed!

His secret, he once told me, was that he never needed more than 4 hours sleep at a stretch.

My first 'Sandringham'

I mentioned earlier of the shunting turn at Broxbourne when we often had engines fresh out of Stratford Workshops well, on Friday, August 9th our engine was an immaculate 'Sandringham' Class B17 4-6-0 no. 61613 carrying the name *'Woodbastwick Hall'*.   She looked an absolute beauty in her fresh, green express passenger livery.   Never in my wildest dreams could I have known that she would be consigned to the scrapheap not too many months later.

Another Firing Examination

Following my appointment to Fireman, on August 20th I was summoned to Stratford for a Fireman's Examination.   Unlike the test I underwent as a Cleaner, I was not given a practical test on a locomotive but simply sat in a classroom with several fellow firemen whilst an Inspector drilled us on the essential elements of our responsibilities. This covered such things as taking care

A rather over-exposed shot of driver Ted Champ (left) and his fireman - Gerald Knight - on the footplate of N7 69680 c. 1956.

of our own safety and that of others, helping our driver in observing signals, keeping our eyes open to ensure nothing is amiss with our train etc. etc.   Most of this was pure common sense, which the various drivers I had worked with had already taught me.

I remember one of the questions the Inspector asked the group was *"What is the first thing a fireman must do whenever he gets on an engine?"*

To which one wag in our group called out "**Go and make the tea**!"   Even the Inspector joined in the laughter.

The correct answer was, as we all knew, to 'check the water-level in the boiler'.

An attack of the Flu'

I had my first ever dose of influenza on Sunday, October 6th and I still remember to this day the effect it had on me.

I signed on duty at 12.45 p.m. on a passenger turn with N7 no. 69687, my driver was Alf Childs.   I felt ok when I signed on but before we left Hertford an hour later I wondered what was happening to me.   My limbs and chest started to ache and my whole body became lethargic, I was finding it difficult even to lift - let alone swing - the shovel.

Fortunately, 69687 steamed well without undue effort on my part, so between bouts of firing I was able to dump myself in the corner of the cab on my little wooden seat and conserve what small amount of energy I had left.

Alf was very sympathetic and helped me with the firing as much as he could. On our return to shed at the end of the shift Alf raked out the ashpan and smokebox while I struggled to clean the fire – I was very grateful for having a good mate that day!

When I finally got home I fell into my bed and stayed there until the Wednesday morning, when I returned to work feeling a whole lot better.

Although the odd injury prevented me from short periods of work, that was the only occasion for many years that I was off work through sickness. Mind you, there were many occasions when maybe it would have been wiser to have stayed at home to recover from similar symptoms, but that was not my nature!

Driver Alf Childs leans out of the cab of Class N7 0-6-2 no.69683 as he starts away from Hertford East with a Liverpool Street train in 1958.

The Churchbury Loop

The week commencing 4th of November found Ted Champ and myself on the 8.25 p.m. Temple Mills goods turn. The week was uneventful until we arrived at Cheshunt on the Thursday evening.

There was some trouble further up the main line, so a Pilotman was waiting to take us through to Tottenham via the Churchbury Loop. This Loop had been closed to passenger traffic for around 40 years but was now being refurbished in readiness for the forthcoming electrification programme which would become the route to Liverpool Street for electric trains.

As it was dark there was not a lot to see during that trip but, although it was the first time Ted or I had travelled that road, I did wonder how many times our engine, Class J15 0-6-0 65440 had been there during her 74 year life.

The next occasion I travelled the Churchbury Loop was as a passenger in an electric train early in 1961, which, due to the many teething problems the new electrics were experiencing, broke down en route.

Coincidentally, the driver (or Motorman, to use his new title) of the blighted electric on that occasion was none other than my old mate, Ted Champ!

I remember leaning out of the carriage window and giving him some good-natured 'stick'!

My first (car) Driving Test

In the hopes of changing my trusty old cycle for a car, I took a driving test at mid-day on 3rd of December. A couple of my pals had already taken the test and passed, telling me how easy it was. I went along to the Driving Test Centre bubbling with confidence – and failed!

In those days you were not allowed to take another Test until at least 3 months from the last one so, what with the long waiting list, another 6 months was to elapse before I tried again.

Into 1958

I had Christmas Day off that year although I did have to work on Boxing Day, but not until 10.30 a.m., which was quite a civilised time of the day for me.

After seeing in the New Year at a party in the home of one of my old schoolpals, I signed on at 11.20 a.m. on New Year's Day, another reasonable time of day!

By this time I had completed 381 firing turns.

CHAPTER SEVEN

1958 – A very chilly start

Snow and more snow

One of the more memorable occasions during the early part of the year was the tremendous snowfall towards the end of February.

It started on Tuesday the 25th and just went on and on. I was duty fireman on 6 a.m. to 2.p.m. shed duties and when I cycled home on Tuesday afternoon the falling snow was already lying pretty thickly. After arriving home, I didn't go outside again until just after 5.30 the following morning, to work the same turn as the day before.

What a shock I received as I stepped outside my back door! The snow must have been over a foot deep and there was no chance of riding my cycle at that stage, so I hoisted it on my shoulder and carried it, expecting better conditions when I reached the main road.

Instead of the improvement I expected, the situation was much worse as heavy drifting had taken place.

I trudged past a couple of abandoned cars and, when I reached somewhere near the halfway stage to Hertford, I came across a single-decker bus almost covered in a huge drift. It was completely iced up and abandoned and must have been the last bus from Hertford the evening before.

It was past 7 o'clock by the time I reached the Shed, but nobody minded, in fact, there was some surprise that I made it at all. Some crews couldn't get in, particularly those that lived out towards Buntingford, which had suffered severely, many roads remained blocked for several days. At least one of Hertford's crew was completely stranded for several hours on a Buntingford passenger train from the previous evening.

Snowploughs were summoned from Stratford to clear the Buntingford branch but the Hertford branch itself managed to keep open, albeit with a skeleton service.

It was several days before things returned to something like normal.

Bitterly cold spells followed the snow and we had to ensure the small braziers were kept well alight beneath the water columns to prevent them freezing up.

Even the injector equipment located just below the footplate was prone to freezing solid and much use was made of blazing oilcloths on the firing shovel, which were held beneath the frozen pipes.

I believe it was some weeks before the last of the snow and ice cleared and things returned to normal.

A visit to Wembley

Later in the year, on May 3rd, I went to Wembley with another of the firemen to see the Football Cup Final. Bolton Wanderers beat Manchester United 2 – 0.

The Bus Strike

Monday, 5th of May was the beginning of a London Transport bus strike that lasted for several weeks.

This obviously resulted in a sudden increase in local traffic on the railway.

The transport situation was so serious that learner drivers - subject to certain conditions - were allowed to use their cars unaccompanied by a qualified driver for the duration of the strike.

National Service

Having now reached my 18th birthday, I was now eligible for being summoned to serve 2 years National Service in the British Army. This arrangement was compulsory until the end of the 1950s.

However, there were exceptions dependant upon what ones occupation was at that time. Railwaymen were classified as carrying out an 'essential public service', so we were one of the exceptions.

It is interesting to note the efficiency of the relevant Records Office even in those days, as exampled by some of my colleagues who decided to leave the railway during that time. In a very short space of time they had received their 'Call-up' papers, and the next time I saw them, they were in Army uniform!

They all seemed to benefit from the 2 years in the military and in some respects I regretted missing it.

By the time I left the railway the scheme had been discontinued.

The BSA 'Winged Wheel'

About this time, to save myself some of the effort of pedalling to and fro from work, I purchased a bicycle that was fitted with a BSA 'Winged Wheel'. This was a tiny two-stroke petrol engine fitted in the hub of the rear wheel which you started by pedalling furiously before engaging the clutch via a lever fitted to the handlebars.

I can't remember whether it required a Road Fund Licence, but it was powerful enough to get up a fair turn of speed – well, about 25mph! - on level ground. For steep hills one was required to pedal-assist the little motor.

It wasn't an ideal piece of machinery as the spark-plug was prone to frequent oiling up which made it impossible to start unless it was taken out and burnt dry using a cigarette lighter. In my naivety, I started to add less oil to the petrol, as it seemed to produce greater speed. The inevitable result was that I blew the engine up in a very short time, so it was back to my old sports cycle.

A much better form of transport was the motor scooter owned by my younger brother, it was a 50cc job and I persuaded him to let me borrow it when I was on late turns. I had to make sure it was there for him when he was due to go to work at around 7.30 a.m.

I used it every opportunity I could and I don't remember ever once letting him down on the arrangement.

The Ware Shunter

I have previously made mention of the yards at Ware and the little 0-4-0 diesel engine used exclusively for shunting that yard. The regular (and only) driver was named Jack Hart and, although it was normally a driver-only operation whilst operating within the confines of the yard, I did have reason to accompany him on one occasion when working a Sunday train on track maintenance out on the main line at Ware.

I don't think anyone knew Jack Hart very well, as he only ever worked the Ware Yard. I believe he was originally from March near Cambridge, and applied for the Ware job because of the attraction of no Sunday workings.

Because he did not regularly work out on the main line, his rate of pay was somewhat less than that of other Hertford drivers, but it obviously suited him.

There was just one other occasion that found me shunting in Ware yard, that was for a couple of hours on 2nd of June with N7 69693. I cannot recall the reason for that unscheduled job – maybe the diesel engine had broken down.

Another Driving Test – another failure!

On Wednesday, 18th June I took my second driving test for a car licence and failed again! I was choked off as it meant another 6 months before I could take the test again.

I came to the conclusion that much of the problem was the fact that the cars I took the test in were not making things easy for me.

They were my dad's cars, which he seemed to change every few months and, as we were not a wealthy family, they were rather ancient pre-war vehicles. Among other things, the steering wheel was an effort to turn and the brakes, whilst perfectly legal, did not stop the car quickly enough to satisfy the Examiner's emergency stop. The M.O.T. vehicle tests had not been introduced at that time.

I vowed that for my next test I would hire one of the modern cars operated by the local Driving Schools.

A change of Driver

At the end of June, my regular driver, Ted Champ was promoted to the Passenger Link, and a newly promoted driver, Dennis Banks, replaced him.

Sorry as I was to lose Ted, I was not disappointed with his replacement.

Although Dennis was a newcomer to Hertford, he was quite a cheerful character. I think he was also an immigrant from Bishop's Stortford, as was Cyril Thomson, who transferred to gain promotion.

Although quite a responsible driver, Dennis was always on the lookout for a bit of fun and I had to watch myself for the little pranks he would play on me given half a chance.

There goes my cap!

A typical example of Dennis' type of humour was on the Temple Mills turn with J15 0-6-0 65464 on Friday the 4th of July. We were just running into Rye House station and I was looking out my side of the cab when Dennis whipped my cap off my head and threw it out on the side of the track!

As we were only travelling at walking pace I was able to leap of the engine and run back and retrieve it, just in time to clamber up onto the Guard's Van as it went past.

We had to stop at Rye House to pick up a couple of wagons from the yard, so I was able to rejoin my engine. While I led off at him for doing such a daft thing Dennis just sat there laughing his head off, he thought it was a great joke!

A beautiful black B1

On July 10th we were on the 4 p.m. Broxbourne shunt turn and that day when we walked across the yard to relieve the Stratford crew we found that our engine was an immaculate black Class B1 4-6-0 express engine number 61360.

It was another engine straight from a major overhaul in Stratford Works and I could not believe how silently she ran. When we did the trip to Waltham Cross and back, all you could hear was the clicking of the rail joints beneath the wheels.

What a change from the clashing rattles and bangs, squeals and groans emitted by other locomotives we usually worked with.

'Off the road' at Hertford

There were many occasions when running at speed on the mainline when I thought the engine would literally fall to pieces beneath us. The noise and vibration – accompanied by swirling coal-dust – has to be experienced to be believed.

There was one occasion when my fear of leaving the track became a reality.

Dennis and I were just finishing our 7.15 a.m. shift on the afternoon of Thursday, 14th of August. Our engine that day was N7 no. 69731.

We had brought our passenger train in, unhooked and run our engine back down the main line to return to the shed.

By this date, alterations had taken place and the old Turntable Road was now the way in and out of the engine yard. The turntable had been removed and the pit filled in, a hole knocked through the end of the shed on the Mead Lane side, and the track realigned so as to run right through the shed.

Well, we stopped past the main-line points on the London side of the Signalbox and waited for the signalman to alter the road to allow us to run into the carriage yard past the box. He would then change another set of points to allow us to reverse back down the old Turntable Road and into the shed.

Having got the ok from the small ground signal to come off the main line Dennis opened up 69731 and we nipped smartly across the pointwork behind the Signalbox.

All of a sudden I thought the world had come to an end! There was this almighty crash and our engine rocked and jumped about like a mad thing, the tool cupboard at the back of the cab above our heads burst open and everything in it crashed to the floor.

Dust was flying everywhere and I felt certain we were going to topple over. After what seemed like ages (but was probably just a few seconds) we came to a stop - still upright I was relieved to find.

Of course, we were well and truly 'off the road' or, to coin a favourite term used at that time for such an occasion 'we were on Old England'.

It appeared that the engine that entered the shed before us had probably reversed back onto the Turntable Road before the points had been reset from the main line, so that engine had 'split them'.

How it happened

In other words, the previous locomotive's wheel flanges had forced their way through the opposite-facing points and bent the blades inward, so that they no longer fitted tight against the rail.

This meant that when we hit those facing points our wheel flanges ran between the slightly open point blades, left the track, and ran onto the wooden sleepers.

Normally, the Signalman gets some indication that something is amiss the next time he operates the relevant levers from his box or, if so equipped, the electric track circuit board above his lever frame will show a fault.

On this occasion he had no such indication that anything was wrong. Furthermore, these points were situated at the unglazed rear of the Signalbox, so he could not have even spotted that an engine had run through them.

Avoiding further catastrophe

When the Shedmaster learnt of the mishap he was in something of a panic as it was just about the time when the passeger timetable started to get busy, it was 3.25 p.m. Every wheel of our engine was off the rails so there was no chance of re-railing us with the limited amount of equipment we had at Hertford, so the Stratford Breakdown Train had to be summoned.

Meantime, the Shedmaster had the problem of how he was to release the engines trapped in the shed, as we were blocking the exit road. Access to and from the main line at the London end of the shed roads had been severed when the alterations were made and the new exit normally used was via the Great Northern track, but we were blocking the way off of there.

As luck would have it, an inspection revealed that we had run just about an engine's length clear of the offending points so that, with a Platelayer operating the points manually with clamps, the engines could be carefully released from the shed by coming back up the old Turntable Road.

As we were already on overtime, we left the engine in the care of the shed crew and went home.   I didn't find out how long it took to re-rail 69731, but it was an experience I am glad to say was never repeated!

A near-miss at Broxbourne

There was an earlier incident that occurred at Broxbourne early one morning when we could have split the points, which would have caused untold disruption – and possibly much worse – on the Down Main line.

We were on the Temple Mills turn and had arrived at Broxbourne at around 4.00 a.m.   We stopped our train in the Down platform and waited for the Guard to unhook the wagons that we were to drop off in the Down Yard.   Several yards beyond the end of the (original) station platform were two sets of points fairly close together, a 'facing' and a 'trailing' set.
The facing points were set for us to draw forward with our rake of wagons and enter the yard sidings, which we proceeded to do.   Having delivered these few wagons, we uncoupled and ran down to the far end of the yard where another set of points allowed us back onto the Down Main.   We then reversed back onto our train, where we had one more wagon to detach and place in the old Cattle Dock bay just to the left of the Down Platform.   This involved pulling forward up the main line clear of the trailing points which, after the Signalman had switched them and pulled off the small ground signal, allowed us to propel the wagon into the bay. We then drew back out onto the main line and waited for the Signalman to reset the points for us to rejoin the rest of our train in the platform.
I would explain out that, as the old Signalbox was almost opposite the end of the Down Platform, the Signalman had a clear view of all the movements which were taking place, so there was no need for whistled instructions to be given.
After we had drawn out of the bay onto the main line I looked out to watch the points change and the ground signal turn to green to let us back onto our train.
As this signal was on my side, i.e. set between the Up and Down main lines, I called across to my driver that all was clear to reverse.
Luckily, and I don't know why, I stretched out of the cab to have another look at the track, and immediately shouted to my mate to stop.
Although we had the 'all clear', for some inexplicable reason, the Signalman had also switched the facing points off of the main into the yard.   Had we ran back onto our train, we would have 'run through' those points or, in other words, split them.
Confusion reigned for the next few minutes, the Signalman had his head out of his window waving us back, with me shouting and waving at the track ahead of us.
Eventually the penny dropped and he quickly disappeared to do some rapid lever pulling to set the track right.
He waved his thanks to me and pretended to mop sweat from his brow as we passed his box!

To Broxbourne with a 'museum piece'

There was one occasion I remember when the 'Mills' engine was needed to work the 8.25 a.m. passenger train to Broxbourne - due to my driver failing our allocated locomotive due to some defect – and that was the only spare available.

This must have been sometime in late 1956 because we brought the engine across from the yard to the turntable, so that we faced 'chimney first' to Broxbourne.

I remember groaning that it was just our luck that, on that particular morning, the engine was the smallest of the 0-6-0 goods – a J15 – the fire had not been cleaned properly and the tender was full of dusty 'slack' rather than good-sized lumps of coal.

Anyway, we pulled her round so that by the time we had hooked on to our train, we had a full head of steam and half a boilerfull of water.

It was not a good trip to Broxbourne, even though the distance was not much more than 7 miles, but we just about made it before the steam pressure fell to the danger level that would automatically apply the brakes.

Although the Up side of Broxbourne station had a long, bay platform, because of the location of the Signalbox, it was not possible to run straight into it from the main line.

The procedure was to run right through the station and reverse back into the bay platform. This must have been rather disconcerting at times for passengers wishing to alight at Broxbourne – thinking that we were not stopping!

Anyway, even this short 7-mile trip was all too much for the old girl and, as we wheezed to a stop in the bay platform a group of businessmen walked up to inspect this grubby little curiosity that was clearly out of her depth. They roared with laughter when they read the legend on the maker's plate attached to the centre wheel splasher above the footplating. It read 'Built 1883' and they remarked that it's proper place was in a museum!

Hertford's Station Pilot engine

As I mentioned at the beginning of my story, another job introduced at Hertford sometime during 1957 was that of Station Pilot.

Up until that time it was usual for us to draw our train out of the carriage sidings and reverse it into the platform in the morning, and put it back in the sidings at night.

In addition, certain trains were shunted during the day to enable the Carriage Cleaners to do their job.

Now we had a little Class J69 0-6-0 tank engine to do all these jobs, plus other duties like bringing coal and ash wagons into the depot etc. Although this Pilot job was only a single full shift, the job was continued until late evening by a couple of other sets of men as part of their duties, so the locomotive actually worked something like a 16-hour day.

Initially, the engine allocated was numbered 68500, to be changed later for another member of the same class, numbered 68600. With just a change of one digit in the number, I often wondered just how many casual observers actually noticed that it was a different engine?

Hertford East station pilot, Class J69 0-6-0 68500 receives routine attention by the Turntable Road water column c. 1957. Regular driver Arthur Tilcock watches from the cab doorway as his fireman – Wally Coleman - refills the lubricator on top of the Westinghouse air pump.

Driver Arthur Tilcock

The regular driver on the Station Pilot for the first year or so was Arthur Tilcock.
Arthur was a rather stern-faced, well-built individual close to retirement, and he was a stickler for having things done correctly.
When he was in the Passenger Link most of us young firemen dreaded being paired with Arthur as we knew we would be pulled up for something or other.
But, as with many of the drivers I have worked with, you cannot go by first impressions and the few occasions I worked alongside Arthur I found quite enjoyable.
I witnessed an entertaining event one morning in the shed when Arthur was preparing the Pilot for the day's work.   His fireman that day was Bill Baugh. Bill had started several months after me and, likeable chap that he was, never exactly set the ground alight with his speed of movement, especially at 4.45 a.m., which was the starting time for this turn of duty.
On this particular morning he was on the top of the tank of 68500 supervising the filling of it from the water column, with Arthur down below waiting to turn the water off as soon as Bill called for him to do so.

Unfortunately, Bill was a bit slow in giving the word and the water overflowed before Arthur could turn it off.   Some of the water splashed onto Arthur's immaculate overalls. However, he managed to stop the flow without getting any wetter.

Arthur muttered some choice words, including something about "B******* standing up there half-asleep" and proceeded to walk to the front of the engine.

As he did so he looked up and saw Bill standing motionless on top of the tank.

*"Don't just b****** stand there"* roared Arthur, " ***chuck the b******* bag out and let's get going***." As he turned away, Bill lifted the leather water pipe out of the filler hole and let it drop over the side.

Although commonly referred to as 'bags', they were in fact thick leather flexible pipes about 12 inches in diameter and between 8 and 10 feet long. Now those bags usually still held several gallons of water and as Bill slid it out of the filler-hole and let it flop down to ground level like an elephant's trunk, it emptied the contents all down poor old Arthur's back.

Well, none of us dared laugh, although we were dying to do so, fully expecting Arthur to go berserk, but amazingly, he didn't utter a word!

He simply squelched off to the locker-room where he had a spare set of overalls, (but no dry underwear I suspect!) came out and stepped up onto his engine and left the shed.

Needless to say, he never said another word to Bill that day, neither did he get offered any of Arthur's tea.   I never did ask Bill, but I did wonder if that little episode really *was* accidental!

Into the Passenger Link

I was promoted to the Passenger Link on September 8th that year.   It didn't carry an increase in pay but it did mean that, with just a few exceptions, I would be working only on passenger trains.

Our passenger routes covered; Buntingford, Bishops Stortford, North Woolwich, Stratford and Liverpool Street.   Of course, by this time I had already covered those routes on many occasions.

The Passenger Train Service at this time comprised something like 28 weekday trains each way between Hertford and Liverpool Street, plus a handful running to and from Stratford.   There were also some trains that ran only as far as Broxbourne, from which passengers could obtain a connection to London.

The operation of these services were shared with Stratford and Bishops Stortford crews of course, but Hertford men also had a small share of services to Bishops Stortford, Buntingford and (once a day) North Woolwich.

Route variations up the line

The first three of our morning trains to Liverpool Street went via Stratford, which meant leaving the main line at Coppermill Junction – about a mile beyond Tottenham station.

For the rest of the day, most of our trains went via Hackney Downs. Although there were 3 stations beyond Hackney – Cambridge Heath, London Fields and Bethnal Green – we were never booked to stop at any of them, they were served by Enfield and Wood Street trains.

There were 14 station stops between Hertford and Liverpool Street as can be seen from the sample 1960 Timetable reproduced in the Appendix Section at the back of this book.

Strange as it may seem, I don't believe any of our return journeys out of Liverpool Street ever went via Stratford, we always branched left immediately beyond Bethnal Green station to head for our first stop, Hackney Downs.

We would occasionally stop at Bethnal Green, not to pick up passengers but to await a path on the fast line to Hackney Downs, perhaps due to a Cambridge express taking precedence.

Sometimes we would take empty coaches from Liverpool Street to Thornton Fields Carriage Sidings at Stratford and then work a train from Stratford to Hertford.

The Channelsea Loop

There was at least one train that was booked only as far as Stratford and returned later in the day. I believe this train went via the Channelsea Loop around the back of the vast Stratford Works and Yard complex. This meant that the engine – and carriages - arrived back at Hertford facing the opposite direction to when it left.

There was always something of interest around Channelsea, maybe an ancient coach or two, some old redundant locomotive tenders used for water-carrying or sludge storage, even the occasional locomotive could be seen dumped in one of those far-flung sidings.

Then there were the little black timber shacks dotted haphazardly along the way, where individuals earned their living performing all manner of tasks, be it repairs to rolling stock or equipment, or some other obscure job of work necessary to the running of the railway.

Temple Mills avoiding curve

The old route from Lea Bridge to Stratford station ran right through the centre of the vast, newly constructed, marshalling yards of Temple Mills. This caused serious operating difficulties as regards to traffic movements between the Up and Down Yards. During the mid 1950s a new set of tracks were constructed which skirted the yards on the right-hand (Up) side.

Although this new line was sharply curved, it was also heavily cambered so it was still possible to run safely at a good rate of speed.

Above. Class N7 0-6-2 Tank engine no. 69682 is seen arriving at Hertford East at the end of her run from Liverpool Street. The exact date is unknown, but the immaculate condition of the engine suggests it must be sometime between October 1958 and January 1959, when she was the author's 'regular' engine. The driver looking out of the cab is probably Charlie Lee.
Below. Class N7 no. 69724 is seen leaving Broxbourne's original station with a Hertford East to Liverpool Street train in June 1955.

Charlie Lee

My new mate in the Passenger Link was Charlie Lee, one of the nicest drivers one could ever wish to meet. My fellow firemen kept telling me how lucky I was, and I fully agreed.

Charlie was getting on in years and I believe he was a widower. I say this because he frequently referred to his daughter with whom he lived somewhere in the Leyton area, but he never mentioned a wife.

He was one of the genuine 'Fireman's Friends' in that you only burnt half the amount of coal when Charlie was on the regulator. As soon as you pulled out of the station with your train, he would wind the gear lever right up so there was little more than a puff from the chimney, as opposed to the fire-eating blast normally accompanying a standing start. Consequently, much less steam, water and coal was required and, even though we seemed to dawdle along between stations, we still kept perfect time.

Charlie's improvisation!

One of Charlie's few delights was his hand-rolled cigarettes, but he was always running out of cigarette papers at the wrong time.

As I only smoked ready-made cigarettes at that time, I was unable to help him when he ran out, and he refused to smoke any of mine.

Instead, he would tear up a piece of newspaper, or a paper bag from his lunchbox, and fabricate a cigarette, using a goodly amount of saliva to keep the paper tube held together.

What it used taste like I can't imagine, but old Charlie would sit contentedly in his corner puffing away, at peace with the world!

69682 – My own regular engine

Charlie's regular engine was N7 no. 69682. I now had the opportunity to fulfil a promise I had made to myself many months earlier, that was to shine her up to match those I had looked upon at Liverpool Street.

I was very fortunate that '82 had recently gone through Stratford Works for a major overhaul - including a repaint - so it was not too difficult to make the bodywork sparkle.

The job of keeping her shining!

The Hertford Fitting crew got me off to a good start by acid-dipping much of the brass and copperwork as well as buffing up the handrails, smokebox outer ring and buffer-heads to make them shine.

Even old Bert Neve always seemed to find extra lumps of tallow and Derby Paste to enable me to keep everything sparkling. An addition to the other bits and pieces in my holdall was a tin of 'Brasso'.

I believe our 'opposite number' who shared '82 was Driver Alf Lee (no relation to Charlie) and Fireman Herbie Howard, who both did their bit to ensure she was kept in pristine condition.

I suppose I was the most fastidious of the lot because maintaining her in that order became a bit of an obsession.

Had we had our own engine every day, keeping her spotless would have been demanding enough, but things didn't turn out that way.

We would 'lose' her for days on end to other crews and when we finally got her back, she would look little different than the rest of her other grubby sisters. It was then a matter of starting all over again. I exaggerate a little because, although she was just as filthy, most of the grime came off much easier because of the highly polished metal beneath.

There was never a spare moment when I was not doing something, like nipping out on to the platform to run a cleaning cloth over the tank and cabsides, or polishing the various cab fittings in between my other duties while we were on the move.

When we pulled into the platform at Liverpool Street, I would waste no time in uncoupling our train, then jumping up onto the side-tank and dropping the leather water bag into the filler-hole. While the tank was filling up, I would clamber over the top of the boiler wiping the paintwork and polishing the safety valves and the twin brass snifting valve covers just behind the chimney.

At the start and finish of our shift I would work through my mentally prepared cleaning programme, but it really was hard graft.

However, the sense of pride I felt from working on the footplate of an immaculate locomotive made the extra effort well worthwhile.

Jealousy?

An extra bonus was the admiring glances from the general public as we drew into a platform, or as they hurried by our engine when we arrived at Liverpool Street.

Some of the shed staff used to refer to 69682 during this period as the 'Hertford Royal' engine.

Strange as it may seem, there was not much in the way of compliments from my fellow enginemen. One or two even went as far as to call me a 'stupid sod' for doing all that extra work, their arguments being that no-one thanked you for it, you were paid no extra and it didn't make her steam any better anyway.

Maybe they were right in their own way, but I did it because it gave me a degree of pride in my job, something that was becoming increasingly rare towards the end of the steam age –and I like to think that she ***did*** steam better!

It also helped to give some dignity to an ageing locomotive that still continued to give loyal and reliable service in all weathers, despite the appalling neglect these engines had to suffer during their final years.

The author's hard effort is reflected in the shining brass and gleaming paintwork of 69682 as she stands over the ashpit in Hertford Loco during the autumn of 1958

Some driving experience

All this was only to last for but a few months, as later on most of our N7 fleet, including 69682, was replaced by the larger, Class L1 2-6-4 tank engines, more of which I will refer to later.

By this time, there had been occasions when I had been allowed to take over the driving for short periods. Most commonly this had been when we were carrying out small shunting operations in the various goods yards, particularly at Broxbourne, and not always because of a kindly driver.

I mentioned some of the ex-Works engines we had at Broxbourne, although they gave a nice smooth ride, much of the mechanism could be very stiff.

Constantly winding a stiff reversing screw back and forth and heaving open and close a 'tight' regulator really could be arm and backaching work.

So it was not unusual for your mate, particularly the older ones, to swap places for the comparatively easy job of the fireman. Still, it was good experience and I certainly never refused the opportunity.

Apart from the shunting, by this time I was sufficiently knowledgeable to be allowed to drive out on the main line.

I used to find it required more skill to manage a loose-coupled goods train than a passenger train, simply because judging stopping distances was much more difficult with the goods because the only braking power was on the engine.

With a passenger train a continuous vacuum brake operated on the wheels of every coach.

With the passage of time I was to act as driver on numerous occasions, but never once did I ever take it for granted.   Each time my driver pointed me to his side of the cab, I felt it a great privilege, after all, he was breaking the rules in order to give me driving experience.

With Charlie Lee and 69682 I started driving on a regular basis, usually every other day.   Old Charlie made firing look as easy as his driving, we were never short of steam, and neither did he waste any through the safety valves.

To help Charlie on my 'driving days', I would shovel a good few hundredweight of coal into the firebox before we set off.

By this time I knew every signal and permanent speed restriction between Hertford, Liverpool Street, Stratford, Bishops Stortford and Buntingford and, along with my driver, studied the daily bulletins pinned above the Signing-on desk to note any temporary changes applicable to our daily route.

These bulletins were very important as there was always something going on in the way of maintenance on the railway system, particularly at that time when preparations in readiness for electrification were in progress.

There is nothing really difficult in driving a steam locomotive, the art is to drive it economically both in terms of coal consumption and wear and tear on the locomotive and your fireman.

The skill came in regulating your speed to maintain correct time, and to start and stop your train smoothly in order to cause minimum inconvenience to your passengers or, in the case of a Goods train, your Guard.

There was no point in dashing between stations at high speed only to have the Guard or the Station Inspector make you wait for a few minutes until your due time to leave, although some drivers did exactly that!   This really was just a waste of fuel and the poor old fireman's energy.

Having said all that, there was a great deal of pleasure to be derived from 'opening her up' now and again.   Even our N7s, small when compared with an express locomotive, were quite powerful engines for their size and were capable of a tidy turn of speed when the occasion demanded.

Waking the babies

A common instance of opening up was on the last leg of a passenger journey from London.   As you left Ware, it was usual to look in the firebox to check the level of fire, knowing you had to clean it when you arrived on shed.

The ideal situation was to run in with barely a couple of inches of red embers over the firebed, which made cleaning it a much easier job than with a white-hot mass of coals.

If there was a surplus, you would ask your driver to 'drop the wheel', i.e. wind the reversing screw into low gear and open up the regulator to it's full extent.

The effect was that the exhaust from the chimney would erupt into a deafening roar, throwing out red-hot cinders as the blast ripped through the firebed. How long this lasted depended on how much the level of the firebed needed to be reduced.

At night this could produce a pretty good impersonation of Vesuvius, with the sound of the exhaust echoing for miles across the watermeadows between Ware and Hertford and probably heard in several of the villages a couple of miles away.

As no member of the public ever seemed to complain of this practice, I suppose it was an accepted part of life at that time.

Smart stopping

Another of the essential arts of driving was stopping you train in the platform at the right place without causing any fuss.

Unlike driving a car, the vacuum-operated brakes on a railway train took several seconds to 'bite' after the brake lever has been operated. By the same principal, it took as many seconds to release them once the brake handle has been returned to the 'off' position.

Added to this - although our usual all-stations timing was not too demanding - it was necessary to arrive and depart each station fairly smartly. In order to achieve this, it was normal not to begin applying the brakes until you were actually running into the station. Then it was a matter of dropping the brake handle into the 'full on' position and leaving it there until you feel the brake begin to bite, by which time you were probably half-way down the platform.

Immediately you felt this, you whipped the brake handle up to the 'full off' position and, if you have judged everything to perfection, your train would draw gently to a stop in exactly the right place, with the brakes just 'rubbing' on the wheels.

The engine brake was not vacuum operated but worked by air pressure, which was supplied by a Westinghouse 'Donkey Pump' situated on the right hand Running Plate alongside the smokebox.

It was possible to set the engine's Westinghouse brake handle in such a position that it operated in conjunction with the vacuum brake.

Important judgement

With our normal length trains, which comprised two sets of 'quad-art' articulated coaches, making eight coaches in all, there was very little to spare in the length of platforms at most of the stations on our route, so good judgement in stopping was vital.

If you stopped short, or overran the platform, valuable time was lost in pulling forward or setting back. This only ever happened on rare occasions, years of practice made all drivers highly skilled in stopping at the precise spot.

On the Chingford and Enfield routes, the Westinghouse Air Brake was used, this, as the name suggests, operated by compressed air rather then vacuum and was a lot more immediate in it's application and release.

Our coaching stock was only equipped for the Continuous Vacuum Brake, so we were unable to use Westinghouse Air Braking other than on the engine. The air pump was the source of the frantic 'panting' you would often hear coming from a stationary locomotive.

This Westinghouse Donkey pump could be very temperamental and often required a hefty clout with the coal pick to persuade it to start. It was very rare to spot a Donkey pump free of dents!

Quite often the pump would decide to stop working during the journey. Then it was a matter of jumping out onto the platform at the next stop, running to the front of the engine and 'waking the pump up' with the aid of the coal hammer.

I guess the sight of a fireman leaping onto the platform with a hammer in his hand must have caused momentary concern to any passengers waiting nearby!

In later years, British Railways converted all it's stock to air brakes and I believe vacuum systems can now only be found on preserved railways.

Getting back to braking methods at that time, the approach into Liverpool Street terminus required a little more skill and respect. To stop too short would be an unforgivable embarrassment, and to overrun would be a total disaster!

On only one occasion did I make a slight misjudgement and smacked into the buffer stops at the terminus a little too hard for my liking, but none of our passengers seemed to take any notice. Causing injury to a passenger in such instances could be much easier than one would at first imagine. Doors are flung open and passengers are leaping out long before the train comes to rest, so a sudden stop, like hitting the buffers hard, could easily cause an alighting passenger to crash against the doorframe.

Conversely, there were the odd occasions when too much brake was applied, threatening to bring your train to a halt halfway into the platform. Then it was a matter of frantically trying to release the brakes, at the same time applying power to the engine to haul the train that last few yards against the brake, because if you came to a stand you didn't dare move again until all your passengers had alighted.

Who lost their garden shed?

A couple of other events come to mind regarding entering Liverpool Street with passenger trains. One was when we were running bunker first into platform 5 (I think) one afternoon. As we rounded the slight curve into the platform a Porter was struggling to pull clear a 4-wheeled platform trolley which had run close to the edge of the platform.

This trolley was loaded with the sections of a wooden garden shed, the panels of which were loaded flat across the raised ends of the trolley.
He had no hope of pulling it clear, and we had no chance of stopping, so we caught the overhanging panels with the corner of our bunker. The force of impact spun the trolley round and smashed the panels to matchwood but fortunately, the Porter had already jumped clear, so nobody was injured.

An emergency stop

On another occasion, we were coasting through the short tunnels beneath Bishopsgate Good Yards on the approach into the terminus. This approach was on a gentle curve and the signalling arrangement was by electric colour lighting, which had replaced the old semaphore type throughout most of the London area.
On the run in, the last two signals were an Outer Home and Home.
If the Outer signal showed an orange light you had to be prepared to stop at the Home signal if it showed red. This signal was situated on a curve at the end of the tunnel complex and couldn't be spotted until you were within a hundred yards or so.
However, if the Outer Home shown green, and it normally always did, you could assume a straight run in to the platform.

On this particular day, the Outer Home showed green as usual but, as we rounded the curve and came in sight of the Home signal, to our horror it was red!
As we were running bunker first, I was the first to spot the light and hollered out "***Whoa, it's a red'un!***" to my mate.
Our engine that day was Harry Curtis's regular N7, 69684 and it was fresh out of the Works, having had a complete overhaul.
Well, as we were expecting a smooth run-in, my Driver had hardly started to apply the brakes but, with a red light in front of us barely a hundred yards away, drastic action was called for. The brake handle was dropped into the 'full on' position, the Forward/Reverse gear wheel spun into the opposite direction and the regulator yanked wide open.
While my mate was doing that, I was frantically operating the sanding gear that ran sand onto the rails to give greater grip. Eventually, the train brake took hold and, with our engine wheels frantically spinning in the opposite direction, we came to a grinding halt just a few feet past the signal.
Now, to overrun a red light was viewed as serious and was usually reported to Higher Authority by the Signalman, the outcome of which the driver concerned was issued with a 'Please Explain' notice, followed by a possible period of suspension without pay.
I jumped off the engine and picked up the internal telephone receiver attached to the signal post.

As soon as it was answered at the other end, I shouted into it *"**What the b***** hell's going on, the Outer Home was green?**"* Passengers were hanging out of the carriage windows, wondering as to the cause of the abrupt stop.
"Sorry mate, we had a conflicting movement in the station, did you stop ok?"
"Eventually" I replied *"but we've overrun a yard or two"*.
"Don't worry about that mate, sorry for the scare, you're ok to come in now." he said. What with that, the light turned orange and we completed the last few hundred yards of our journey, never knowing the exact reason for the emergency.
I wondered how much strain we put on the mechanics of old '84 by the way we had to treat her that day, but she didn't appear to have suffered unduly from the ordeal.

Staying alert

Another occasion with a red light occurred one day towards the end of October 1958 on a passenger train from London. We had just passed Wormley level crossing, a mile-and-a-half from Broxbourne station and were running at a fair pace, when I noticed the Outer Home signal at red. This was another electric colour light and usually it was never at red. The fact that it was at Danger on this occasion suggested that Broxbourne's Down platform was still occupied by a train.
Now my driver that day, who shall remain nameless, was nearing retirement and physically was not the most robust of men.
I always knew he was very hard of hearing, but I didn't suspect there was anything wrong with his eyesight.
We were running chimney first towards Broxbourne and, having spotted the red light, I glanced across the cab to my mate, expecting him to shut off steam and prepare to slow down. Although he was looking straight ahead, he seemed oblivious to the signal and made no attempt to adjust our speed.
*"**Red light up ahead, mate**!"* I shouted across the cab but, what with the rattle of our engine and his poor hearing, he neither looked over at me nor changed his position.
By now we were fast approaching the signal, still at red, so I just stepped across the cab, slammed the regulator shut, and reached across the front of my drivers face and dropped the vacuum brake handle to full on.
I think I frightened the life out of him for a second or two, but he soon realised the situation and quickly assumed control. I had acted in good time and we stopped ok without any real effort.
He didn't say anything to me, I reckon he was a little embarrassed. I believe he may have nodded off for a moment, but I never did know for sure.

Finchy's lemon squeezer!

On a lighter note, there was a brief period when one of the drivers, Vic Finch, had in his bag one of those little yellow plastic 'Jif' lemon-shaped squeezers filled with water. He took great delight in giving you a squirt down the back of your neck when you were least expecting it.

I suppose it was harmless fun but eventually I, among others, got a bit fed up with it.

One morning early in November, we were running into Hertford with a passenger train when, from the opposite direction, a train was just leaving for London.

"*Hey Albert*" my driver, Ted Govier shouted across,"*that's old Finchy just coming up, watch out for his squeezer!*"

With us running in chimney first and him approaching bunker first, both Vic and I were on the same right-hand side of the track.

I quickly whipped the lid off our tea can and filled it with water out of the bucket, which was part of standard equipment on the footplate.

As we approached each other, old Vic had his head stuck out of the cab and was just about to wave a friendly greeting. Although he didn't have his 'squeezer' that morning, it was too late for me to stop what I was about to do.

At precisely the right moment, I emptied the lid of water smack into poor old Vic's smiling face!

At the same time as I let fly, Ted was looking across the cab and couldn't help but see the expression on Vic's face suddenly change from a smile to one of shocked surprise.

Ted roared with laughter, and was still chuckling away long after we had stopped in the platform. Passengers walking past must have thought he was going mad.

I thought I was going to get some trouble from Vic the next time he saw me, but no, he didn't mention the episode, and we never saw the lemon squeezer again neither! As for Ted, for days afterwards, he related the episode to anyone prepared to listen, and he always ended the tale with great guffaws of laughter.

North Woolwich

The final event worth mentioning in 1958 was on Boxing Day when I was doing the 10 p.m. till 6 a.m. shed turn. Herbie Howard didn't turn up for his shift, so I teamed up with driver Alf Lee on the 6.18 a.m. passenger train to North Woolwich. I believe this was the only turn we had to Woolwich, which ran every day except Sundays. Because Woolwich was in the London Docklands, some wag nicknamed it 'The Boat Train'!

As it was after the end of my normal shift, I could have refused to work it. Being Boxing Day, there were no spare men available so, to avoid the possibility of cancelling the train, I volunteered to carry on working.

Although I was feeling a little jaded, it was quite an easy working, all stations to Lea Bridge, after which we would take the Channelsea route around the back of the vast Stratford Works and Depot complex and end up at Stratford Low Level station.

It was a strange route along to North Woolwich, much of the line running alongside the road, through Silvertown Tunnel (where poor old Charlie, our ex-Coalman, met his untimely end) and along to the North Woolwich terminus.

As soon as we had come to a stand I dived between our engine and the first carriage, unscrewed and unhooked the coupling, brake and heating pipes and clambered back on to our engine.   Before we backed off our train, Alf said to me, in his gravelly voice, *"I'll fill the tank and run round"* ('running round' meaning going up the slip road and reversing back onto the rear of our train in preparation for the return journey) *"go and get some breakfast."*

'Hair of the dog'

I knew exactly what he meant, and didn't need twice telling.
Just down the road outside the station was a pub – I can't recall the name (was it The Angel?), that was open for the dockworkers from about 7a.m. till 9 a.m.
It was quite a novelty to find a pub packed out before 8 o'clock in the morning.
'Breakfast' was in the shape of a pint glass filled with dark mild beer, lovely!
By the time I returned to the engine, feeling a lot better – mentally if not physically! – Alf had done everything necessary and we were ready to go.

14 Hours at premium rates

I believe we went back empties carriages to Stratford and worked the 10.57 a.m. local passenger back to Hertford, arriving at 11.59.   As I had already been on duty for 14 hours, I signed off as soon as we arrived in the depot, leaving one of the shed staff to dispose of the engine.
With it being a Bank Holiday paid at premium rates, my earnings that day probably made the Taxman very happy with the day's work - with no complaints from myself, neither!

Heavier trains

During 1958 most of our old coaching stock, which comprised sets of 4 articulated carriages mounted on 5 sets of bogies (called 'Quad Arts') were replaced with more luxurious, but heavier, coaching stock displaced from the recently electrified Southend service.
With the old stock, our normal off-peak loading was just 4 coaches and 8 during peak periods. The loading changed with this new stock.
This was due to a lower seating capacity per coach so, instead of 4 during off-peak, the loading was increased to 6.   At peak periods this load increased to 8 carriages, which really did put a strain on our N7s.   If you happened to have an engine that, for one reason or another, had difficulty maintaining steam pressure, then you were in serious trouble.

Steam and water

A brief explanation on the basic workings of the locomotive may help the reader's understanding of the importance of steam and water.

First and foremost is the importance of ensuring there is water in the engine's boiler at all times.   The crown of a steam engine's firebox is fitted with a 'fusible plug' i.e. a hollow steel plug that has its core filled with lead.
Now, as long as there is water covering the top of this plug, the lead will not melt.
If the boiler is allowed to run dry, then the lead will instantly melt allowing steam to rush into the firebox to help douse the fire.   If the fire is not thrown out or extinguished immediately, then there is a high risk of the boiler exploding with dire consequences.
It was regarded as the ultimate crime to blow a fusible plug and fortunately I was never to experience it but must have come pretty close on several occasions.
The other essential is the level of steam pressure.   The full working pressure of an N7 was 180 lbs. per square inch (on the L1 Class it was 225 lbs.)
Any excess pressure was released through the safety valves (i.e. 'blown off') which was avoided as much as possible as it was a sheer waste.

Class N7 69710 was often on loan to Hertford East. Here she is photographed at Stratford Low Level station in October 1959, with a train to North Woolwich. *(J.P. Mullett/Colour-Rail/BRE306)*

Steam pressure and the Vacuum Brake

Although the engine could function at a lower pressure, the vacuum brake (which released the brakes through a 'suction' method) depended upon a certain amount of steam pressure to ensure the brakes of the train were kept fully released.   The exact steam pressure required was subject to some variation, but if it fell below 80 lbs. then there was the danger of the vacuum being destroyed thereby allowing the brakes to be applied. When that happened there was nothing you could do about it, you were simply brought to a stand until you could raise sufficient steam pressure to fully release the brakes again. This event was commonly known as 'stopping for a blow-up'.

The dreaded 'blow-up'

To delay the event of a 'blow-up' if the engine was not steaming properly, you could 'mortgage the boiler' which means delaying the injection of fresh (cold) water into the boiler. The act of injecting cold water into the boiler retarded the generation of steam until the water came to the boil again - much the same effect as pouring cold water into a boiling kettle.

Meanwhile, you would be working hard raking through the firebed to liven the fire up sufficiently to generate a greater steaming rate.

If you were successful, you would be able to restore the boiler water level to the ideal level, which was about three-quarters full.

The danger level was reached when the water level in the boiler disappeared from sight in the very bottom of the water-gauge glass, then you just had to turn the injector on, or stop at the next station for a 'blow-up'.

I remember one occasion in my early days as a fireman when we were having a really rough trip on a passenger train to London. I can't remember who my driver was but I know he appeared somewhat less agitated than I was about our situation.

Steam and water was getting dangerously low and, between trying to rake some life into the fire, I was anxiously glancing at the water gauge where the level was occasionally disappearing from view.

Each time my hand hovered over the injector handle, he would shout out *"**Not until I say so!**"*

Although we were losing time, we managed to creep from station to station by the skin of our teeth – about 90 lbs of steam pressure and water only making an occasional appearance in the bottom of the glass.

Eventually, my nerve couldn't stand it any more and I turned the injector on without my mate's say-so.

"*Oi, I told you!*" he hollered across the cab. "***Now turn it off!***" "But I can't see any water in the gauge...." I protested.

With that, he stepped across to the centre of the cab, threw the cloth he had in his hand over one of the twin gauges, took off his cap and hung it over the other one.

"*Now you can't see anything to worry about, so now shut the injector off and leave the bloody thing alone!*" he said, giving me a steely glare. For the rest of the trip he worked the injector on his side of the cab. Somehow we made it to London without blowing the fusible plug.

Platforms too short

In addition to the increased demand for steam power, another problem that arose with an 8-coach train of this ex-Southend stock was that many of the station platforms were not long enough to accommodate the full length.

Maintaining the timetable became that much more difficult, as it was even more important to stop at the very end of the platform in order to allow any passengers in the rearmost carriage to alight. As I mentioned earlier, valuable time could be lost in reversing or drawing forward as a result of a misjudgement.

Even so, some platforms were just not long enough to accommodate the whole train, so sometimes the need to pull forward or set back was inevitable.

If the coaches were of the corridor type – which unfortunately they weren't – this problem would not have arisen.

Over a period of time, many stations had their platform lengths extended. These alterations were not just for our benefit, but were part of the preparations for the forthcoming electric trains.

A High-flying City Gent

I remember one particular occasion on a busy peak-hour train out from Liverpool Street when we slightly overran the platform at Tottenham station.

Normally, anyone in that coach wishing to alight would stick their head out of the window and wait until we set the train back.

On this occasion as I watched, the door of the nearest compartment swung open and a bowler-hatted city gent, complete with briefcase and rolled-up umbrella, stepped smartly out into mid-air!

Well, it was about a 6-foot drop to ground level and the poor chap landed in one almighty heap, I was sure he had broken both legs at least.

But no, he picked himself up, slapped the dust off his pinstriped suit and marched stiffly up the platform ramp without a backward glance - perhaps he saw service in the Parachute Regiment!

An unusual passenger!

On one of the late trains to Hertford one evening, we had a special pick-up at Broxbourne. We unhooked our coaches on the mainline and picked up a long Parcels Van from the Cattle Dock.

It contained a full-grown elephant on its way to Hertford for the circus being set up on Hartham Field.

It had a keeper with it of course, but it was quite funny to see a foot or so of the elephant's trunk waving out of the window now and again during the journey. The way the van rocked quite alarmingly from side-to-side on several occasions brought home to me the enormous weight of these animals. We reached Hertford without mishap but were not allowed to wait to see it unloaded, as we had to get our engine out of the way in case the noise panicked it.

Lineside fire

Another 'one off' was encountered on the 11.33 p.m. out of Liverpool Street one evening. We were stopped just after leaving Enfield Lock station due to a Platelayer's lineside cabin being on fire.

Those cabins were made of old railway sleepers liberally coated with tar. We could see it up ahead blazing away, the wind blowing the flames straight across our path.

The signalman said he had called the Fire Brigade and we would have to wait until they arrived to put it out.

By now it was well past midnight and the few passengers we had were hanging out of the windows having a right old moan at the delay.

After a while, there being no sign of the Fire Brigade, we decided to make a dash past the fire. The guard went down the train telling everyone to keep the windows closed and away we went past this blazing inferno at a fair gallop. We got by without incident and carried on our way.

Introduction to Welsh coal

When we talk about coal, the ordinary person could be forgiven for thinking that all coal was the same, just that some may be a different size than others.

This is far from the case and I must mention of Welsh coal, which was supplied to Hertford for a period sometime between 1957/58.

Up until that time we had used various types of steam coal from (presumably) the coalfields of northern England.

I believe Welsh coal had been in use for many years on the Great Western Railway but, of course, their locomotives had been specially designed to burn that type of coal. However, it was completely alien to us and had some very unusual properties that we would learn of the hard way!

First off, it would crumble to dust when smashed with the coal-pick, whereas our normal coal would just break into smaller lumps.

Secondly, it gave off very little smoke, which, as London was fast becoming a Smokeless Zone, may have been a reason that we were made to use it.

Thirdly, it took a lot longer to fully ignite, which is where we were caught out, coupled with the fact that the damned stuff actually melted!

This melting process occurred when the firebed was not hot enough to instantly ignite the fresh coal being added.

The serious problems this caused was that this molten matter ran between the firebars where it was instantly cooled by the incoming draught of air underneath and set solid between the bars.

This effectively cut off all air currents beneath the firebed that was essential for ignition, the result was that the fire went 'dead' and steam pressure plummeted.

Even lighting up an engine became more difficult, no longer could it be achieved with rolled up newspaper and oily rags. To overcome these problems, two other essential items were supplied by the wagonload to Hertford.

Firstly, there were small bundles of wood coated with some crystallised substance, which were firelighters to aid the lighting-up problem.

The second thing was an ample supply of near walnut-sized pebbles, a few shovelfulls of which were to be spread across the firebars prior to adding coal.

The idea was that, as the fire got hot, so did the pebbles which then exploded and kept any molten residue from solidifying between the bars.
That was the theory, I was not convinced that it always worked in practice.

I do know that we were constantly running out of replacement firebars due to them becoming deformed and melted together by the residue from this Welsh coal.
Another peculiarity, which I haven't mentioned, was that as it got hotter it swelled up. I wouldn't say it doubled in size but it certainly swelled significantly.
This caught out many a fireman for the following reason:

'Lazy' firing

Apart from the orthodox method of firing, there was a cruder method known as 'boxing it up'. This simply meant that you filled the firebox right up before the start of the journey and, provided you had timed everything perfectly in that it had burned through sufficiently enough to maintain steam pressure, further firing would not be required for quite some time. In fact, with a driver who was not too heavy-handed on the regulator, a boxful on an N7 could see you right through an all stations to Liverpool Street.

With Welsh coal however, if the boxful was too solid it would not burn through, then the trip would become a nightmare rather than a doddle.
The quantity was also important, several Firemen in the early days caused the brick arch above the firebox to collapse due to the swollen firebed pushing against it – a bit like a Yorkshire pudding swelling in the oven.
Eventually we got used to it, the secret was to fire little and often on a white-hot firebed to ensure instantaneous combustion. The calorific value of Welsh coal was tremendously high, and was economical and extremely effective at maintaining good steam pressure.
Even cleaning the fire took on a different form. Instead of a thick layer of ash and clinker, which could sometimes be a foot deep, plus a full ashpan underneath to rake out, all you normally had to remove was a thin layer of clinker.
Most times this thin layer would come off the firebars as easy as anything, but very occasionally it would cling to the bars, requiring the long-pointed Pricker tool to lever it off.
Unfortunately, there were occasions when the Fireman disposing of the engine at the end of his shift was unable to clean the fire properly, so just left the job part-done. The next crew could then be saddled with the problem of blocked firebars before they even started their day's work.

Just as soon as we got used to it, supplies gradually dried up and we went back to the original types of coal. Its withdrawal may have been because too many delays through steam failure were occurring or through acceptance that our engines (and crew) were just not suited to it.

She wouldn't steam on anthracite!

One evening we were required to do a special trip to Broxbourne with a few wagons. We had just completed a London run and most of the coal left in our bunker was little more than dust. Just as we hooked up to these wagons, we noticed some handy sized coal in a truck standing alongside the adjacent track.

Thinking that it was part of a consignment for locomotive use, I jumped across with the firing shovel and quickly transferred a couple of hundredweight into our near-empty bunker.

What a mistake that was! It transpired that this stuff was anthracite, which was totally unsuitable for an N7, and just lay on the firebed like little black pebbles. What should have been one of the easiest of trips turned into a nightmare!

We returned to Hertford light-engine with barely 50 lbs of steam on the pressure gauge and about an inch of water in the boiler – and a fire that would not have toasted a slice of bread!

I left what remained of this coal in the bunker and wondered how the next fireman would get on with it! However, by this time the bunker would have been topped up with the proper coal so the anthracite was well 'diluted'.

Looking towards Hertford East station from the Signalbox in 1964. Although steam has long since gone, the mushroom-type water tower adjacent to the Great Northern branch is still in situ on the far right of the photograph.

CHAPTER EIGHT

Into 1959 and from N7s to L1s

Monday the 12th of January 1959 was something of a 'red-letter' day for Hertford when we took delivery of our first batch of Class L1 2-6-4 tank engines that replaced most of our overworked N7s.
These L1s were really powerful locomotives that were quite capable of – and often were utilised for – running express passenger trains.
They had quite spacious cabs, with doors that even had windows in the upper half that could be closed against the elements in bad weather.
Our initial allocation was made up of engines displaced from sheds at Lowestoft, Ipswich and Yarmouth, as well as a couple from Stratford.
Not all of our N7s were replaced, a small number were retained for working the Buntingford branch, from which the much larger and heavier L1s were prohibited.
I believe the only N7 of our original allocation among those left was 69684.

Goodbye to 69682

Sadly, I lost 69682 as she was among those transferred back to Stratford. I used to see her occasionally out on the open road but by then, being just a 'common user' engine, she was as neglected and filthy as the rest of them. I was never pleased to see her on those occasions – preferring to remember her in the pristine condition when she was my 'regular'.

Trying to polish an L1

The 'regular' L1 allocated to Charlie Lee and I was 67706 but by that time, having a regular engine allocated became a bit of nonsense. You were lucky if you had it allocated to you for one week in a month!
Still, I retained the cleaning habit and always did the best I could, but it was a bit of a hopeless task. The surface area of the side-tanks and bunker of an L1 was over twice that of an N7 so most of my spare time was taken keeping the paintwork clean, let alone paying attention to brasswork.
Nonetheless I did try, in fact, I used to attempt to at least wipe over the side-tanks of any engine I was working on. Even this token effort, which brightened up the number and revealed the coloured lining, made an enormous difference to the appearance of an otherwise grimy workhorse.

Monday morning grime

I used to dread the Monday morning shift, when the fire had been re-lit after the Sunday rest. Everything in the cab would be covered with a layer of oily black soot, which had to be wiped off with cotton waste and old newspapers.
It was very difficult to wipe the higher parts of the cabfront controls without collecting the odd burn or two from one of the many steam pipes.

Above. Sometime early in 1959, captured coming off shed via the Great Northern branch at Hertford East is Class L1 2-6-4 67734 .... *Below.* .... Not long after, she's away with a train to Liverpool Street.

155

The L1's rocking firegrate

Cleaning the fire on an L1 was made easier by the use of a rocking firegrate. First you would open the louvres in the ashpan with the aid of a crank-handle which fitted into a square pivot between the driving wheels. Then it was a matter of raking about in the firebed to get all the clinker over the rocking area of the grate and dropping it through into the ashpit. This was effected by tipping the grate by levering with a special bar fitted into sockets set into the cab floor either side of the firedoor.

Occasionally, due to distortion or fracture, the whole grate area would follow the clinker into the pit, then you had a problem! These rockers were quite heavy and had to be replaced using a pair of long, iron tongs which required a skill which very few of us possessed. The engine usually had to be set aside to be dealt with by the shed staff the following day, unless of course they happened to be on duty at the time.

The other problem was that, although each engine should have had it's own rocker lever on board, there never seemed to be enough to go round. Some firemen were in the habit of hiding them away for their own exclusive use, so you arrived on shed hoping to borrow one from another engine, but if you couldn't find one, then you had no choice but to clean the fire the hard way using the long shovel.

I believe it was the habit of some men to hide these tools that created the shortage in the first place.

Although the rocking firegrate made life somewhat easier for us firemen, it certainly was not the case for the Yardman, Don Walls, whose job it was to shovel the ash and clinker out of the ashpits.

When cleaning - or throwing out - the fire on an N7, all the clinker was drawn out through the firedoor and thrown onto the growing heap beside the tracks in the Depot.

With the L1s, everything was dumped into the ashpits, and from then on they always appeared to be full.

Of course, we still had a few N7s that had to have their ashpans raked out from underneath. On those occasions I could find myself in the pit underneath amid piles of red-hot clinkers giving off choking, sulphurous fumes – just to add a bit more 'flavour' to the fine ash swirling around as it cascaded from the ashpan!

Speedometers

Another refinement on the L1 was the provision of a speedometer, although I don't believe all of the class was fitted with one.

Even on those that were, they seldom worked properly and their accuracy was always doubtful – unless one believed you really could reach 75 mph between stations!

Still, they were a novelty to us and it was fun at times seeing what speed we could get it up to.

Back with Ted Champ

My initial efforts at 'tarting up' 67706 turned out to be a waste of time, as within the space of a couple of months (during which we had worked 67706 on no more than 7 occasions) I parted with her and Charlie Lee.

On March 15th, resulting from a reshuffle in the Passenger Link, I found myself back with Ted Champ as my regular mate, along with L1 No.67704 as our allocated engine. Strangely though, it wasn't until the 21st of May that we actually had 67704 rostered to us, on that occasion Ted promptly failed her after inspection due to a bent connecting rod!

Electrification looms closer

By this time, work on electrification was well under way, with regular weekend gangs of workmen on BICCC (the British Insulated Calendars Cable Company) trains in evidence every weekend. First they bored holes at intervals by the lineside, filled them with concrete and erected the steel uprights that would carry the overhead power supply.

The long road to the Driver's seat

You may already have guessed that the steps to promotion to Engine Driver are Cleaner, Passed Cleaner, Fireman, Passed Fireman and then – all being well – Driver. Even then, drivers were categorised by Seniority, starting in the lowest Link and gradually working his way upward.

A man could be a driver of many years standing before reaching the top Passenger Link in his Depot.

At the time I began my railway career, promotion to driver was much quicker than it used to be, due to the acute shortage of footplate staff at that time.

Even so, getting beyond the Passed Fireman stage at the same Depot could take a long time – unless you moved to another location.

This was due to the railway policy of advertising every Driver's vacancy throughout the Region, so a Passed Fireman from another Depot could apply for the position and, if he was a more senior man in terms of length of service, he would be entitled to the job.

Many of Hertford's drivers started their railway career elsewhere and ended up at Hertford East via this system.

How Frank Tarry – father of John – came to Hertford East is an example of just how long and hard a road this could be.

After he came out of the Army in 1918, Frank started as an engine Cleaner at Lincoln MPD.

17 years later, in 1935, Frank moved his family to Bishop's Stortford to gain promotion to Passed Fireman.

During the 18 months he was at Bishop's Stortford, Frank and his family moved home no less than 4 times!

157

In those days, promotion to driver always necessitated moving, in the first instance, to Stratford. So, around Christmas 1936 Frank and his family moved to a house in Dagenham to enable him to take a Driver's position at Stratford.

A few years later Frank was taken into the King George V hospital at Ilford for an operation on a duodenal ulcer, which very nearly cost him his life.

Ulcers and other related complaints were not uncommon among footplatemen in steam days, considering their irregular mealtimes and the horrendous conditions they had to work under.

Whilst he was recovering, Frank's doctor advised him to take up alternative employment. Jobs in those days were hard to come by and Frank told him it was out of the question. As a compromise, the doctor suggested he obtain a transfer to a country location where life would be less hectic and the air pollution less dense.

In 1942 Frank applied for a vacancy for Hertford – even though it was a fair distance from his home in Daghenham.

Here's where he had a little bit of good fortune. It happened that there was a Stratford driver living at Hertford, so it suited both parties to swap houses, to which the respective Council Authorities readily agreed.

Frank never looked back after that and spent 18 happy years at Hertford, retiring in 1960.

A few of Hertford's Drivers

During my period of over 5 years at Hertford, I remember at least 30 drivers, all of which I fired to on at least one occasion. Of course, they were not all allocated there at the same time, some transferred in to fill vacancies created through retirement or, in at least 2 instances, through bereavements.

I believe the usual compliment was around 20 sets of men.

I would like to devote this section to just a few of those wonderful characters, sad to say many of them have now passed on.

Quite a few had nicknames – bestowed by their colleagues because of certain mannerisms or as a result of a memorable event – but very few of these nicknames were uttered within earshot of the individual!

Some I remember were; Nibbo Lee– Slasher Green – Farmer Brown – Taiters Bass – Dadda White – Brother Black – Gubby Allen – Bottles Wench and Buck Storey, the last name is the only one that was freely used to address Roy Storey.

I never saw them grow old, so I am able to remember them exactly as they were some 40 years ago.

George (Ernie) Castle

Ernie, as he was always known to his fellow railwaymen, is happily still with us and in good health. During the writing of this book I was able to make contact with him after a gap of over 35 years and he has been invaluable in helping me to remember the characteristics of many of our old colleagues. I was fireman to Ernie on many occasions and he finally retired in 1987.

Above. Hertford East MPD in 1955. Pausing from their discussion beside N7 no. 69684, from left to right are drivers Charlie Lambert and Ted Champ. The third member of the group – with a shirt and tie far cleaner than his overalls – is fireman John Shelsher.
Below. Driver Ernie Castle cautiously smiles at the camera from the cab of N7 69683 as it waits in the platform at Buntingford ready to depart with a passenger train to St. Margarets during 1958.

Above. Driver Frank Tarry watches the cameraman from the footplate of his regular engine – N7 0-6-2 no.69688. *c.* 1958.   *Below.* Driver John Tarry looks happy in his work as he stands alongside Class J69 0-6-0 no. 68600 in the carriage sidings at Hertford East in November 1960. By this date father Frank had retired.

Frank Tarry

I remember Frank as a 'coal-miners' friend, whose usual driving technique was regulator wide open and reversing screw only wound partway up. The result was a continuous blast at the chimney and cinders sometimes shooting a mile in the sky!

I'm sure Frank loved the sound the engine made, as he would sit there staring straight ahead with a contented smile on his face.

I have heard of occasions when a stroppy fireman would glare at Frank and tap the steam pressure gauge, but it never got them anywhere.

More than likely I would think Frank would just give an extra tug on the Regulator handle and wind the lever out a little more!

His favourite phrase was "Cane-em, matey!" - and he wasn't necessarily referring just to his driving technique!

Frank was an absolute wizard at squeezing every last ounce of overtime out of a turn of duty. He would hang about wherever he could, e.g. if there was an opportunity to make an extra stop to take on water, he would take it, irrespective as to whether it was necessary.

After 'putting his train to bed' at the end of the trip to Hertford, he would take as long as he could in returning his engine to the MPD. It was practice for the Signalman to log the time an engine returns to the Shed and Frank has even been known on occasions to get the Signalman to book him in a bit later!

Of course, us firemen never complained when we were with him – his overtime was ours also!

Another memory of Frank is the lovely silver badge he wore on his cap, which I think was the 'Dragon's Wing' of the old Great Eastern Railway Coat-of-Arms, I never saw another cap badge like it.

He was the only driver I ever remember who spurned the railwayman's satchel and carried his lunch – and everything else – in one of the original driver's black-painted metal boxes with an oval hinged lid – inset with a brass handle and nameplate.

This box must have been quite old because they were usually associated with footplatemen of the old pre-Grouping days of railways.

As I mentioned earlier, Frank retired in 1960. His son John, who was a Passed Fireman at Hertford at that time, continued as a driver until he too retired in 1990, after 47 years service, this meant father and son put in over 90 years railway service between them!

John Tarry

Frank's son and a real lover of the RAF – in which he served before joining the railway – start talking to him about aircraft and he would go on forever!

John spent some time in the Railway Police at Liverpool Street and elsewhere before finally joining his father on the footplate at Hertford East. Interestingly, there was a local arrangement that John and his father should not be rostered to work together as driver and fireman – and they never were.

Like Ernie Castle, John Tarry is alive and well and likes nothing better than to sit and chat about the good old days of steam.

A close-up of N7 69681 with driver Eric Wrangles in charge, waiting to depart from Hertford East with a train to Liverpool Street in 1957. The engine's bunker contains Welsh coal.

Charlie Lee

I have already mentioned Charlie whose driving style was completely opposite to Frank's.
I never once remember Charlie being anything other than a quietly spoken, unflustered individual.

George Dawson

George was quite a young-looking driver for his age – probably in his late 40s at that time – and always immaculately turned out.
I don't know if George was a religious man, but he never used strong language. The worst you would hear from him were words like '*blooming* 'and '*flipping*'!

He was a bit of a worrier in that he had this habit of double-checking everything. As an example, if I told him a ground signal on my side had given us the all-clear, chances were he would hop over to my side to check for himself.

Driver Ron Hopkins leans over the cab door window-frame of L1 2-6-4 no. 67731 at Hertford in this 1959 photograph. The fireman looks very much like Jim Hadland.

George was very much a stickler for doing everything 'by the book' and recently, retired driver Bob Smith, recalled the following occasion when one of the drivers really wound him up.

George had just signed on duty at 6 am as the morning Shed Duty Driver and he was told that the fireman for one of the early trains had failed to turn up.
The night Cleaner was assisting the driver in preparing the engine, which was about to leave the Shed in order to join its train up at the station.
Now, as with most of us young Passed Cleaners, we were always in the market for some overtime and this one was no exception.
However, this particular Cleaner was not officially qualified for mainline firing duties so, when the driver indicated that they were ready to leave the Shed, George said, *"You can't take him, you just can't, he's not passed for the mainline."*
The driver casually replied, *"Hell be ok, no one'll know any different."*
But George was adamant, *"You can't, he's not allowed"* he replied, raising his voice a few octaves, *"He can go with you up to the station and that's it!"*
What George didn't know was that this driver knew his own fireman was going to be a bit late and that he would join him up at the station, which he duly did.

163

As the Cleaner was now off duty and he would be catching this same train home, he remained on the engine with the crew.
When the train left, the driver made his fireman crouch down behind the door and for the Cleaner to stand by the cab doorway as they passed the Enginemen's Restroom.
Sure enough, old George was staring out of the window to check who was on the footplate.　When he saw the Cleaner he went into a fit of rage!　He started to wave his arms in exasperation at the fast-disappearing train, spluttering *"You blooming.....What the.....Gerrofff there!!"*, but of course, they couldn't hear him.

When the engine returned to the Shed about 3 hours later, George was out after the driver like a shot.
"What d'you think you're playing at" he fumed *"you know you got no right to take him – you know he's not passed out – you know the rules, if anything had happened to him...."* And so he went on for several minutes.
After he had blown himself out, the driver enlightened him as to the true situation, but somehow George failed to see the funny side that he had been the butt end of a joke!

John (Jack) Black

Another immaculately dressed driver, with a pencil-thin moustache, Jack was a Special Police Constable and I often used to see him in uniform on Traffic Duty on speedway racing days at Rye House Stadium.　In general conversation, Jack had this habit of addressing everyone as 'brother', as a consequence, many of the men used to refer to him as 'Brother Black'.

Bill Bright

As previously mentioned, Bill was the local ASLEF Union Branch Representative and secretary of the Local Departmental Committee (LDC).
It was from Bill that I would purchase each year the ASLEF Union diary - which I still have - for the princely sum of 2/6d (12.5p).

Ted Govier

Another I have already mentioned, Ted was a really cheerful man in his 50s, albeit a little overweight.　He always had time for a game of cards in the messroom, or a game of dominoes over at the Great Eastern Tavern.　I had many happy times with dear old Ted.
A humorous tale was related to me concerning Ted when Hertford was electrified. The new working rosters for Motormen were pinned up on the Notice Board, and several of the Drivers were gathered round discussing them.
Ted happened to look round and spotted this man in a blue suit sitting quietly at the back of the room. Knowing that Stratford men at that time were a common sight at

Hertford while men were being trained, Ted called out to him, *"Ullo bruvver, you come dahhn to 'elp us out?"*
The man in the suit said, *"Do you know to whom you are talking?"*
"Nope" replied Ted *" I ain't never 'ad the pleasure."*
"And who are you?" the man asked.
"I'm Ted Govier – one of Hertford's drivers."
The man in the blue suit stood up and said,*"Well, Ted Govier, you'll know me next time, because I'm Mr. Hardy, District Running and Maintenance Engineer."*
In the world of railways, a mere driver meeting 'Hardy' was about as near as he would get on this earth to meeting God!
Poor old Ted went a bit pale and replied *"Well, I'm very sorry Guv'nor, but I didn't bleedin' know, did I!"*
It seems the great man took it all in good part because when they met again a couple of days later, he smiled and said *"Hello, Ted Govier, do you remember who I am?"*
Driver John Tarry related this tale to me and I could just picture old Ted dropping himself in it and digging the hole even deeper!
On another occasion, when doing the Night Shed turn, Ted's fireman was a chap on loan from Stratford. Apparently, this youngster turned up with a guitar under his arm.
Ted gave one look and said, *"If you're going to play with that bloody thing all night, you can go down the other end of the shed!"*
It was said that the fireman was none other than Joe Brown, who later became a famous 'Pop' star!
Yes, Ted really was one of the nicest men you could ever wish to meet.

Roy (Buck) Storey

Buck was another jovial character was, an avid cowboy fan who used to draw cowboys in wide Stetson hats on the mess-room Formica tabletop.
He had a habit of only hearing what he wanted to hear, and shrugged off any arguments with a loud chuckle and a disarming wave of the hand.
Ernie Castle quoted a typical example to me, when Buck was his fireman on a job at Temple Mills one day.

Having waited some time to dispose of their engine in Stratford MPD, Ernie eventually decided to leave it in Temple Mills Yard.
The Yard Foreman was one Arthur Andrews, who had been one-time foreman at Hertford East, so he and the crew were not entirely unknown to each other.
As Ernie and Buck were walking away from their engine, Arthur came running out of his little office shouting *"Hey, you can't leave that there!"*.
Buck gave him one of his big grins and replied *"Yeah, yeah, okay – cheerio Arthur"*, and with a casual wave of his hand, they were gone, leaving the engine exactly where it was! That example was typical of Buck – water off a duck's back – but because of his likeable personality, he invariably got away with it.

Eric and Charlie Wrangles

Eric and Charlie are brothers, I believe Eric is the eldest. They both started their railway career at Hatfield – Eric transferred to Hertford as a Fireman sometime during 1955.

I didn't know Charlie quite as well as he arrived a few years later at Hertford, also transferring across from Hatfield in order to get his promotion to driver.

Both of them were cheerful characters and ace darts players for their local team.

Eric recently related a little tale of when he was required to tow one of Wickham's rail-coaches on a trial run over the Buntingford branch.

His engine that day was N7 69685, and Eric takes up the story....

"When we got to St. Margaret's, one of the Wickhams chaps came up and said. *"We've got some leads we're going to fit up between the coach and your cab with a microphone, because we want to tell you what speed we want you to do. When we tell you, we want you to slow down to 20 mph or speed up to 40 mph."* Well, I thought, I don't know how we're going to do that seeing as we hadn't got a speedometer on the engine! Anyway, we did a couple of trips and we speeded up and slowed down when they said, and we eventually got back into Ware sidings, where we had to shove this coach back into their private siding.

Being eager to get finished, the shunter uncoupled the coach and said *"Away you go"*, we forgot about the microphone and cable.

Of course, as we pulled away, this cable stretched and stretched until it broke – course, that caused a job for the Wickham people who apparently had to spend all the next day getting it sorted out!"

Charlie went on to become a Number One Link driver on the electric expresses out of Kings Cross prior to his retirement in the 1990s.

Ron Hopkins

I believe Ron was still a Passed Fireman during my time, but I did fire for him on more than one occasion.

Ron's mother was Crossing Keeper at Mead Lane just a few hundred yards south of the Loco Shed and the family lived in the railway cottage next to the line. Rumour had it that very few vehicles got to use the crossing as Mrs. Hopkins usually managed to persuade would-be customers that it would be quicker for them to go round via the Station!

The crossing was eventually closed to traffic and is now for pedestrians only.

I believe Ron also had a bit of a smallholding as he could occasionally be seen around Hertford on a small horse-drawn cart collecting food waste for some pigs he kept.

Arthur Tilcock

I have already given some description of the sort of character Arthur was, but another yarn I picked up concerned a time when Arthur was in the ashpit oiling underneath his engine.

He was quite a tall man and he happened to crack his head on one of the heavy steel big-end cotter pins attached to the inside crankshaft.

He staggered out from underneath and hauled himself onto the footplate. He rummaged in his bag and produced a little bottle of brandy.

On the engine in the adjoining road was Driver George Cousins who, seeing what was going on, promptly moved nearer to Arthur expecting to be invited to partake of the bottle in easing Arthur's pain.

Imagine his disappointment when all Arthur did was tip some brandy onto his handkerchief and dab it on the sore spot on his head!

Arthur *never* drank on duty.

Jimmy Pratt

A small, wizened man, little old Jim could be craftier than a cartload of monkeys! His favourite tactic was when he was oiling up and it came to oiling the big-end cranks located beneath the boiler of an N7. This involved reaching up between the cranks from the ashpit underneath the engine, or stretching across a dirty running-plate from above. Although lying on an old piece of sacking helped to avoid getting too messed up, there was still the risk of rubbing your back on the underside of the boiler cladding as you stretched across.

When I was with him, Jimmy would sidle up to me and say *"As you're a bit smaller than me,"* (which I wasn't!) *"you can squeeze underneath and oil those ends, can't you?"*. Like a mug, I used to do it for him, but I know some of the older firemen used to tell him where to get off!

I recall one occasion when a fireman got his own back on Jimmy. It was during the return trip on the Temple Mills goods, which, as I previously described, was a long, slow haul down to Broxbourne.

On this particular morning, having got his train under way, with green signals showing as far as the eye could see, old Jimmy gradually nodded off with his arms folded across the reversing-screw wheel.

His fireman (I'm sure it was Pete Nolan) crept out of his side of the cab and made his way along the running-plate and around the front of their slow-moving engine. On the way round he lifted the headlamp off it's bracket and changed the light from white to red (those lamps had red and purple filters fitted in them). He made his way down the driver's side of the engine, held the lamp right up against the little round window in front of the cab and screamed out *"**Jimmy!!!**"* Well, poor old Jimmy woke with a start to be faced with this huge red light right in front of him. I don't know exactly what happened after that, but it must have almost frightened the life out of the poor old chap!

Whilst Jim may have been hard of hearing, there certainly was nothing wrong with his memory. He never did forget the time I lost the bag of stores at Liverpool Street, because on meeting him by chance a few years later, after he had retired, his first words to me were *"Remember that time when you just went for a cup of cawwfee?......"*

Bob Smith

Here was another great character – always full of energy and ready for a bit of fun. Although he was several years older than firemen such as myself, Bob was always regarded as 'one of the lads' – in fact – he didn't look any older than most of us.

During his early days as a driver, a number of the London Guards would think he was having them on when they asked who the driver of their train was!

A typical snippet of Bob's character was told to me on the closure of the Buntingford branch in 1965. Several of the drivers gathered for a farewell party in the *'Shah of India'* pub outside the station. Before the end of the evening, Bob was up on one of the tables giving his impression the 'pop star' Freddy, of *'Freddy and the Dreamers'*!

During an interview just after he retired, Bob related a tale of an event that occurred a short while before the closure of the Buntingford line.

The driver of a 3-coach diesel railcar overran the platform after coming down the bank at Hadham station. About that time, in the early 1960s, the Space Programme was in progress with the returning Space Capsules splashing down in their scheduled spot in the Pacific.

Young Driver Bob Smith looks down on the photographer from his lofty perch aboard L1 2-6-4 67731 at Hertford East in 1959...............

..........35 years later, in armchair comfort, Bob Smith is in control of a Class 31 Electric locomotive on a Kings Cross – Newcastle 3-hour express. The speedometer on the right of the panel confirms that the photograph was taken whilst the train was travelling at the maximum permitted speed of 123 mph!

On this particular morning, after the driver had reversed his train back into the platform, the Stationmaster went up to the cab and quietly said to the driver, *"D'you know, after travelling hundreds of thousands of miles, they can land a Space Capsule within a few hundred yards of its target. So why do you find it so difficult to stop your little train of 3 coaches in this platform?"*

Together with Charlie Wrangles, Bob graduated to the Number One Link at Kings Cross driving East Coast expresses as far as Newcastle on the 140mph Class 91 Electric trains.
His day's work was a round trip of 540 miles – a distance that could have taken well over a week to clock up in Hertford's steam days!
Bob Smith retired in 1997 with almost 50 years service!

Vic Finch

I've already related the tale of Vic and his lemon squeezer, but here was another of the railway's great characters, smashing sense of humour, and one who was just as ready to accept a joke played on him. It was typical of Vic to see the funny side the day I threw a cupful of water in his face, instead of knocking my block off for doing such a thing!

Vic also had other talents as, during my period at Hertford, he built himself a beautiful bungalow in the village of Amwell, just outside Ware.

During the writing of this book, I learnt that Vic had recently passed away at the ripe old age of 91 years.

Driver Alf Childs pauses during his task of 'oiling up' L1 67739 in Hertford Loco sometime during 1960. Comfortably framed in the cab window is Alf's regular fireman, Johnny Hawthorn.

Fireman Herbie Howard

There is just one particular fireman I would add to this list because, although many of them were great characters, Herbie really was a 'one-off'.

I have already mentioned his prank that backfired with the Night Cleaner at Buntingford.

Although he was one of the very small minorities in the depot who didn't smoke, he made up for it with his enormous appetite for beer.

He had a terrific thirst and could be found in any number of local inns during his off-duty periods.

My first experiences with Herbie were, as mentioned earlier in this book, when I was an Engine Cleaner.

As soon as he arrived on shed at the end of his shift, he would look around for one of we Cleaners to dispose of his engine so that he could get over to the pub that much earlier! As payment for performing this favour, Herbie would give any number of things except money – which he needed to buy beer.

Driver Ernie Gray enjoying the sunshine outside the Enginemen's rest-room at Hertford in 1957.   The handsome face on the left belongs to fireman Don Cordwell.

Apart from promised footplate trips, I remember receiving from Herbie such things as, an old BR issue Serge Fireman's jacket, a battered 'Sausage Logo' BR cap-badge and a tatty old Rulebook.
Even so, there were occasions when I would insist on nothing but money. It depended on how his finances were whether he would reluctantly part with a couple of shillings, or simply dispose of the engine himself.

Although I don't believe Herbie ever reported for duty in an incapable state, there were occasions when he was pretty well 'frayed at the edges'!
He would get no sympathy from his gravelly-voiced regular driver, Alfie Lee, who would give poor old Herbie a merciless tongue-lashing to start the day.
However, Herbie was such a likeable character that by the time they finished their shift they were the best of pals again.
I recall one occasion on an early-morning passenger train when poor old Herbie connected all the piping between coach and engine, but forgot to hook-up the coupling.   Consequently, when they got the 'Right Away' and Alf opened the regulator, the engine pulled away from the carriages and produced a loud bang when the brake-pipes parted!
There followed a fair amount of delay whilst a new vacuum pipe was found and fitted.   I think the air was blue that morning as Alf told Herbie his life's history!

On another occasion when I was on Night Shed Duty, Herbie arrived on the last train ready for his early morning shift (he never possessed any kind of transport) and came weaving into the rest-room asking to borrow a handlamp.

Apparently he had managed to lose his false teeth down the carriage toilet somewhere between Ware and Hertford.   It was the type of toilet where the pan emptied straight onto the track below!

Off he staggered into the darkness carrying an engine headlamp that emitted just a pencil-thin beam of light.

I don't know how far he walked, but he did manage to find his teeth that night!

Sadly, Herbie passed away some years ago at a comparatively young age.

It was a great shame as he really was one of life's great characters.

These then, are just a few of the colourful characters that helped to make a railwayman's job so rewarding.   Several more are mentioned in other parts of my story.

Although their individual characteristics varied greatly, there was one thing that was common to every one of them.

That was their dedication and responsibility towards their job.   However much we may have had our little jokes and pranks in our spare moments, nothing concerning the job was ever treated with anything less than the utmost seriousness.

Most gave extremely long service to the railway, it was not uncommon to find employees achieving up to 50 years service.

In these days such continuous service is extremely rare, many Companies don't seem to survive as long as that, aside from whether Company loyalty is anywhere near as strong as it was then!

A local Railway Historian?

One more character I remember wasn't a railwayman at all.   He was an old man who used to wear one of those heavy khaki army greatcoats, a black felt hat and leather spats around his lower legs. He was a real railway fanatic and used to come into the restroom from time to time for a cup of tea and a chat to anyone who cared to listen.

He must have lived quite close to the line as he used to know more of what went on than most of us did!

To us youngsters he seemed a bit of a bore and we avoided him as much as we could.

One day he brought in a whole pile of ancient Great Eastern Railway Magazines that lay about the restroom for weeks afterwards.

Before they were eventually thrown away I retrieved two of them, one copy dated 1915 and the other 1925, I still have them to this day.

I believe this old chap's name was Jim Brightwell (or Brittwell?) and I am sure he must have kept very detailed notes of his observations.   I have often thought that somewhere in Hertford may lie a comprehensive history of Hertford East and it's locomotives just waiting to be discovered and published!

Above. Fireman Jim Hadland poses for the cameraman from the footplate of Class L1 no. 67731. *c.* 1959
Below. . Class N7 0-6-2 no. 69686 at Hertford MPD in 1957. Her regular driver, Frank Clarke, is on the footplate whilst his fireman, John Shelsher, leans casually against the cab steps.

Above. A group of railwaymen relaxes on a platform seat at Hertford East.   On the left is Passenger Guard Fred Eusden, off-duty Driver Frank Clarke, Fireman Geoffrey Suckling and a member of the Station Staff.
Below. The rather murky interior of the locomen's rest-room reveals driver Buck Storey checking the contents of his satchel, while in the far right corner driver Frank Clarke has vacated his seat on the station platform (previous photograph) and is enjoying a cup of tea

The Great Eastern Tavern

As you may by now have gathered, there was a great camaraderie between the railwaymen at Hertford.

After working all day in front of a white-hot furnace within the confines of a small cab, it was natural that one lost a good deal of body fluid that needed to be replaced.

It was therefor not surprising that we were in the habit of drinking copious amounts of liquid, of which many of us preferred it to be good old English Ale!

The regular home watering hole for many of us was the Great Eastern Tavern, a small public house situated on a corner of Railway Place just opposite the Goods Yard entrance. Mine hosts were Eric and Jean Taylor.

We would congregate after the end of our shifts at all times of day (subject to opening times) and play darts, dominoes and cards whilst satisfying our thirsts.

This old Inn must have seen generations of railwaymen and passengers back in the 1800s, as the original Hertford Station entrance was just across the road from where it still stands.

Class N7 69684 at Hertford Loco *c.*1957. Fireman John Shelsher, typically dressed in a dazzling white shirt, clings to the window frame from his position in the Driver's seat.

A crafty pair of Bills!

There was one pair of pensioners we used to meet during the lunchtime openings who always looked forward to a game of dominoes with any pair willing to take them on.
They were Bill West and Bill Barr, the former was, I believe, a retired Senior Police Officer, whilst the latter was a retired London Bus Inspector.
They were two great characters, both of whom sadly passed away many years ago.
They were also crafty pair as we found out to our cost on many occasions!
We would play for half-a-pint each to the winners and, although we were no slouches at the game - whoever I had as a partner - we always seemed to lose.
Eventually we twigged on that these two had played with those dominoes for so long, they knew every number by the scuffs and scratches on the backs of them.
So, apart from selecting the best scoring 'cards' at the start, they could read the backs of ours when we stood them on edge on the table during play!
It was the same as playing with a marked deck of cards.
After we eventually sussed them, we would quietly ask Eric the landlord for another set of dominoes to play with.
This gave us a level playing field and a fighting chance. The two Bills used to mumble and grumble but they couldn't really make too much fuss.
The Great Eastern is still there, little changed from those days, but there was another pub opposite that has long since been demolished.

A popular 'watering hole' for many of Hertford's enginemen was the Great Eastern Tavern in Railway Place, happily, still there today.

With their steam days almost at an end, a group of Hertford's drivers during training at Stratford for their new role as 'Motorrmen'.   From L to R are Bernard Ansell, Cliff Lockhead, Ray Staniland, Tom Sydney and Tom Gray. In the cab doorway of the diesel railcar is their Instructor, Charlie Cheater. Soon they would go to Clacton to receive instructions on driving electric trains.

Gerry Wade and the 'Albion'

This was called the Albion and the only occasions I used that pub was well after closing time.

I remember the landlord was Gerry Wade who I think had a wooden leg, so he couldn't get around all that well.

There was a standing arrangement between Gerry and some of the railwaymen that he would leave the back door unlocked overnight. If any of us fancied a nocturnal pint we would slip in the back entrance, draw our own beer from the pump and leave the money on the top of the till.

We were forbidden to make any noise in case we woke up Gerry's wife, who would not take too kindly to it.

It was a very trusting arrangement but I am certain Gerry never ever lost out, I was not the only one who always left a bit extra on top of the till.

For a long time, one of the Albion's rooms was used for Union Meetings.

There are several houses on the site of the Albion and the Goods Yard that was directly behind it.

The Goods Offices were part of the original Hertford East station, which was replaced by the current station in 1888.

Part of this development carry the names Albion Close and Holden Close (Holden was a Chief Mechanical Engineer of the old Great Eastern Railway). I wonder how many of the residents are aware of the historical significance of those names?

The characteristics of the L1s

Getting back to day-to-day working and the Thompson L1s, they were generally a poor old batch of engines as regards to condition. As the end of steam was fast approaching, I suppose they suffered their share of mechanical and visual neglect the same as everywhere else.

They clattered and banged so loudly that they were often referred to as 'concrete mixers' on account of the noise they made.

Mind you, they were immensely powerful locomotives, but had a bad reputation for slipping – later on in my story I will give an example of just how bad they could be.

Conversely, if you were lucky enough to get one recently out of the workshops, she would be a completely different performer.

One of their good points was that they were generally good steamers. The only occasions I was ever short of steam on an L1 were when I failed to keep up a fast enough rate of firing – or when I put the fire out, as I'll explain later!

Initially I, along with my colleagues, was very pleased to get the L1s as at last we were getting an engine with enough power to cope with the heavier type of passenger coaches that we were now hauling

However, we had not anticipated the extra work required when compared to that on the N7s. I mentioned earlier that with some of the N7 engines, you could fill the firebox at Hertford and not have to pick up the shovel again all the way to London.

I cannot recall any such feats being performed with an L1, firstly because they did not take kindly to anything other than a thin fire at the front end of the firebox, and secondly because one boxfull of coal would never be enough.

These new engines were real coal guzzlers without a doubt and I believe they doubled the fireman's daily workload.

I would estimate that their average fuel consumption was approximately 56lbs of coal and 45 gallons of water per mile, so on a trip to Liverpool Street and back a fireman would have fed a ton and a half of coal into the firebox. Their bunkers held about 4 tons of coal and 2,000 gallons of water in the side-tanks.

Some experts on railway locomotive history have said that the Thompson L1 Class engines were far too powerful for their size, which resulted in them appearing to shake themselves to pieces soon after a heavy overhaul. I'm inclined to agree with this theory as the deafening crescendo of noise one experienced at speed almost defies description.

But there is no denying that, even in an extremely rough condition, these locomotives were still quite capable of running well in excess of 70 mph, providing the driver had the nerve to let it clatter along at such speeds!

I can recall seeing an L1 racing through Sawbridgeworth one evening on the down *'Fenman'* express, complete with the *'Fenman'* headboard on the smokebox. No doubt it was substituting for a failed Class B1 4-6-0 or a Britannia Pacific, which were the usual locomotives for this prestigious Great Eastern express.

One alarming habit of the L1 was that the reversing lever-retaining ratchet was prone to working it's way out of the toothed locking wheel, which resulted in the lever running into full fore-gear. When this happened the noise was absolutely deafening, even more so if the driver was unlucky enough to get his knuckles in the way of the spinning lever!

Class L1 no. 67709 tops the bank at Bethnal Green with a train bound for Hertford East early in 1960. By this time the overhead wires are up and electrification is imminent.

Mechanical coaling comes to Hertford

A change in the ages-old hand-coaling arrangements became necessary soon after these L1s arrived. Apart from the fact that they burned a great deal more coal than the N7s, their coalbunkers were much higher. It was a hard enough task for the Coalman to heave lumps of coal into the bunker when he was standing on a full wagon of coal alongside. But when he had dug down to anywhere like floor level of the wagon it became an impossible task to heave supplies that high, particularly if he was shovelling small stuff.

179

Class L1 no. 67727 passing Broxbourne Junction Crossing and Signalbox at the head of a train for Bishops Stortford in 1952.

So we had a mechanical shovel permanently allocated to the shed, hired from an outside firm called Greenham & Co. This used to operate alongside the spur that used to give the Great Northern track access to the main line and was now used as one of the routes in and out of the MPD. Locomotives requiring coal would run up the Engine Road past the Locomen's restroom, over a set of points, and come back on the GN spur on the opposite side of the building. Alternatively, it would pause as it came up the GN track. A number of wagons of coal used to be parked on part of the siding that led to the crossing over Mead Lane and the Greenham's Shovel would be situated in the inverted 'V' area.

From there it would scoop coal from the wagons on its right and swing across to the waiting bunker of the locomotive on the left.

Traffic along the G.N. track had access only to the Tar Works sidings on the other side of Mead Lane, so the coal wagons were removed from there on the evenings that traffic was due to use the loop.

The time taken to replenish the bunker of an engine was only a fraction of that required before, a couple of bucketful's swung across from wagon to engine, and the job was done.   Mind you, on a windy day, the dust that blew from the load as it dropped into the bunker could be pretty evil.

It was for this reason that we usually vacated the footplate and retreated into the messroom while the engine was being coaled-up.

The Greenham shovel driver

I remember the Greenham's driver was a wiry little man who always wore a brown Trilby hat.   He used to come into the Enginemen's Restroom while awaiting the next engine, and sit in a chair beside our stove and drift off to sleep.

We young firemen used to take great delight in surreptitiously filling the indentation in the crown of his hat with water.   As he drifted into a deeper snooze, his head drooped forward spilling the water into his lap, waking him up with a start!   Of course, by the time that happened, nobody was anywhere near him so he was unable to identify the culprit.

He used to work very long hours and during the week, instead of going to his home in the London area, he would sleep in a Guard's van over in the Goods yard.

When we were on nightshift, we fireman would occasionally lob a lump of coal at the side of the van out of devilment!

Although this digger operated over 12 hours a day only, a certain amount of hand coaling was still required on the late shift.

Messrs. Greenham's mechanical shovel is at work replenishing the bunker of an L1 in 1960. The locomotive is standing on the Great Northern branch and the wagons of coal are on the Mead Lane Tarworks spur.

Nearly out in the road!

As we ran into Hertford on Thursday, April 16th on 67726 with an evening train, we saw another L1 had come to grief on the catch-points coming from the carriage siding adjacent to Railway Street. The unfortunate engine was 67709 with driver Alf Childs and his mate Johnny Hawthorn. They had shunted their train in there for the night, uncoupled and reversed straight out, expecting the road to be kept open for them. It obviously wasn't the case and she had run off onto 'Old England'.

When I saw her, she was leaning over at quite an acute angle into Railway Street, with the corner of her front buffer-beam forced through the green painted iron-railing fence.

Those bent railings were never replaced, and for many years afterwards, whenever I drove down Railway Street past that spot, I could picture that L1 hanging over the edge of the road.

The entire fence has since been replaced and so another link with the steam-age has disappeared.

A 'foreigner' from the LMS

The week commencing May 24th 1959 produced a couple of noteworthy events.

I was on a 4 p.m. turn all that week except for Tuesday which was my Rest-day, which I worked on a 12.30 p.m. special ballast-train working. On that day we had a 2-6-0 tender locomotive no. 43150. Although this carried an LMS Railway number, it was built by British Railways after 1948 and was a forerunner to the BR Standard Class 3 engines built between 1953 and 1957.

These locomotives were quite a novel experience for us, as the cab was higher from ground level than anything we had had before!

A number of these types would visit Hertford East in the remaining few months of steam operation.

Off the road in the shed

On the Thursday we came off the rails in the shed yard with 67706 due to an excess of ash and clinker cascading onto the rail from the accumulated pile beside the track.

It was only the rear pony wheels that came off but, to avoid delay, we abandoned 67706 and took sister engine 67725. The shed staff managed to re-rail 67706 with the aid of cast-iron ramps specially designed for dealing with such minor mishaps.

An 'Austerity' WD 2-8-0

Early one week in September I was on a 7 a.m. passenger turn and for the entire week we had our own 'regular' engine 67704, which was something of a rarity by this time. On the Friday there appeared at Hertford a Class WD (ex-War Department) 2-8-0 Austerity locomotive no. 90508.

I have no idea how it came to be there, only that the Shedmaster was looking for a volunteer crew to take it back to Stratford. I volunteered but cannot be certain if my mate Ted Champ accompanied me or not. This was the largest locomotive to date that I had worked on, but as we were just running engine only ('light engine' in railway parlance) there was no demand for any particular firing skill. We clanked our way to Stratford without incident.

The effect of Driver Training

By this time the electrification scheme was well progressed and drivers were beginning to disappear from time-to-time to attend instruction courses in their forthcoming roles as Motormen. It meant that we firemen didn't always know which driver we would be paired with from one day to the next.
It even meant that drivers from Stratford were drafted in to cover some of the gaps.

Bang goes the 'regular engine' policy

During week commencing Monday 30th November I was teamed up with Stratford driver Harold Sutheren for the 6.45 a.m. shift. Also that same week we had no less than **seven** different locomotives, which were as follows:
Monday: 2-6-0 no. 43037. Tuesday; 0-6-0 no. 65555, which proved defective, so we exchanged for 2-6-0 no. 76030. Wednesday: 0-6-0 no. 64708. Thursday: no. 43151. Friday: no. 43105 and Saturday L1 2-6-4 no. 67735.
This was a pretty sure indication that the 'regular engine' policy had now fallen apart.

We pass up some 'Hot Tips'

Before I move on from 1959 there was another occasion that sticks in my memory of a golden opportunity missed when we were on the Broxbourne Shunt job.
I have mentioned previously that this job included a run to Waltham Cross. Well, on this particular day one of the wagons we had to pick up at the 'Cross' was a horsebox, complete with racehorse and groom.
 I believe this was during the racing season at Newmarket and this box would be attached at Broxbourne to a northbound express.
While we were waiting for the shunter to hook up this wagon in the loading-bay, we ambled down to the box to have a look at the magnificent racehorse.
Not being much of a horseracing fan I didn't ask the groom what the horse's name was, but my mate did ask the groom if he had any worthwhile tips.
At first he hedged, saying he wasn't allowed to give 'inside information', so we didn't get any Newmarket tips.
However, he eventually gave us the names of two horses for two of the Classic races coming up later in the season. The two names he gave us were 'Marshal Pil' and 'Oxo'. *"Put your shirts on 'em mates, but remember, I ain't said nothing – OK?"* he said.
Now, at that time there were no such things as Betting Shops, where you could just wander in and place a bet. You had to use what was known as a 'Bookies

Runner'. This was a person who collected the bets and placed them with a bona-fide Turf Accountant.

How it actually worked I don't know, all I do remember was that there was a house in Railway Street where a Runner lived. You wrote your bet out on a slip of paper, wrapped your stake inside it and dropped it through the letterbox of this house.

I never found out how to collect any winnings as, on the few occasions I had a bet, I never won anything. In my naivety I used to bet on the outsiders, because they offered much bigger odds. In those days I certainly was the bookie's 'friend'!

Anyway, having got these tips, my mate and I agreed to go ten bob (50p) each on an 'each-way double'. By placing our bets early we could be sure of getting good odds. Well, we forgot all about it until 'Oxo' won the Grand National!

We deliberated on whether to place a bet on the remaining horse, but decided it wouldn't be our luck for that one to win as well, so we let it pass.

I can't remember which of the other Classics it was, but 'Marshal Pil' won. We cursed ourselves for ages after that, bemoaning the small fortune our 'each-way double' would have given us had we not dragged our heels at the outset!

An unidentified N7 standing on the Great Northern branch behind the carriage cleaner's 'offices' at Hertford East. As there is no electrification paraphernalia in evidence, the date is prior to 1960.

CHAPTER NINE

1960 – Final Year of Hertford Steam

In comes 1960

At the end of 1959 I had the luxury of Christmas and Boxing days off, but I was on a 4 a.m. shift all the following week, including New Year's Day, so I didn't see much of my bed the morning after seeing in the New Year!

By the end of that first week in 1960 my tally of Firing Turns had climbed up to 990.

The electrics are coming

Although I could not have known for certain at that time, this was to be my last year at Hertford East, as the Electrification Programme was quickly gathering pace. It became commonplace to see electric trains running up and down the line on trials.

It brought with it the added danger of overhead live wires, with 25,000 volts running through them.

All locomotives had postcard-size warning plates riveted to them at each location where there were steps. These plates carried the legend "DANGER – OVERHEAD LIVE WIRES" in red lettering on a white background.

Such was the force-field around these wires we were informed that, even getting too close to them carried a high risk of electrocution – a bit like the effect of a magnet I suppose.

The strange thing was - that with all the terrible power those wires carried - they looked so innocent. They didn't buzz (except when it was raining) or give off any sparks to let you know they were active, so it was perhaps inevitable that something was bound to happen, sometime.

One day during the early part of 1960, we were talking to a young Stratford fireman who was on loan to us on a day when we were short staffed.

Apparently, just before the end of steam on the Clacton line, he climbed up into the tender of his engine while at Clacton to pull some coal forward for the return journey to London.

Thinking the overhead power was off, his back touched the live wire and the force threw him back into the cab. He was badly burned and spent a lot of time recovering in hospital.

He stripped off his jacket and shirt and showed us the long, white livid scar all the way down his back. He was very lucky to be alive – and he knew it!

He owed his life to the fact that, at that time, the voltage used was *only* 1,500 - had it been the 25,000 volt system later used across the entire Region, he would not have been so lucky – as we were soon to find out.

At the time I didn't know who this young fireman was, but years later – in R.H.N. Hardy's book *"Railways in the Blood"* – he relates a similar accident to fireman

185

Ray Rowe on a B17 at Clacton in August 1959, so it could well have been the same person.

A tragedy at Hertford East

Some of my colleagues were to witness the terrible power of the electricity coursing through those wires sometime later on in the year when Enfield Fireman Chris Chapman climbed up onto the bunker of L1 no.67735 to trim the coal whilst standing in Hertford East platform.

I was in the shed at the time that it happened and several of my mates ran up to the station to see. I didn't go but one of them told me of the terrible injuries that this poor individual had suffered.

No doubt he made the fatal mistake of thinking that the power was switched off - as indeed it often was during those early days when trials were taking place. But we had been warned to treat the 'wires' as live at all times.

This demonstration of the terrible consequences of forgetting the warnings certainly shook us up and made us all ultra-careful thereafter.

Class L1 2-6-4 67735 about to depart from Stratford on a Hertford East train on 6th March 1958. This locomotive was involved in the tragic accident at Hertford in 1960 when an engineman was electrocuted while climbing onto the bunker. 67735 was also the locomotive on which the author worked on his final day at Hertford East – Sunday, 20th November 196. *(R.C. Riley)*

Never too careful

My mate, Ted Champ, usually so quiet and placid, threw a fit one afternoon as we stood waiting to leave with a London train from the platform at Hertford.

I was starting to climb the bunker steps of our L1 to brush off some small coal and dust from the ledge in line with the window. Although I was conscious of the 'wires' and had no intention of getting too close, Ted would have physically pulled me from those steps had I not responded immediately to his urgent shout of "***Get down you silly bugger!***".

Initially we had some worries as to how we would be affected on the footplate of an engine that was blowing off steam directly under a live wire. We were assured that, as the whole locomotive was earthed, there was absolutely no danger to us.

The Liverpool Street Pilots

Back to the steam scene, I must mention the 2 Liverpool Street pilot engines. These were Class J69 0-6-0 Tank no. 68619 and N7 0-6-2 Tank no. 69614.

The J69 had been around the station area for many years and was joined by the N7 during 1956/57, when both of them were finished in appearance to exhibition standard.

These locomotives were beautiful to behold, I believe enthusiasts came from miles away especially to see them. They were kept absolutely immaculate inside and out, with every conceivable piece of copper and brass sparkling. The black-cherry paintwork shone like coloured glass.

The crews received special time-allowance just to keep these engines in that condition – more than I received for my efforts on 69682 I might add!

The J69 was allocated to the East Side of the station, with the N7 situated on the West (suburban) Side.

Apart from displaying an attractive image to the general public, their main jobs was to perform small shunting movements within the station limits – like transferring special coaches and wagons from one train to another etc..

In the case of 69614, she also acted as a standby engine for the suburban services should one fail. On the occasions that she was called upon for such duties, the crew was never too happy about letting her go. It usually meant that by the time they got her back, much extra cleaning would be required – for no additional pay!

Although 69614 often acted as replacement on suburban workings, I never saw 68619 on such duties but, as this class used to be regular operators of the Enfield services in their time, she would probably have been well capable of standing in on those trips.

In 1959 the J69 was repainted in the old Great Eastern Railway blue livery, she remained in that condition until she was withdrawn and scrapped in 1961. Her immaculate appearance must have belied her general condition because it was one of her sisters (68633) that was eventually chosen for preservation and is currently displayed at York Railway Museum.

Even 69614 was scrapped eventually, but fortunately a member of the class (69621) has survived into preservation.

On one of her occasional visits to Hertford East, Liverpool Street's immaculate West Side Pilot, N7 no. 69614, is receiving a fresh supply of coal in the Loco.

Liverpool Street's West-Side Pilot

On Wednesday, 27th January I had my first trip on 69614. I had worked a morning train into Liverpool Street with Driver Bob Smith and L1 no. 67714. Our normal duty on that shift was then to take a train of empty coaches back to Thornton Fields Sidings at Stratford, and work a train from there to Hertford.

When we arrived in London that morning, a Bishops Stortford crew whose engine had failed commandeered our engine, and we had to use 69614 for our Thornton Fields working.

However, to ensure the Pilot's crew got their 'pride and joy' back pretty quickly, we were relieved of 69614 when we arrived at Stratford and took charge of another L1 no. 67705.

Another Driving Test - third time lucky

It was now over 18 months since I failed my second attempt at passing the Driving Test for a car. I had decided to try yet again and was given a Test date for Thursday 28th January.

This time I was determined not to fail again and had taken steps to ensure success, as I mentioned when reporting my second failure.

I enlisted the help of a locally recommended Driving School Instructor. I booked 3 lessons with him at a cost of 15 shillings (75p) a lesson.

The car was one of the - then - new Ford Anglia 105E models which drove like an absolute dream compared with what I had been used to.

The Instructor took me round each of the known Test Routes in Hertford and gave me useful tips on reversing and the 3-point turn, which had been a couple of my faults.

It proved to be money well spent as I sailed through the Test with flying colours, I wished at the time that I had taken lessons in the first place.

The author's 1939 Wolseley 14 photographed just off the A303 opposite Stonehenge in June 1960. 14 miles to the gallon and built like a tank!

My first car

Some time previously father had changed cars yet again, and we had jointly purchased (for the princely sum of £45) a 1939 fourteen-horse power Wolseley saloon, in which I had gained considerable experience - driving on L-plates – with dad present, of course.

Upon passing my test he allowed me to 'buy out' his share of the car for £20 (at a £1 a week – such high finance!) so now I had my own transport. I was yet to find out what the joys of running a car would cost – particularly with a car that barely managed to travel 14 miles on a gallon of petrol!

Fortunately, with dad's help and tuition, I was able to carry out virtually all maintenance work -- even heavy repairs – without incurring garage costs.

Even so, spare parts didn't 'grow on trees' and still had to be paid for.

However, it did mean I could venture a little bit further than the County cinema at Hertford on my evenings off.

One of my first drives to London was to the Ambassadors Theatre in Cambridge Square, the date was the 27th of February. My old schoolpal Tony Liles and I saw Agatha Christie's *"The Mousetrap"*, then advertised as in it's *"7th Fantastic Year"*. Incredibly, that that same play is still running at the time of writing - 46 years after it first started!

Water problems

Back to the work scene, a persistent problem with one of our L1s – 67714 - was that of leaking water tanks.

This was due to the working loose of the bolts that secured the side tanks to the footplate framing. No matter how much the Fitter tightened these bolts, within a very short time they would work loose again, ultimately leaking more water than was actually used on a run.

This created other problems. As we ran into a station water would spray out on to the edge of the platform, to the annoyance of passengers waiting to board the train.

Even more annoying was that water would pour onto the rail, causing the engine to slip violently. The L1s were notorious for slipping anyway, so this made the problem even worse.

It became quite common for drivers to refuse to take 67714 out of the shed for fear of running out of water during a journey. To give an idea as to the extent of the problem, on a run to Liverpool Street, about 1,000 gallons would have leaked onto the track! The Fitter would retighten the bolts, but within just a few days they would be as loose as ever.

Although one or two other L1s suffered from similar problems, they were quickly remedied. It was strange that the problem seemed incurable on that particular engine.

The steam-driven dynamo

Some of the L1s were fitted with electric lighting, which was quite a novelty.
Electricity was generated by a steam-operated dynamo located on the framing to the right of the smokebox.
Bulbs seemed to fail fairly regularly but we soon discovered that they were the same size as those fitted to the reading lights in the carriages of the ex-Southend stock, so a ready supply of replacements was guaranteed!
Whether it was because these bulbs were not quite the same voltage, or because the dynamos were erratic in their power output, they never seemed to last very long. Added to that, the dynamos were very unreliable so the benefit of electric lighting was not enjoyed very often.
Occasionally, a good clout with the hammer encouraged the dynamo to stir itself into life, but even then the chances were that the motor would make such a racket that it would have to be turned off.

A burst water-gauge

I mentioned earlier the glass-tube boiler water gauge, there was one occasion we had one burst.
We were just approaching St. Margaret's station with a passenger train from London, when there was this terrific bang and the cab was suddenly filled with steam.
I didn't realise what had happened at first until my mate shouted out for me to ***"turn the cocks off"***.   I then knew what had happened but I could not get near the gauge due to the rush of 220 lbs pressure of scalding steam and water that was erupting from the broken tube.
My mate was referring to the isolation cocks fitted above and below the gauge-glass to close off the flow of water and steam.
 We were quickly getting soaked and as we ran into the station, I saw my mate was hanging to the outside of the cab of our L1 with his arm through the window operating the brake!   As soon as we came to a stand he grabbed his gabardine raincoat and used it as a shield to get near the gauge and succeeded in shutting the steam and water cocks off.
There was no delay for repairs as these engines (along with most classes) were fitted with twin gauges, so we still had one to read from.
From there to Hertford we were showered with drops of dirty water dripping from inside the cab roof.   That was the only occasion that I experienced the failure of a water-gauge glass.   On our preparation checks it was standard practice to renew a gauge-glass and it's rubber washers if it showed any signs of leakage.

Looking out for dad

Mention of St. Margaret's station reminds me of the occasions when I looked for my father during my morning trips.

In his job as milk-roundsman for United Dairies, he served in and around Stanstead Abbotts, the village in which the station was situated.

Having helped him on his round many times as a youngster – and still did occasionally on my days off – I knew roughly where he was likely to be at a certain time, so I used to look out for him.

He was often spotted making his deliveries in one of the cul-de-sacs on our left as we pulled away from the station heading for Hertford.   A couple of blasts on the whistle brought a friendly wave from him.

Not so friendly were the occasions we were on a London bound train, we would come to a stand straddling the level crossing at the end of the platform.

Like numerous railway crossings on busy roads all over the country, they were a curse to highway traffic, causing infuriating congestion and delays.

If my father happened to be one of the unfortunates in the long queues, and he spotted me on the footplate, he would leap out of his cab into the road and shake his fist at us in mocking threat.

I used to wonder what the other motorists made of this seemingly demented milkman!

If I happened to be in the driving seat on those occasions, I would yank the regulator open a little quicker than usual to purposely make the engine slip for a second or two, sending smoke and ash shooting high into the sky, just a bit of showing off, really!

Enginemen's outings

Apart from the occasional pint at the local pub, the only fireman I mixed with socially on any sort of regular basis was Mick Chapman, but on Sunday 24th of April a whole group of us went on a day-trip to Southend-on-Sea.   I cannot remember whether we went by coach or train, but I do know we had a great day. I still have a faded group photograph to record the event.

You occasionally read of 'railwaymen's outings' but there were only two occasions that I remember a group from Hertford East going on a trip together.   The other occasion was another day at Southend on July 22nd 1961 – several months after steam had gone from Hertford.

69614 – not as good as she looks!

Returning to the Liverpool Street West-Side pilot engine - 69614 - Friday 8th July was the next occasion I worked on her, this time all the way to Hertford.   We had failed with 69688 for some reason and were given the pilot for our return working that evening.

I have to say that her good looks were certainly not matched by her performance!

We had a pretty rough trip due to her inability to steam freely, by the time we reached Hertford East I was of the firm opinion that I would be quite happy if I never saw 69614 again.

Would you believe it, when we signed on for duty at 5.20 p.m. the following evening, the Shedmaster had 'kindly' kept 69614 in reserve especially for us to work our train back to London!

Despite the time of year, a group of Hertford East enginemen enjoyed a day at Southend on 24/4/60. From L to R they are: John Shadbolt, Sid Heath, Mick Chapman, Dennis Clarke, Colin Clarke, Bob Smith, Eric Wrangles, Wally Coleman, Tony Parrot and the author.

Were they happy to have her back?

After an equally rough trip back, we changed over at Liverpool Street for sister engine, 69675. I remember the glum look on the faces of the pilot's crew as they cast their eyes over the tarnished copper and brass fittings and dusty paintwork of their beloved engine, she certainly had had 'a dirty night out'!
I wondered how much hard graft they had to exert before they restored her to her usual pristine condition.

Water leaks - a suggested cure!

The last occasion I worked on 69614 was on the 10th of August when we failed in Liverpool Street with good old 67714 and her leaking side-tanks. I believe my mate's thinking was that if she went back to Stratford workshops, maybe they would effect a more permanent cure for this ongoing problem – *"Like making razor blades out of her"* he muttered. But no, she was back in Hertford shed waiting for us the following morning!

193

Good days – Bad days

To illustrate the characteristics of the L1 class engines, I can recall 3 particular occasions that show what Jekyll and Hyde locomotives they were.

A very good morning

On the morning of Saturday, 16th of July, we were working the second train of the day, the 5.24 a.m. to Liverpool Street via Stratford.
My driver was Geoff Codling and our engine was L1 no. 67709.
The following intermediate times are approximate as I didn't write them in my diary at the time, but the events are true as I remember them.
67709 had only recently returned to Hertford after a major overhaul at Stratford Works and ran like a proverbially well-oiled sewing machine.
Our train was quite light with just 5 coaches and this trip would normally be a doddle with such a powerful locomotive.
However, we were stopped at Broxbourne Junction by adverse signals just before joining up with the main line.

We hung on the whistle to no effect and, after a few minutes I used the telephone on the signal post and was informed by the Signalman that he had a points failure on the junction, but that it was being dealt with.
After waiting a few more minutes with nothing happening, I walked the few hundred yards to the Signalbox to carry out Rule 55, a procedure that ensures our train is protected from the rear. Having signed the register I remained in the box until the maintenance crew hand-clipped the points over and we were given the green light to continue on our way.
We drew into Broxbourne station at around 6 a.m. which put us 16 minutes late.
Now it so happened travelling in the coach nearest the engine was one of our regular passengers - Ernie Beauchamp - who boarded the train Hertford every morning. He travelled to Stratford where he caught a connection to his place of work somewhere near Ilford.
I believe this connection arrived at Stratford at 6.33 so, if we were running to time, he had around 5 minutes to make his way via the underpass to reach the mainline platform to make his connection.
He knew many of us railwaymen, as he was a regular at the *Great Eastern Tavern* in Railway Street.
On this particular morning he stuck his head out of the window at Broxbourne and shook his fist at us.
I turned to Geoff and commented *"We're for it the next time Ernie sees us in the pub, he's going to be late for work".*
Geoff got up from his seat and unbuttoned his jacket. *"Let's see if we can make his connection then."* He replied, throwing his jacket onto my seat.
"You've got to be joking" I said, knowing we only had 26 minutes to cover the 15 miles to Stratford – instead of the usual 43 minutes - stopping at all stations along the way.

He picked up the shovel and waved me into the driving seat.

I should explain that Geoff had only recently transferred to Hertford to get his driver's promotion, having spent his firing career at Melton Constable where he had gained a great deal of experience working with the L1 class engines.

Other factors in our favour were a bright, dry summer morning, and our engine was chimney-first to London, which meant the station platforms were on the driver's side.

Our Guard was an uncle of mine - George Felstead - which meant I could hustle him along if need be without fear of being reported for Guard 'harassment'!

I slipped into the driving seat, popped the whistle and gave an impatient wave to Uncle George. He got the message and promptly waved his green flag.

I heaved the regulator wide open and we shot out of Broxbourne like a bullet from a gun.

I glanced across at Geoff who was shovelling coal into the firebox for all he was worth, he looked up and grinned, then frowned and shook his head as I wound the reversing gear lever up to reduce the shower of sparks that were erupting from the front end.

So I dropped the gear down again and he returned to his task of trying to keep pace with what was disappearing out of the chimney!

L1 no. 67734 waits for the signal to join the mainline at Broxbourne Junction with a Hertford to Liverpool Street train in June 1955.

We roared into Cheshunt station and screeched to a halt.   There were very few passengers about at that time on a Saturday morning, so as soon as I had blown the brakes off I popped the whistle for George to wave his flag.

I didn't need to remind him to move smartly after that, and we went like the wind in and out of every station.

Although I opened the regulator wide with the engine in full forward gear on each occasion, 67709 never once slipped and the needle on the steam-pressure gauge never wandered far from the 220 lbs full-pressure mark.

A humorous incident occurred as we ran into Angel Road station.   It was customary for the Station Porter to have a cup of tea ready for the Guard.

As we came to a stand, the Porter had just descended the steps from the overbridge at the London (engine) end of the platform carrying the cup of tea. Unfortunately for George, the Guard's Van was at the rear end of our train and, as we paused only for a few seconds, the Porter had only just made it alongside our engine as we pulled away.

By the time the Guard's van came abreast of the Porter we must have already reached around 30 mph and as I looked back down the train I could see George's outstretched hand hopelessly trying to grab his cup of tea.

My final glimpse was of the fast-receding Porter standing by the edge of the platform drinking the tea himself!

Here is the star performer of my exhilarating run on 16/7/60, Class L1 2-6-4 no. 67709, photographed the same month at Broxbourne station during construction. As the track has yet to be re-aligned, a temporary 'fillet' has been attached to the new platform.

We sprinted into Stratford just over a couple of minutes behind time, having made up about thirteen minutes since leaving Broxbourne.

We got a thankful wave from Ernie as he dived out of the carriage and hurried down the subway to get his connection, which he confirmed he caught ok when I next saw him in the pub.   I also got a pint from him for the 'quickest run of his life'.

Furthermore, we arrived at Liverpool Street 'right time'- we had regained all of the 16 minutes - some achievement, even though the original time allowed may be considered as pretty generous.

I suppose we were fortunate that it was a Saturday morning, when there was less traffic about to impede our efforts. Also all the Signalmen along the route guessed what we were about and did their best to ensure we had green lights all the way, which indeed was the case.

I think the performance of 67709 that morning, it's beautiful riding with a total absence of slip, knock or rattle, illustrated what excellent locomotives the L1s could be when in fine fettle.

With such a light load for so powerful a locomotive, the only strain suffered that day was on my 'fireman' who thoroughly enjoyed every minute of it.

Of course, the coal consumption would not have pleased Company officials, but there was a lot of pride at stake in these twilight months of steam on the Hertford branch, as I knew there was right across the railway system.

Also, we must have given many residents along the way an unexpected 'early morning call' with the continuous roar emitting from 67709's chimney!

Nonetheless, our run that morning was not too far away from the time allowed for an express from Broxbourne to Liverpool Street travelling non-stop via the shorter, Hackney Downs route.

I am not aware of that run ever being bettered and I doubt if the modern-day electric trains could equal that all-stations timing of almost 40 years ago.

A bad afternoon

Probably the worst problem with the L1s, from the driver's point of view, was wheel-slip.   As I mentioned earlier, the rougher they became, the more they slipped – due to excess wear in the axleboxes.

This problem was not helped by the fact that the steam-operated sanding gear rarely worked properly, invariably placing a nice jet of wet steam between wheel and rail – which just made matters worse! An example of severe slipping was on one rainy Saturday afternoon in October 1960.

We left Liverpool Street on an 'all-stations' to Hertford with 67735, which was in appalling mechanical condition.   This was during the final few weeks of suburban steam operation and maintenance was almost non-existent.

We were in trouble even before the last coach of our train cleared the platform, the engine slipped uncontrollably and it was a full 15 minutes before we finally made it to the top of Bethnal Green bank, a distance of just over a mile.

The sanding gear had no effect at all, for the very reason just explained.

There were times when I didn't think we would make it at all.   My driver was Don Wench who was quite a fit man, but he was absolutely dripping with perspiration from his constant struggle with opening and closing the regulator.

Had it not been for the continuous cacophony of noise coming from 67735 – and had I been a lip-reader - I do believe I would have learnt a few new choice words from Don during that battle!

Although there were special procedures in force in the event of a train stalling on Bethnal Green Bank, I cannot recall one single occasion when a Hertford train failed to make it to the top, but that day it was a pretty close-run thing.

A nightmare!

My nightmare happened one evening during the second week in August 1960, I can't be certain of the exact day, but it was on a turn that involved working up to London with the 6.30 p.m.   Our engine that evening was 67706.

After arriving London just after 7.30 we were not scheduled to leave again until 10.28.

So, after we were released from our train, we parked in the bay at the end of the platform and prepared to 'bed' our engine down for a couple of hours while we had a stroll around town.

Having filled the boiler right up, I banked the fire under the door and smothered it with dusty coal.

To ensure that it did not burn through too quickly – thereby raising steam pressure to blowing off point – I dampened the coal down with the water-hose.

Off we went for a walk around part of the Metropolis, ending up at the *'Baker & Basket'* at the end of Sun Street Passage for a nice pint of Watney's Ale.

When we got back to our engine just after 10 p.m. I discovered to my horror that I had done too good a job of damping-down the fire – it was out!

There was still plenty of water in the boiler, but only about 50 lbs. of steam pressure. The next few minutes were spent darting across the tracks desperately trying to find some firewood in the shape of wooden rail chair keys or something similar that would burn quickly, but to no avail.

At 10.15 the signal came off calling us to back on to our train which, with only 50 lbs. of steam, we just about managed to do.

I always knew the firegrate of an L1 was pretty big, but when there is no fire in it at a time when there was supposed to be, it looked twice the size!

Our efforts at getting the fire going using oil-soaked rags were having very little impact and the situation was now very serious indeed.

To have to report to Control that we needed another engine at that time of night because I had let the fire go out was unthinkable!

Fortunately, at that moment an Enfield train was just pulling out of the adjacent platform so we waved down the N7 that had brought it in and scrounged a few shovelfuls of burning coals from his fire, which at last started to pump some life into our firebox.

By the time our signal to leave came off at 10.28 we had barely raised the 80 lbs. of steam required to release the brakes of our train, we could not even contemplate tackling Bethnal Green bank with less than 160 lbs. 'on the clock'.

So I had the embarrassing task of phoning the Signalman with the half-truth that we had a problem with the vacuum brake and were not yet ready to leave – I omitted to say that the problem with releasing the brake was due to a shortage of steam! He returned the signal to red, with the instruction that I was to let him know when we were ready.

We finally got away at 10.45 and struggled for steam all the way to Hertford without being able to make up any of the lost time.

I know I cannot blame the engine for this episode but had we had an N7 with it's smaller firebox, I am sure we would have left London right time with very little trouble.

Stratford-based N7 no. 69643 arrives at Broxbourne's original station with a shuttle working from Bishop's Stortford in May 1956.

For a brief period during the construction of the new station at Broxbourne, some Sunday trains from Hertford East were terminated at Broxbourne. In August 1960, a trio of locomotives is coupled together for the return trip to Hertford. From L to R they are N7 no. 69684, L1 no. 67706 and a BR Standard Class 4MT no. 76034.

A typical run to London

A routine trip for me to Liverpool Street with an L1 on an all-stations passenger train would go something like this;

Having prepared our engine I would let the Signalman know (via the internal telephone) that we were ready to leave the Shed. This would be no less than 15 minutes before the train Departure Time.

During winter months we had to allow another 15 minutes in order to steam-heat the carriages in the platform.

Slowly approaching our train waiting at the platform, we would 'buffer-up' to it and I would duck under the buffer-beam of our engine and the first coach and heave the engine's coupling on to the hook of the coach. I would take up any slack by turning the screw device in the centre of the coupling. A short bar with an iron knob on one end is fixed in the middle of the threaded section to make it easier to turn.

I would then probably shout to my driver to 'ease-off' – releasing the compression on the buffers – allowing me a bit more space to connect the vacuum-brake piping. These were thick, flexible hoses that clipped together and held in place with a wire pin. There was a knack in snapping these hoses together and I would automatically check that each hose face had its rubber-sealing ring in place.

If it was wintertime I would also connect the steam-heating hoses and open the steam-cocks attached to the coach and engine.

It was usual for tank engines to run 'bunker first' to Liverpool Street as it was reckoned that any risk of slipping during the climb up Bethnal Green Bank was much reduced running 'boiler first'.

Having coupled up, it was round to the rear of the engine to put the destination discs on the appropriate brackets, in our case it was a purple disc at the top of the bunker and a white disc on the left-hand (facing front) bracket.

Occasionally, we would have a destination board to hang on brackets fitted to the smokebox door and the bunker. These were made of mild steel painted black with yellow lettering – LIVERPOOL STREET on one side and HERTFORD on the reverse. However, very few of these were available so their use was limited.

Meanwhile, my mate would have turned on the steam-heating cock and the vacuum brake valve to test the brakes. If he was unable to raise 21 inches of vacuum on the gauge, it meant there was a leak somewhere. First place to check would be the opposite end of the engine to ensure the pipe was secure on it's seating. After that, it was a matter of walking along the train checking each hose coupling between the carriages. It was usually quite easy to identify a leak by listening for the telltale 'hiss' at the faulty connection.

By the time we were ready to go, I would have a full head of steam, about three-quarters of a boiler full of water and a fire which is just turning from a dull orange glow to a brighter red colour. Once we have got the 'right-away' and my mate opens the regulator, the draught on the fire soon turns it from bright red to an iridescent white. It is while the fire is this colour that the opportunity is taken to put half a dozen shovels full of coal around the firebox. Although the steam pressure has not started to fall it is bad practice to wait for it to do so before putting on more coal, as this would only serve to 'cool' the fire at a crucial stage.

I replenish the boiler water by turning on the injector the moment the driver shuts off steam prior to a station stop. This action counteracts the sudden rise in steam pressure that would otherwise be wasted through the safety valves. I turn the injector off immediately we start off again.

Repeating this operation as we approach each of the 14 stations on our route is usually sufficient to keep the water level in the boiler at a safe level. On some engines, it was possible to 'fine-tune' the injector to pump a reduced amount of water into the boiler continuously, which eliminated 'on and off' routine. Not all engines had injectors that would take to this 'trickle' method.

Every now and then, I will have a look round the firebed to ensure that it is burning evenly, and that there are no holes or dead areas. To enable me to inspect the firebed through the wall of white flame, I will rest the firing shovel on the rim of the firehole and turn it upside-down. The incoming draught below the blade of the shovel clears a narrow tunnel through the flames, and by altering the direction of the blade, this tunnel can be guided all over the firebox, enabling me to inspect the bed of the fire.

Little or no conversation is possible whilst we are on the move as the entire cab is filled with a great deal of noise originating from a number of sources.

There is the muffled, staccato roar from the firebox, the whining of the injector and the rumble, shake and rattle from the moving parts of the locomotive. Then there are the sounds of the wheels running over the tracks beneath our feet – in those days a constant 'clicketty-clack' of the rail-joints – magnified much more every time we pass over a bridge, a junction or a set of points.

When I am actually firing, there is the added noise of the shovel scraping on the metal plate near the coalhole as I take up fresh coal and the crash and clang as I 'bounce' the shovel off the edge of the firehole door. All the time the engine is swaying, jumping and jerking at every turn of the wheels and I have to concentrate to maintain my balance while swinging the shovel from bunker coalhole across and through the firehole door.

In addition to all this, coal dust is constantly being whirled around the confines of the cab – whipped up by the draughts that are finding their way in through every nook and cranny.

My mate and I may exchange the odd shouted word or two during our brief stops at the stations. All the time when we are running I am constantly on the lookout to ensure all is well with our train. I am frequently sticking my head out of the cab and looking back down our train to check that nothing is amiss e.g. that a door has not come open on any of the carriages.

Then I look ahead, not only to check the signals, but also the track ahead, just in case something – or somebody – is blocking the line.

Of course, my driver is doing the same thing and I am merely assisting him in his vigil – all part of the teamwork essential for efficient working.

After we leave Clapton station and head towards Hackney Downs – our last stop before Liverpool Street – I will not do any more firing. I will also allow the boiler water level to fall, so that we arrive at the terminus with little more than a quarter reading on the gauge-glass, and the fire burnt down to a dull-red glow. This will ensure that I am able to avoid the possibility of blowing off excess steam whilst in the confines of the station, a practice much frowned on by the Authorities, not to mention the discomfort to passengers who may be showered by sooty smuts cascading down upon them.

If steam pressure does become uncomfortably high, I will be able to 'knock it back' by injecting cold water into the boiler.

Fortunately, we are never too long at the buffer-stops in the station. Usually, by the time I have topped-up our water tanks, washed my hands and had a cup of tea, our train will have left again and we will move down to the far end of the platform and into the waiting bay. This end of the station is in the open-air so if we were to blow off steam it is unlikely to cause any discomfort to the travelling public.

I now start to build the fire again in readiness for the return journey. I have to be careful, as this is a Smokeless Zone and if I do happen to create anything more than a light blue haze, we could be reported by one of the 'beady-eyed' Smoke Inspectors. One way to build the fire without causing excessive smoke is to leave an area of the firebars open – a hole in fact – and either fill it in or spread the fire over it at the time of departure. The sharp haul out of Liverpool Street and up

Bethnal Green Bank will create a tremendous pull on the fire and ensure that it reaches its optimum thermal capacity very quickly.

My description is of a trip that goes as smooth as silk, with an engine that behaves impeccably. Unfortunately, this was not always so, I have had my share of 'nightmare' trips where everything that can go wrong – does!

Ware Signalbox and station looking towards Hertford, a mid-1950s view.

Views along the route

I enjoyed many, many good trips along the line and there was always something of interest to see.

Most of the 3 miles between Broxbourne and Cheshunt was Nurserymen's country and we passed scores of glasshouses along the route. One of them at Wormley was where I worked and watched the trains during my school holidays.

At Waltham Cross there was the huge scrapyard of Mr. Jones where I used to go for spare parts for my old Wolseley. One of the workers would direct me to where one of my particular models lay, and leave me to unbolt the parts I needed. I admit to slipping a few spare lamp bulbs into my pocket during the process!

Moving on up the line, we passed hundreds of small businesses set up in rows of old sheds and garages – 'Industrial Estates' and 'Business Parks' were fancy terms for the future. In those days they were known simply as factory sites.

Between Ponders End and Angel Road stations is an area known as Picketts Lock - where there is a huge Recreation Centre - which is part of the Lea Valley Regional Park. During steam days this was nothing but a bare stretch of waste ground and occasionally, during school holiday periods, youngsters would appear out of the bushes and fire catapults and air-guns at passing trains.

203

For a time, we nicknamed this stretch of line 'Gunman's Gap' and kept a wary eye open as we passed by! However, I believe the police put a stop to those dangerous activities and I have no recollection of any crew or passengers getting injured.

At Northumberland Park the extensive Goods Sidings were on our left, I also seem to remember that on occasions, over on the far side, the red coaches of an Underground Tube train could be spotted.

One big factory that sticks in my mind was just before we got to Tottenham station. It had a huge sign facing the railway proclaiming "DUSMO, THE DUSTLESS SWEEPING POWDER". Believing that all powder was dusty, I used to wonder what 'dustless powder' looked like – and I still do!

Beyond Tottenham was Coppermill Junction, which was in the middle of marshland. Straight on at the junction led to Lea Bridge and Stratford, while branching off right took you to Clapton. After passing through the short tunnels beyond Clapton station, the line climbed up to Hackney Downs, our last stop before Liverpool Street, although there were 3 more station along the route. From Hackney Downs the line runs along one continuous viaduct until it joins the Ipswich mainline at the junction just before Bethnal Green station. This viaduct is almost 2 miles long and carries 4 sets of tracks – Fast and Slow lines each way.

The mind boggles when trying to imagine how many bricks went into making this viaduct – all laid by hand all those years ago and still giving service to this day!

And this is only one of many similar structures in and around the London area. It makes you realise what vast undertakings our Victorian forbears embarked upon when they built the railways.

Although there were 2 other stations along this bit – London Fields and Cambridge Heath – our tracks by-passed them on the left.

Along this part of the route I would watch the hustle and bustle of everyday life along the High Streets of Mare Road and Cambridge Heath. As we rounded Bethnal Green Junction, over on the right was the huge red-brick building of Allen & Hanbury, this name always stuck in my mind because at the time that company had another huge factory at Ware, not very far from where I lived.

Of course, the line is still there today and maybe also some of the factories we used to pass – I wonder if the 'DUSMO' company still exists?

Ancient Lights?

Running along the viaduct after leaving Hackney Downs, in the London direction, there were many views of the rear gardens of row upon row of Victorian terraced houses. I have a clear memory of a black-lettered sign upon a white background fixed on a tall post in the rear garden of one property close to the line. Written in Gothic-style lettering, it contained the legend 'ANCIENT LIGHTS'.

I had no idea as to what it meant until recently checking it up in a reference book.

I found it is a legal term which means that, as the occupier has had an uninterrupted view from the window for at least 20 years, no-one may erect a building or fence which blocks this view. To this day, I have never seen a similar sign – anywhere.

Foggy memories

On some trips, the view would take on a completely different form – that of a blanket of fog. On those occasions the journey could be an absolute nightmare, as anyone old enough to remember the 'pea-souper' fogs will know!

For those who don't know, this type of fog contained all the dirt, smoke and grime of countless tons of pollution that hung about in the air during those times. In those days, nearly every house and factory burnt coal for heating, so smoke was everywhere. Controls on the exhaust emissions from lorries, buses and cars were non-existent so they were constantly belching out black, oily smoke.

On really bad days the fog took on a sickly yellow or green colour – hence the term 'pea-soup'.

On days like this it became very difficult to know exactly where you are for much of the time, as the very presence of the fog seemed to deaden all sound, resulting in an eerie silence. We would crawl along from signal to signal with both the driver and myself hanging out of the cab, eyes straining to recognise some familiar landmark that would tell us where we were.

Of course, we were also ever watchful of the few feet of track ahead of us, ready to brake instantly should an obstruction appear. Fortunately, our train always arrived safely at its destination – a fact not always noticeably appreciated by our passengers – albeit much later than scheduled.

Having said that, there were rare occasions when a grateful individual would press half-a-crown (12.5p) in the driver's hand as he passed by the engine at Liverpool Street.

I recall one amusing incident during very foggy day early in 1960. Traffic and timetables were in absolute chaos and I was working my Rest-day on a goods turn at Broxbourne. To avoid the delay in waiting for a train to take us to Broxbourne, I decided to make my way there in my car, along with my driver. When we eventually got to Broxbourne we were told that our engine was stuck at Waltham Cross and would likely remain there for some time.

So it was back in the car and on we crawled to Waltham Cross. Visibility was down to a few feet but I knew the road very well and we made steady progress without any hold-up. As we approached the railway bridge at Waltham Cross I swung left into the slip-road which took us into the Down Yard. Unbeknown to me, a convoy of half a dozen cars had been on my tail for some time and followed me right into the Yard, thinking we were still on the main highway!

Having parked the car, my mate and I trudged over the tracks to find our engine, chuckling to ourselves at the antics of those drivers trying to turn their cars round to get back onto the main road.

A close call at Hertford

I recall another, more serious, incident that happened during the late 1950s in dense fog at Hertford East station. Normally, following arrival and once all passengers had alighted, the train would shunt back a few yards to clear a set of points which allowed the engine access to the middle road for returning to the Shed.

Above. Class L1 2-6-4 no. 67715 spent part of her life at Hertford East during 1959/60. Here she is seen under the coaling tower at Norwich MPD in November 1961. *(A. Doyle/Colour-Rail/BRE302)*
Below. In the carriage sidings at Stratford is N7 0-6-2 no. 69713 – fresh out of the Paintshop for probably the last time in her life. *(F. Hornby/Colour-Rail/BRE135)*

The 'wires' are up and Hertford's N7 69680 is almost at the end of her life as she climbs the bank into Bethnal Green station in late 1960. Her brass 'Built at Gorton' worksplate has already been removed (stolen?) from the side of the front sandbox. Within a short number of weeks she would be just a memory.

On this occasion, due to the conditions playing havoc with the timetable, an engine was already waiting to take the train back to London, so the arrival engine simply waited a few minutes until the train had departed. Then, instead of running down the middle road as per normal procedure, the light engine made it's way down to the end of the platform and waited for the signal to proceed to the Shed, much the same movement as at Liverpool Street. Somehow the Signalman must have forgotten about this change from the norm as suddenly, out of the thick fog, another train from London appeared on the same track!

Fortunately, because of the weather conditions, this train was travelling no faster than walking pace. Nonetheless, the impact when the two engines collided was sufficient to catapult the light engine back down the platform, severely shaking up the unsuspecting crew, who I believe were driver Vic Finch and fireman Mick Chapman. Luckily there were no injuries to passengers or any damage to engines and carriages.

Fog on the railways was a terrible thing and it is a great credit to all of Hertford East's Enginemen that their passengers always arrived safely at their chosen destinations.

Almost the end of Hertford steam

Eventually, the last summer of steam on the Hertford branch came and went. Towards the end it was very difficult to establish exactly which engines were allocated to Hertford MPD as, according to my diary, I worked on about 30 different class L1s and over 60 N7s which could not possibly have been Hertford based all at the same time.

One of my last duties at Hertford was riding 'shotgun' on the rear of a string of 3 locomotives, only the first of which was in steam, making their final journey to Stratford for scrapping.

I remember feeling quite sad about it at the time, knowing how those neglected old workhorses had given sterling service right up to the very end.

Derailment at Picketts Lock

There was serious disruption on the main line on the 13th of September due to a goods train coming 'off the road' at Picketts Lock.

The Goods Loop between Ponders End and Angel Road was quite lengthy, so if your train was turned off the main to allow another to pass, it was usual practice to slow right down to walking pace. By the time you approached the end of the loop, chances were that the faster train had passed through and you would be switched back out onto the main without all the bother of having to stop altogether. This Northbound goods was being hauled by one of the new Brush diesels and was rolling slowly down the Loop but, on this occasion, it didn't get the signal to go back out onto the main line and failed to stop at the signal. The result was that it went off the catch-points and spread its wagons all across the main lines. Luckily the Signalman was able to stop any other trains piling into the mess. I never did learn the real cause of the accident.

A turn on the Ware Shunter

Talking of diesels, on the 25th of September I had my only turn on the Ware-based diesel, no. D2956 (by this time renumbered from 11506), with driver George Cousins. As this engine only usually operated in the confines of Ware sidings, it did not normally require a fireman – or 'Second Man' as we were called on the diesels. That particular day was a Sunday and we were out on the main line on a track maintenance train.

A medical at Marylebone

On the 28th of September I was summoned to Marylebone for my 5-year medical and eyesight test, which I passed without any problems.

Redundancy Notices

With the planned implementation of the full electrification of the Hertford East/Bishops Stortford/ Liverpool Street lines set for late November, it must have been around this time that Redundancy Notices were issued.

Those affected at Hertford were all the firemen and Passed Firemen, I don't think any full-time drivers were given Notice.

From what I remember, there was no question of Redundancy Payment offers, you were required complete a form stating your new location preference or be given a week's notice.

I was required to choose between Stratford, Kings Cross and Hornsey Motive Power Depots, the form required me agree a transfer to whichever of these could accommodate me.

As there were ample opportunities on the job front at that time, an awful lot of men simply left the railway at that time, but a few of us decided to stay with it to see how things worked out. Of course, everyone opted for Stratford as it was the most convenient to get to, being on a direct rail route from Hertford East, and Kings Cross had only limited vacancies. Unfortunately, Hertford was not the only country shed to be closing, so the numbers of vacancies were limited. They were allocated on length of service (seniority) of the applicant, so we younger firemen had no chance of getting a transfer to Stratford.

The rear of Hertford East Engine shed in 1957, showing Apprentice Fitter George Don's immaculate Triumph motorbike parked alongside a pile of firebricks used for making the brick arch in the firebox of locomotives Just behind the bike is an iron stove recently removed from the old Enginemen's rest-room on the opposite side of the shed. The Fitter's storeroom on the right survived demolition and was being used as a shed in retired Driver Bob Smith's garden in 1999!

CHAPTER TEN

Final months spent on the Great Northern

Hornsey it has to be

So I was automatically appointed to Hornsey, which is on the old Great Northern mainline out of Kings Cross.

A couple of my colleagues did the smart thing and applied for a transfer to Stratford before the Redundancy Notices were issued, so they got in before the rush. One of them - Johnny Shelsher – transferred to Kings Cross Top Shed during 1958 and graduated to Top Link fireman on the East Coast expresses, a dream I was never to fulfil.

Sunday November 20th 1960 - the final day – and L1 67735

My last day as a fireman at Hertford East was on Sunday, 20th of November when I signed on at 6.17 a.m. with L1 no. 67735. That was also the final day of regular steam passenger working on the branch.

Looking back, it is strange how that particular engine holds more than just a passing thought in my memory.

It was the engine that had played a part in the tragic death of the Stratford fireman electrocuted earlier in the year in Hertford station.

It was also the same loco that had caused driver Wench so much trouble the previous month in our struggle to climb Bethnal Green Bank on that Saturday afternoon.

Now it was to be the last locomotive I would work on before saying cheerio to Hertford East.

A final week at Stratford and a spell on 68619

On the Monday I, along with the rest of my mates, was required to report to Stratford MPD on standby duties for the one week only.

Most of that week was spent playing cards in the restroom and occasionally being called upon to carry out disposal duties on an incoming engine.

It was on the Thursday of that week that I worked a shift on the other Liverpool Street pilot, the immaculate little Class J69 0-6-0 tank, no. 68619.

First day at Hornsey

At 8.45 a.m. on Monday 28th of November 1960 I reported for duty at Hornsey MPD. My new regular mate was Freddie Wray, a dapper little man who walked with a limp.

We were in the Bottom Link which comprised mainly of shunting movements in Bounds Green Carriage Sidings and working into Kings Cross with empty coaching stock for the Northbound expresses and bringing empty trains back to

Bounds Green for servicing. We also worked the Snow Hill banking engine at Farringdon.

On my first morning our engine was a Gresley Class N2 0-6-2 tank no. 69579, similar in power to the N7 Class that I was so used to, but bigger and heavier by around 8 tons.

Our duties were that first week involved ferrying coaching stock between Bounds Green carriage sidings and Kings Cross station, each day we had a different N2.

The South London freight trains

The following week I was placed with several different drivers and covered various freight trips over the South London area, which constituted a large chunk of Hornsey's workload.

It was on these trips that I clocked up enormous amounts of overtime, as these trains, traversing as they did, through extremely busy parts of London's rail network, were subject to long periods of waiting for a clear path through to our various destinations.

For example, on Monday 5th of December I signed on duty at 6.40 p.m. and booked off the following morning at 6.40 a.m. – exactly 12 hours.

We had been on freight working to Hither Green and were delayed through fog.

The Lewisham Flyover

I will always remember the part of that trip, after we had passed through Nunhead Station, my mate stepped over to my side of the cab and said: *"The bridge we'll be going over in a few minutes is the one that collapsed in the Lewisham smash."*

He was referring to the iron girder bridge that collapsed onto the Cannon Street to Ramsgate express in the terrible Lewisham disaster on December 4th 1957, in which 90 people lost their lives. It was almost 3 years to the day and, in the darkness, the bridge still seemed a temporary arrangement constructed with what looked like huge baulks of timber – there was certainly a speed restriction in force for trains crossing it.

Battersea Power Station

On the Tuesday we took a train of coal wagons into the huge structure of Battersea Power Station, with its 4 massive imposing chimneys, one on each corner.

How different it was then to the silent, empty shell that stands today.

Nearly always in the dark

I made 3 further trips to Hither Green that week but, as it was dark, I was not able to take in very much of the new territory I was passing through.

Apart from the summer evenings, and maybe a rare few daytime trips – particularly on Sundays - most of this cross-country freight could only be moved during out-of-peak times, i.e. at night.

It is for this reason that my memories of the various journeys I made during my brief time at Hornsey are very vague. Unlike my recollections of the routes from Hertford East, which I travelled several hundred times, my travels across the South London lines came in disoriented snatches.

Some South London destinations

Some of the yards we worked between, in addition to Battersea and Hither Green already mentioned were; Feltham, Norwood, Clapham, Herne Hill, Acton and probably others that I never got to visit, or have forgotten.

By the time the lighter nights came in late spring, I had moved up the Links and was travelling more in the opposite direction on passenger trains, more of which I will cover later.

Most of the South London goods routes all travelled the same tracks until Loughborough Junction, where we branched off to our assigned destinations.

The Underground 'Widened Lines'

To reach the Junction, we took the slow (Goods) lines from Ferme Park Yards at Hornsey down to Kings Cross, where we dived down into part of the Underground system via the York Road spur. Our route was over what are known as the 'Widened Lines', i.e. lines specially suited for our use, as the normal 'Tube-train' tunnels are too narrow to allow the passage of British Railways rolling stock.

I found it quite eerie down there, probably because it was, for me, a completely new experience.

Great skill was required from the driver down in those dark tunnels. The track was far from level and the driver had to avoid any violent snatch on our loose-coupled wagons, which could have easily resulted in the train breaking apart.

The Snow Hill Banker

After we passed through the back of Farringdon Underground station we entered a tunnel on a sharp uphill gradient, known as 'Snow Hill'.

Here you were usually required to stop and wait for the banking engine to buffer-up to the rear of your train.

There was an opening between the tunnels and I would take the opportunity to stoke up the fire ready for the quick dash that was to come.

I remember that directly above us in the open air was a tall office building and I used to wonder how much of our soot-laden smoke penetrated those offices!

The banker's crew would let the Signalman know when they were ready and the red signal would change to green. We would give a pop on the whistle and open up the regulator fully for a good run up onto Blackfriars Bridge.

The banker would be pushing hard until we were well on our way, then it would fall back and return to await its next duty.

Across Blackfriars Bridge

Once over the bridge we would trundle along on a viaduct running alongside Walworth Road and then Camberwell Road. I remember that somewhere along on the right we would pass the renowned 'Elephant and Castle' pub.

Class J50 0-6-0 no 68894, often referred to as a 'U Boat' or 'Ardley Tank'. *c.* 1948.

The 'U Boats'

The locomotives we normally had for these trips were Class J50 0-6-0 tanks, which railway enthusiasts also knew as Ardsley Tanks, but locally had the nickname of 'U Boats'. I never quite knew what the connection was, although they did have an unusual look due to the front few feet of their side-tanks ending in a sharp downward slope, presumably to improve the driver's view of the front end of the engine.

Another reason for the name may have been the fact that they spent most of their lives diving down York Road tunnel into the underground system, and resurfacing at the Hotel Curve on the way back!

Although these locomotives were about 6 tons lighter than the N7 class I was so familiar with, they were much more powerful due to their smaller driving wheels and larger steam cylinders.

The Forward/Reverse mechanism on the J50, instead of a worm-screw wheel as on the other engines I had worked on, was a huge ratchet lever – a bit like the handbrake on old-fashioned cars.

213

A scary experience

The engine brake was steam operated which, in my experience, was invariably useless, as experienced by an incident that caused my mate and I some consternation one evening after leaving Ferme Park with our train of loaded coal wagons.

I don't have the exact date, but it must have been sometime in 1961 after I had been there a while and was becoming familiar with the route, as the young driver I had that night invited me to take over from him.

Well, we left the yard and slowly ambled down the falling gradient, through Harringay and on towards Finsbury Park on the Goods line.

At some point, I can't remember if it was at Finsbury Park or Holloway, the Goods line terminated and all trains had to be switched on to the Slow (Suburban) line.

On this particular evening, as we approached the end of the Goods line, our signal was at red, meaning the path was not clear for us to go out onto the Suburban line.

I had seen this red signal in plenty of time and slowly applied the brake. Although we had a very heavy train, the only braking power available to us was the engine brakes, but as we were moving at no more than walking pace I was quite confident we would stop in plenty of time.

However, when I applied the brake fully, nothing happened! True, we were only moving at a snail's pace but nonetheless, we were still moving towards that red light.

I glanced across at my mate to check his reaction, but he was staring unconcernedly ahead enjoying a smoke, oblivious to the first signs of panic that were beginning to grip me.

I knew that beyond the signal was a set of Catch Points which would send us off the track and several yards beyond that, was a small wall behind which was a massive drop into the road below!

Clearly we were not going to stop at the signal in time, so I heaved the lever into reverse, opened the regulator and worked the sanding gear to improve the grip on the rail. My mate, seeing my predicament, disappeared off the footplate, shouting that he would pin some wagon brakes down.

Eventually, to my enormous relief, we came to a stand just a couple of yards past the signal.

Knowing what the consequences could have been had we been travelling any faster, I was quite shaken and immediately offered my mate his own seat, but he would have none of it. *"It happens to us all one time or another."* he said, *"You carry on mate, I know you won't get caught out like that again."* He was right, I didn't.

Watch out for the third rail!

Another thing new to me on those trips was that we operated over lines that had an electrified third rail. On the Underground sections this was not usually of any concern, as we did not have reason to leave our engine. Mind you, you had to remember not to empty a bucket of water out of the cab as you could be in for one nasty shock!

It was on the Southern Railway sections, such as at Hither Green, where you had to be ultra careful.   Here I would quite often leave the engine to walk across several tracks to a Shunter's cabin in search of some boiling water for a brew of tea, or to find a toilet.

In the engine depot itself there was no immediate danger as the third rail was not present, the power was switched to overhead gantries for the benefit of the electric locomotives that shared the depot with steam.

Pity the lineside residents

Apart from the poor braking power of the J50 Class, I cannot recall having one that wouldn't steam freely, they were excellent locomotives in that respect.

The routes we took were very undulating and it always seemed to me that we were either coasting downhill, or thrashing our engine like mad on an uphill gradient.

I remember another evening when we were climbing hard, up toward Nunhead I believe, I watched the white-hot cinders shoot high in the sky from our chimney and cascade onto the houses and cars far below us.

I mentioned to my mate about our hot ashes not doing the cars' paintwork much good, he replied, *"Oh, claims against the railway for compensation for damage to cars, washing hanging out and the like are always coming in, it's a way of life."*

I used to wonder how the people that lived in the countless houses alongside the lines of those South London routes managed to sleep, with the constant racket of our passing at all hours of the night.

Smoke was another factor that must have caused a lot of grief to the public – especially on washdays!   Whilst the J50s were undoubtedly good steamers, they burnt a lot of coal in the process, much of which went up the chimney in the form of cinders and smoke.

Still, I suppose that as it had been that way for over a hundred years, people just accepted the dirt, grime and noise of living beside the railway as a way of life.

Excessive hours

Returning to my first few weeks at Hornsey at the latter end of 1960, during the second week – on the South London trips – I clocked up 66 hours for the 6 days worked.

These sort of hours were to become commonplace during the months to come which, added to the time spent travelling to and from Hornsey, amounted to an enormous amount of time spent away from home.

Having said that, my third week there was a straight 8-hour day, as we were on carriage shunting duties in Bounds Green sidings, signing on at 1.15 p.m.

My first taste of Diesel

For this duty I spent my first ever week on a diesel locomotive – number D3711 – one of the ubiquitous little 0-6-0 400 horsepower shunting engines, many of which are still employed today.

My initial reactions were rather mixed, it was novel sitting there with practically nothing to do apart from relaying the Shunter's instructions to Freddy.   It also became rather boring after a while, whilst the horrible smell of diesel oil began to percolate into my overalls.   Of course, the same thing happened with the smell of coal dust and engine oil but it was, in my opinion, much more pleasant on the nose than the smell of diesel.

I remember D3711 made quite a loud grinding noise and was very jerky in its movements.   Overall, I was not particularly impressed with that first introduction to the diesel locomotive.

The following week we were on the same duties, this time on the morning shift (5.45 a.m.) with D3712. That was the week immediately before Christmas.

My first taste of diesel fumes at Hornsey was on one of these ubiquitous 0-6-0 370 bhp diesel/electric Shunters in the carriage sidings at Bounds Green. Here ClassD3/5 no. 13307 takes a rest in the goods yards at Kings Cross-in 1959.

The impressive 1,000 h.p. Brush

As with the previous year, I had the luxury of both Christmas and Boxing days off, reporting back at work at 10 p.m. on December 27th. It was a 'stand-by' duty and soon after signing on I was paired up with a different driver on D5594. Now this was a different diesel altogether, being one of the larger "Type 2" 1,000 horsepower locomotives built by Brush Traction Ltd and weighing in at 104 tons and somewhere around 60 feet in length.

To be precise, these locomotives were diesel/electrics i.e. their diesel engines generated power for electric motors, which in turn powered the wheels.

For ease of reading, I will simply refer to them as 'diesels'.

I was very impressed with my first trip on one of these, sitting in a soft 'armchair style' padded leather seat in the sound-insulated cab, the engine glided along as smoothly and quietly as a Rolls Royce.

Mind you, it was only the very effective sound insulation that made it so quiet.

Once you opened the door and entered the Engine-room the sound was absolutely deafening. The pounding of those huge engines, together with the intense heat they generated in such a confined space and the stifling smell of hot oil, was something never to be forgotten.

They even had a small Belling cooker installed, complete with hotplate and kettle, so that we could make our tea and toast!

I quite liked this particular class of diesel, they had clean lines, rode beautifully and possessed a fair turn of speed. I believe the first batch of this type were not so impressive as regards overall performance, but most of the teething problems had been ironed out on the later productions which I worked on.

Many of the class are still in service nearly 40 years after they were built – albeit much modified – but I much preferred them in their original BR Green livery with the wide, cream band around the middle.

Our duties on D5594 that night involved running in and out of Kings Cross-with empty carriage stock.

On the Snow Hill Banker

For the rest of the week Freddy and I were on the 10.55 p.m. shift of the Snow Hill Banker at Farringdon.

For this turn, the Timekeeper in the office where we signed on for duty issued us with Train Passes for Underground travel between Kings Cross and Farringdon.

Unlike the British Railways practice of a uniformed railwayman just nodding his head to the Ticket Inspector on his way through, these London Transport Inspectors always demanded to see your ticket!

Our engine that week - strangely enough - was D3711 which had made its way down here from the carriage sidings of Bounds Green where we had her a couple of weeks previous.

It was on this turn one Saturday night that I learnt a bit about rats, from my driver who was, I think, Bill Andrews.

After the initial flurry of trains going up the bank and onto Blackfriars Bridge, things became pretty quiet during the last few hours before dawn. Even more so on the Saturday night turn, as very little traffic moved about during the early hours of Sunday mornings.

So we would be parked up in the short spur at the end of the tunnels with our diesel engine shut down. Everything would be deadly quiet with just the occasional break in silence by the passing of a tube train over on the far side of the cutting in which we were situated.

Class D13/1 1354 bhp Brush diesel/electric no. D5610 on a freight working near Welwyn Garden City. This is one of several that the author worked on. They were very comfortable locomotives.

A rat's tale

I believe it is commonly known that places such underground railway tunnels are often home to some of the rat population, and Farringdon was no exception.

One small pastime to break the boredom of long waits between trains was to try to kill a rat. This was done by baiting the ground immediately below the cab window with one or two crusts of bread.

If it was a moonlit night in the cutting, it was possible to see the 'bait' without the need of artificial lighting.

You would sit with the window open, armed with a couple of heavy stones or bricks picked up from the trackside earlier and wait soundlessly for a rat to appear.

They must have a wonderful sense of smell to detect a small piece of bread from wherever they normally patrol because, sure enough, after a time one or more of these huge brown creatures would be seen slowly approaching the bait.

Then it was a matter of dropping a stone onto your quarry. At best, you only got one chance because at the slightest sound, the rat would disappear like lightning and you would perhaps not get another opportunity for the rest of that night.

It was also very necessary to stay alert at all times, there have been several occasions where I have dozed of for a minute or two, only to wake and find the bait gone!

Fact or fiction?

Anyway, Bill told me that rats always buried their own dead, which I found difficult to believe. But he was serious, pointing out that rats were very much community dwellers rather than 'lone wolves' and emphasised his point on the way they steal chicken's eggs. I had heard of this method whereby one rat clasps the egg in its four paws lying on its back, whilst another rat pulls it along the ground by its tail.

But burying their own dead took a bit of believing!

However, one night I was lucky and caught a rat fair and square on its head, killing it outright. *"Keep watching,"* my mate said, *"pretty soon his pals will come along and carry him away."*

So I watched for a long time, but none came. Then I happened to doze off for a few minutes and, when I awoke, the rat was gone.

So I had to believe that other rats took him away, but whether it was for burying or eating I have yet to be convinced!

1961 – a move up the Links

At the start of 1961 my tally of Firing Turns had risen to 1,296 and on the 9th of January I moved up another Link with a new regular mate, Bert Sims who was the Branch Representative of the NUR (National Union of Railwaymen).

However, whether it was because his shifts were re-scheduled to fit in with his duties as a Union representative, other drivers were constantly taking his place.

A variety of places

This new Link involved regular workings of empty coaching stock in and out of Kings Cross, sprinkled with some Local Passenger working between Moorgate, Kings Cross, Hertford North, Hatfield and occasionally to Welwyn Garden City.

The bulk of the work was on diesel locomotives, mainly the Brush Type 2s, with the occasional, smaller, Sultzer diesels (horrible engines), although we still had the occasional N2 Class steam engines, but only on the movement of empty stock.

I don't remember any occasion when I worked an N2 on a local passenger train.

In fact, the Hertford North branch was mainly worked by diesel railcars, apart from those trains that went down the tunnels into Moorgate, these were standard coaching stock operated by Brush diesels.

Working the 'Mainliners'!

In a way, over a period of time, I worked all the famous East Coast trains, like the *'Flying Scotsman'* the *'Elizabethan'*, *'Aberdonian'*, *'Queen of Scots Pullman'*, *'The Night Scotsman'* and many others, albeit only as empty trains between Kings Cross and Bounds Green storage sidings!

Steam-heating boilers

Whenever we took empty carriage stock into Kings Cross, it was our responsibility to ensure that the train heating system was in operation.

At that time, although the transition to diesel traction was well progressed, carriages were still heated by steam. To facilitate this, all mainline diesels were fitted with an oil-fired steam boiler. We were given tuition on how to start these up when required, also a set of simple instructions were attached to the boiler casing.

As soon as we coupled up at Bounds Green we were expected to fire up the steam heating boiler and keep it running until we were released from the train at Kings Cross.

On the Brush diesels they were not too much trouble, but the boilers installed in the Sultzers were extremely temperamental. Sometimes they totally refused to ignite and there were many occasions I was still trying to get it started when we arrived at Kings Cross. At other times we may be spewing out great clouds of stinking black diesel smoke due to only partial-ignition of the fuel oil.

Waiting at Kings Cross

As we were effectively 'trapped' at the buffers at Kings Cross, we had to wait until the express departed at its scheduled time before we could move on to our next duty. During this time passengers often asked us if they could step up for a 'look round'. Most times my driver would refuse but, if I had a young driver and an attractive young lady happened to make the request, then it was the full tour!

Incidentally, another change from my Hertford East days was that coupling and uncoupling of trains was mostly carried out by Shunters on hand in the yards and at the stations, whereas I had been used to doing it myself.

A week on the 'Dustbins'

I was on a completely different duty in the last week of January running the 'dustbins' to Holwell Tip. After signing on at 4 a.m. and meeting my driver for the week, Jack Freeman, we made our way to Kings Cross Top Shed and picked up our engine. For the whole week we had L1 2-6-4 tank no. 67779, a class of locomotive very familiar to me, of course.

A June 1957 scene from the end of the platform at Kings Cross station looking towards Gasworks Tunnels. To the left can be seen the Passenger Loco Servicing Depot, while on the right a northbound express is just leaving, hauled by a Class A4 Pacific.

Shed staff had already prepared 67779 so we went straight round to the Goods Yard and picked up our train, which was made up of around a dozen huge steel covered container vans, each of which held several tons of household rubbish.

These vans were fitted with a continuous vacuum brake throughout, so we would not have the same difficulties in braking as I had experienced on the South London goods trains.

As soon as had we coupled up we were given the 'green light' and we were off, first stop, Welwyn Garden City. In order to avoid delay to passenger train schedules on the busy main line, we were booked to run at express speed to Welwyn, so we really did fly.

I found this engine ran much smoother and quieter than most of those we had at Hertford East. The bunker had been filled with a good quality coal so I had no trouble in maintaining a full head of steam, despite the fact that the line was on a rising gradient as far as Potters Bar.

After we arrived at Welwyn we were put into a siding to await a path over the single line of the Welwyn to Hertford North branch. It was on this branch that the Holwell landfill site was situated – the final destination of our 'dustbins'.

Soon we took delivery of the Single-line Pass and a couple of padlock keys.

It was a fairly short trip to Holwell, where we stopped just short of the siding that led off to the tipping area. We pulled forward after unhooking and a small industrial diesel locomotive appeared out of the siding, coupled on to our train and took it away to be emptied.

Holwell Tip had been there for several years, as I was told that Hertford East men used to take rubbish trains into the same tip. At that time there was no industrial locomotive and Hertford men used to push their train right up to the pit edge over temporary track. I don't know how our empties got back to London – or what happened to the Guard, if indeed we had one from Welwyn – because we carried on down the branch light engine, to Hertford North.

There were, I think, two level crossings on the way where we had to stop while I unlocked the gates with the keys provided, wait for my mate to draw our engine through, and lock them again before continuing on our way. This branch incidentally, was also known as the Cole Green branch which was made famous in the old Will Hay film of 1938 vintage called 'Oh, Mr. Porter', part of which was filmed at Cole Green Station. When I travelled the line, it had closed to passengers several years earlier and Cole Green station was rather dilapidated. The only other station along this line was Hertingfordbury.

After we arrived at Hertford North station, we reversed on to the main line and made our way back to Kings Cross Top Shed. After disposing of the engine, we hopped a train back to Hornsey and signed off duty at around 2 p.m., making it a 10 hour shift, which was the general pattern for the remainder of the week.

Clouds on the horizon

I had now been at Hornsey for 9 weeks and trouble was brewing at Hertford North over the parking of my car, which I left in the station Car Park while I caught a train to Hornsey.

Although I was a Company employee, there was no provision for free parking for someone in my circumstances, other than at Hornsey. I had been issued with a free travel pass from Hertford North to Hornsey, but I was being asked to pay a Car Parking fee, which was about a quarter of the full public rate.

At first I ignored the messages being stuck to my windscreen, expecting that, as soon as the staff realised whom I was, they would turn a 'blind eye'.

No such luck, apparently the Stationmaster was in the habit of checking vehicles in the Car Park and felt he had to stick to the rules.

For a short time I purchased a monthly parking pass, but after a while decided – as a matter of principal - I would not continue to do so.

Unpaid overtime

The reason I objected was that I was already 'giving' the Company many hours a week for which I did not receive payment.

For example, on early turns when I was required to report for duty before 5.20 a.m. – when the first morning train reached Hornsey - meant that I had to catch the last train from Hertford the previous night. This train left at 11 p.m. arriving at Hornsey at around 11.40. So, on the 'dustbin' shift for example, where I had to sign on at 4 a.m., meant that I had to kick my heels at Hornsey for over 4 unpaid hours, having left my home at 10.30 the previous evening.

Finishing a turn in the early hours was equally as bad in catching a train home.

Above. Class A1 4-6-2 Pacific 60178 *'Bongrace'* is ready to leave Kings Cross with a Down express, while alongside Class N2 0-6-2 tank engine no. 69501 prepares to take a train of empty express coaches to Bounds Green carriage sidings for cleaning and servicing.
Note the unorthodox 'parking place' for the fireman's shovel on the N2!
Below. The very first Gresley Class A4 4-6-2 Pacific locomotive, no.60014 *'Silver Link'*, introduced in September 1935 and still heading the East Coast Line's premier expresses.   Here she is at the head of the Flying Scotsman at Kings Cross-in June 1957.

223

Expensive motoring

I did occasionally drive the 19 miles to Hornsey from home. It didn't take too long, but with my old Wolseley doing no more than 14 miles to a gallon of petrol, it was quite an expensive journey. At that time the cost of petrol was around 4 gallons for £1 which, ridiculous cheap as it may seem now, was relative to earnings at the time.

I often had an unplanned journey, when I would have that extra five minutes in bed and dash up Hertford North station steps only to hear the roar of the diesel railcar's engines as it pulled away! Then it was back in the car for the drive to Hornsey, but it was costly.

At that time, my limited income made exchanging my car for a more economical model impossible.

No help from the Union

I put my problem to Bert Sims but, as I was a member of the ASLEF Union (Associated Society of Locomotive Engineers and Firemen) and he was NUR, he didn't really want to know – even though I volunteered to change Unions.

The stigma of being an ASLEF man

While on the subject of Unions, it was a strange situation over on the old Great Northern line. A large number of railwaymen, not just in the Locomotive Department, took an instant dislike to you as soon as you revealed that you belonged to ASLEF.

Apparently, the ASLEF Union was predominantly Great Eastern Railway based.

The cause of the animosity occurred many years previously when the ASLEF Union refused to support the NUR when they took industrial action over a particular issue. It was silly really because the issue that caused the rift happened many years earlier and the likes of myself could not possibly have been one of the non-supporters.

Nevertheless, the stigma was still there, and maybe still is even to this day!

Another peculiarity that seemed unique to the Great Northern enginemen was that they always referred to Signalmen as 'Bobbies'. This was a term perpetuated from the very dawn of the Railway Age when Signalmen actually were Railway Policemen.

It was to be another 3 months or so before the outcome of this parking debacle finally emerged, so I will return to the subject later on.

My first trip beyond Welwyn

A short while after the Holwell job, on Saturday February 11th, I was assigned to Class WD 2-8-0 no. 90129 on a goods trip to the brickyards at Yaxley, near Peterborough. I believe we took empties up and brought loaded wagons back.

It was the first of my longer trips on the G.N. mainline (about 60 miles from Ferme Park Yard, I think) and we took the Hertford Loop from Wood Green and rejoined the main line at Knebworth on that occasion.

The only thing I clearly remember was the interminable dust-cloud that filled the cab, no matter how many times I sprayed the floor over with the hosepipe.

I also recall the aching bones caused by the jarring rocking and rolling of the locomotive with each revolution of its wheels.

Good old reliable workhorses they may have been, but the WD Austerity Class must have been one of the most uncomfortable engines to work on.

The following day – the Sunday – found me on another WD 90613 on an engineer's special train. This time we didn't travel very far up the line, so the experience was a great deal better than the previous day.

Trips to Top Shed

On some occasions I found myself doing an extra few hours taking express engines to Top Shed at Kings Cross. These were usually ones that had failed along the way and found short refuge in Hornsey MPD.

As they were minor jobs I did not usually bother to record of them in my diary but I note that on the 18th of February we took B1 4-6-0 no. 1179 back, and during the following week we took back Class A3 Pacific 4-6-2 no. 60036, named '***Colombo***'. I remember that the latter's firebox was full to overflowing with ash, so it had probably failed through poor steaming.

That same week I also noted that I worked 75 hours, which no doubt was due to the many delays due to foggy weather conditions.

The fastest of them all! Class A4 4-6-2 Pacific no. 60022 *'Mallard'* waiting to leave Kings Cross-with an express to the North in June 1957.

Firing on a 'Spaceship'

I had my first firing experience on one of the huge Standard Class 9F 2-10-0 locomotives on Saturday, 29th of April.

These monsters weighed in at 139 tons and had earned the nickname 'Spaceships'.

I believe the name came about, not just because of their huge size, but because when viewed sidelong their boilers resembled one of those giant spacerockets lying on its side on a multi-wheeled Transporter.

Anyway, that day I had 92147 and my driver was Stan Jeffries. Our duty was a freight train to Peterborough. The engine was already prepared for us when we signed on at 1 p.m. and we moved out of the shed to pick up our train in Ferme Park Yard.

To reach the down yard without disrupting the flow of traffic on the main lines, a single-track flyover had been erected from the London end of the MPD across on a skew to the down yard.

This always looked to me to be a bit flimsy, especially when looking up from below and seeing a 9F 2-10-0 making its way across this spidery structure. Still, it must have been up to the job because it stayed firm until it was finally dismantled during the 1960s.

As this was my first trip up the main line with a fast freight on a 9F, I was very green as regards the preparation of the fire prior to leaving the yard.

My mate was less than helpful although he must have noticed that I was not adequately prepared, but he never said a word. In fact, he was not the most communicative person for the whole of the trip.

A 'Spaceship'! An unidentified Class 9F 2-10-0 is photographed working a northbound mixed freight near Potters Bar in 1956.

Too thin a fire

What I should have done was shovel a couple of tons of coal into the huge firebox right at the start. I also learnt afterwards that the fireman who prepared the engine should have given me a good start as regards to the fire.

Instead, by the time we pulled out of the yard, I suppose I had about half a ton in the firebox that was well burnt through already.

We started in fine style, a full boiler of water and steam pressure just about on the blowing-off mark at 250 lbs.

The problem, which I was going to find out within the next half-hour, was that the steady, uphill pull was going to demand more steam than my meagre fire could produce.

On this occasion, instead of taking the Hertford Loop as I did earlier on the Yaxley trip, we went straight up the mainline.

For the 10 miles or so to Potters Bar it is a continuous climb then, after a respite of maybe 5 miles through Hatfield, it is all climb again until the approach to Knebworth.

Pretty soon, despite my shovelling coal into the box for all I was worth, holes began to appear in the firebed - I could not keep up the required firing rate.

My mate just kept staring at the track ahead and, as the boiler pressure slowly fell back, he just yanked the regulator open a bit more to compensate for the loss of power!

I began to mortgage the boiler in order to maintain pressure - allowing the water level to drop – but, as the reading in the gauge-glass sank lower and lower, I knew I was slowly losing the battle.

A lucky break

Then, just when I was thinking of committing Hari-Kari, a miracle happened! My mate eased the regulator closed and as I looked out I could see up ahead that we were being put into a Siding, I think we must have been somewhere around Welwyn.

As we drew to a stand at the end of the loop my mate (lazy sod!) suggested I nip up to the Signalbox to make a can of tea. I left the injector running to fill the boiler now that steam pressure had recovered.

When I returned, the boiler was full and the steam pressure was around the 200-lbs. mark.

As we sat there drinking our tea, Stan said, "*Not used to working on these, then?*" "*No, first time.*" I replied. I then set to with the shovel again, determined not to get caught out a second time. "*Don't go too heavy,*" Stan said, "*It's not too hard a run from here*". The rest of the trip passed without incident.

I worked really hard that day, but had my mate been more helpful in putting me wise at the outset, things could have been a lot easier.

His attitude that day put me in mind of the words of a Fireman's Ballad which I heard many years ago, it went something like this;
> *"The driver sits there like a God,*
> *A decent mate but a lazy sod.*
> *He likes to think he runs the show,*
> *But if I'm not there, the train won't go!"*

A silly little verse, but it highlights the importance of the footplate crew working as a team.

Driving a diesel

The next few weeks were spent mainly ferrying coaching stock in and out of Kings Cross, plus frequent Local Passenger workings as I outlined earlier.

Some of the stock workings out of the Terminus were extremely heavy, particularly on the morning jobs when the train would be made up of Sleeping Cars.

Luckily, there were not many occasions when we were allocated a steam engine (maybe an N7 or N2) for these jobs.   With the Modernisation Plan developing there were more and more diesels taking over, so the work became much easier – but also very boring

Soon I was given opportunities to drive in and out of Kings Cross and I must say it was quite a thrill to have the 1,000 horsepower of a Brush diesel at my fingertips.

How much easier it was compared to the physical effort required to drive a steam locomotive!   Just an effortless turn of the Power Control Lever would evoke a mighty muffled roar from the locomotive's twin engines as the train slowly glided out of the station.   The carriage braking was much more positive and powerful than what I had been used to on the Hertford East suburban stock.   These diesels also had very powerful air brakes.

Bounds Green Carriage Sidings were on the Up side of the main lines, so when we reached Wood Green we were directed over the Flyover onto the Hertford Loop, which passes over all the mainline tracks.

Once over the Flyover, and as soon as we had cleared the points leading into the Sidings, we would be brought to a stand by the Guard operating the brake valve at the rear of our train.   Then we would set the train back until, again, we were brought to a stand by the action of the Guard.

A hard 'bump' at Kings Cross

On a busy railway, where the smooth running depends on the co-operation and diligence of a number of people, occasional accidents are inevitable – you just hope it doesn't happen to you!

Sometimes the old saying 'familiarity breeds contempt' becomes a reality when you least expect it.

I was caught out in this way one dark evening in Kings Cross, where we were waiting to remove the coaches of a recently arrived express.

That evening I was in the driving seat of a Brush diesel so, as soon as we got the 'all clear' from the grounnd signal, I 'blipped' the throttle and we glided smartly out of the bay and into the platform.

The platform was on a slight curve and, as we backed out of the bay, the rear of the train was on the driver's 'blind side'.

Although I was unable to see the distance available before we made contact with the train, I wasn't unduly concerned as it was a procedure we had done each evening that week and I could judge by our surroundings roughly where we needed to stop. My driver also did not bother to lean out of the window on his side of the cab to guide me either, for the same reason.

Just as I put my hand on the brake to slow us right down we hit the rear coach with one almighty crash!

Our 104-ton locomotive shuddered as it was brought to an abrupt halt. Well, I applied the brake and shakily climbed down to the track on my side and walked back to se what damage had been done.

I expected at least to have derailed the coach, with possibly the rear bogie wheels of our locomotive off the track also.

I hardly dared believe what I saw when I arrived at the other end. The small, wiry Shunter was in between coach and engine coupling up as normal. I was still staring in silence when he crawled out from under the buffers, straightened himself up and said, "*She's all yours mate*," and disappeared into the night!

Where I had been caught out was that, either the train had had an extra coach added that day or, the driver had stopped well short of the buffers at the opposite end of the platform.

I felt I was a very lucky fellow that night, had there been damage to report my mate, as driver in charge, would have had to take the full blame.

Only seeing is believing

If that was an amazing escape, it was nothing compared with an event I, and others, witnessed at Harringay early one evening a couple of weeks later.

We had taken a train into Kings Cross and were returning 'light engine' to Hornsey. As usual, we were in charge of a Brush diesel.

At Harringay we were sidetracked to make way for a northbound train and had come to a stand at the signal a few dozen yards from the Signalbox.

While we were waiting, a long train of empty steel Grain Hoppers was coming around the curve on the far side of the goods yard, from the Feltham direction.

As we watched, one of these huge hoppers midway down the train began to buck wildly, it was obvious it had become derailed. I immediately leapt off our engine and sprinted toward the Signalbox to raise the alarm. However, by the time I arrived, the train had been brought to a stand by a red signal.

My mate and I hurried across the yard to see the extent of the damage, on the way we were joined by a couple of yardstaff who had also witnessed the incident.

When we reached the train we found, to our utter disbelief, that every wagon was sitting correctly on the rails!

However, when we reached the spot behind the train where we first saw the incident, there were the splintered wooden sleepers and a few broken rail-chairs as evidence to prove that we had not all been imagining things!

The odds against a derailed wagon jumping back onto the rails must be phenomenal, but that is exactly what had happened that evening.

Off the road at Hitchin

Well and truly off the rails was the 9F 2-10-0 which we relieved on at Hitchin on June 20th.

We had signed on duty at 1.10 a.m. to work a Special goods out to Hither Green.

After a few hours hanging about, the job was cancelled so we returned to the Enginemen's mess to await further orders.   At around 7 a.m. the Duty Foreman instructed us to make our way to Hitchin to relieve the crew on a derailed 9F.

So we hopped on a local train into Kings Cross where we knew there was a Newcastle semi-fast express due to leave at 7.50 a.m., first stop Hitchin.

Another Hornsey crew, who was bound for the same destination to take over a southbound freight, joined us on the platform.

An opportunity missed

The engine in charge of the express was one of Gresley's magnificent A4 Pacifics and the other Hornsey fireman in our party promptly stated that he was 'going up front' to do the firing as far as Hitchin.

Being a newcomer, I didn't know that it was common practice for 'local boys' to take such opportunities to experience a trip on the 'elite' locomotives.

I made a mental note that, when the next opportunity presented itself, I would be there.   Alas, as it turned out, it was never to be.

A precarious position

We arrived at Hitchin and walked down the end of the platform into the Down Yard.   Up ahead we could see the stricken 9F - no. 92145 - nose-down into the dirt, with her 'tail' up in the air.

We relieved the crew and I gingerly climbed up into the cab to check the boiler water level.   It was quite eerie standing on that steeply sloping cab floor and, after checking the condition of the fire and steam pressure, I hastily climbed back down to ground level.

Eventually, the Breakdown Train arrived from Peterborough and backed its crane toward the front of 92145 on the same track.

After hooking chains into the special lifting-holes located above the front buffer-beam it hoisted the 86-ton locomotive up off the ground as if it were a toy.

It was soon back on the rails and appeared none the worse for wear.   My mate and I were preparing to take it on to Peterborough MPD, when another crew appeared on the scene to take over from us.

We caught a diesel railcar back to Hornsey, which took the Hertford Loop at Knebworth. Had I realised before we left Hitchin I could have asked the driver to slow right down at Hertford to enable me to jump off. As it was, we sped through Hertford North and it was best part of an hour-and-a-half later that I returned on my way home.
After signing on duty at 1.10 a.m. we eventually clocked off at 12.30 p.m.
I finally arrived home at 2 p.m. having left it at 10.30 the evening before – an absence of fifteen-and-a-half hours!

Old enough to become a Driver

When I reached my 21st birthday at the beginning of May I knew the time was getting close when I could be summoned to attend an examination for promotion to Engine Driver.
In recent weeks I had been fireman to a couple of young drivers who were my juniors in length of service, but had reached driving status because they were older. According to a leaflet issued by the British Transport Commission during the late 1950s (which I still possess) the minimum age for a driver was 23, but I am fairly certain men were being passed for driving at the age of 21.
This same leaflet gives the minimum age for Mainline Firing Duties as 18 years, but of course, Cleaners such as myself were on the footplate at 16.
It was possibly the acute shortage of footplate staff at the time that forced the BTC to (temporarily?) relax its rules.

By this time I had acquired a great deal of practical experience and was well versed on the Rulebook. I had been given some books on the steam locomotive and its working parts, plus some other information relevant to the Driver's Examination.
Although diesels were fast replacing steam, at that time it was still the steam locomotive upon which the examination was based.

Losing the magic

Although I felt well prepared for the test, my enthusiasm for the railway had begun to waver, just when I was on the brink of achieving my schoolboy ambition.
There were several factors that contributed to the way I was feeling at the time.
One was that, with the fast approach of dieselisation, experiments were being undertaken with 'Single Manning'.

Single Manning

This was a system where, provided the train had a Guard in attendance, certain trains could dispense with the services of a Second Man.
However, when the engine was travelling light from one train to its next duty, then a Second Man was required – it was all very Unionised.

So, on certain days, firemen would be given a 'shopping list' containing train arrival times – e.g. at Kings Cross – where we had to meet the train and accompany the driver to his next duty. Then we would say a fond farewell and return to await the next train.

This was all very nice on paper, but if a train happened to be delayed, which was often the case, the whole system broke down and chaos reigned because you were unable to meet your next train at the scheduled time.

The old and the new. The signal gantry obscures the identity of the A4 Pacific just leaving Kings Cross in 1958. Over in the Passenger Loco Servicing Depot lurks an English Electric Class 40 2,000 bhp locomotive.

No light at the end of the tunnel

No job satisfaction could be gained from this arrangement but I was not totally disillusioned, as I knew I was due for promotion into the Top Link, which involved regular fast goods working between Peterborough and Ferme Park.   Soon I would be firing on the Standard 9F 2-1-0-0s on a regular basis.

Having said that, I could see that more and more of these, and other steam workings, were being replaced by diesel power and that did nothing for my enthusiasm.

The prototype English Electric 'Deltic' 3,300 bhp locomotive is seen backing onto its train at Kings Cross in 1958. The production class of this type were magnificent locomotives and were the mainstay of East Coast express power for many years.

Those boring diesels

After the novelty of sitting in the padded chair of a diesel had worn off, I found myself becoming extremely bored and was constantly looking for something to do to keep me occupied.

After tidying up the cab and cleaning the windows with damp newspapers, I usually filled in the time by doing crosswords in the daily papers.

It became my usual habit, when we arrived with a passenger train at Kings Cross or Moorgate, to run down the train, diving into any compartment in which I spied a discarded newspaper.

But this was not job satisfaction and I didn't like it.

Another problem was that the inactivity was doing nothing for my waistline, I quickly put on over a stone in weight!

233

Back to the Car Park

Then of course, there was the ongoing hassle over the Car Park at Hertford.
By the end of June my Monthly Pass had run out and I had decided that if British Railways were not going to compensate for all my extra travelling time, I sure as hell was not going to fund their Car Park! Most times the parking area was only half-full, so it was not as if I was depriving the railway of revenue by taking up a parking place which would otherwise have been used by a member of the public.
Soon, notices started to appear on my windscreen once again, with messages like: 'Please see the Stationmaster before you leave.'
I sometimes managed a wry smile when reading that message as I returned to my car at 2 0'clock in the morning – would he be there now, I wondered?

One notice too many

The last straw came late one evening in July when I returned from Hornsey feeling particularly jaded after another 12-hour shift.
When I got to my car another notice - twice the normal size - had been fixed to my windscreen with thick, white glue. It was stuck immediately in front of my driving vision and was almost impossible to remove. Normally I am the mildest of individuals but I was suddenly boiling with anger.
I strode into the station Booking Hall and shouted out "**What B******* stuck that notice on my car?**" The Station Inspector took one look at me and dived into the Booking Office and bolted the door. *"Come out here and I'll knock your damned head off."* I shouted through the Ticket grill.
He declined to take up my offer, instead muttering something about *"only doing my job"*, so, after making my intentions very clear to him should it happen again, I let the matter rest.
I eventually managed to remove the mess with a petrol-soaked rag.
No more notices were stuck on my car after that.

Up before the Gaffer

A couple of days later a message was left in the Timekeeper's office for me to see the Shedmaster before going off duty.
During all my months at Hornsey I had never met the Shedmaster, although his office door was directly adjacent to the main door when you came in from the road. Anyway, I kept my appointment and he said that he had received a complaint from the Stationmaster at Hertford that a Hornsey fireman had threatened one of his staff, could it have been me?
I replied that it certainly was and explained the circumstances to him.
I said I was aware of the normal policy but that I would leave rather leave the railway than make any further payments. His reply was *"Why don't you drive to work, you can park outside here for nothing"*.

The stupidity of that remark left me speechless, I stood up, bade him good day and stomped out of his office. That was the one and only time I ever saw him.

Enough is enough

I arrived home in a bad frame of mind. My father knew of the hassle I had been having and had already suggested I pack the job in and join him as a milkman at the local dairy. It was a job I felt quite capable of doing, but had no real enthusiasm for the work. On the other hand, I dreaded the thought of being out of work, so this would suffice until something more appealing came up.

On this occasion, as soon as I arrived home I said to him, *"Let me know when another job comes up at the dairy, I've had enough."*

The final days

Of the handful of Hertford East firemen who initially went to Hornsey, I believe I was the only one still there after Wally Coleman had left several weeks earlier.

Well, things were brought to a head very quickly after that. A few days later the Dairy Manager came to see me at home with the offer of a job, provided I could start within a week or so.

I was in a bit of a dilemma as I had just learned that the following week I was to be promoted to the Number One Link and was looking forward to a spell on the mainline freight trains to Peterborough.

However, I was loath to miss the opportunity so I gave a week's notice and left the railway on Saturday, 29Th July 1961. I had completed 1,448 firing turns and just over 6 years service.

That final Saturday was spent diving around Kings Cross on one of those 'Second Manning' jobs.

I can still recall the miserable feeling I had when travelling home that afternoon. My lifelong ambition of becoming an Engine Driver had come to an end after just 6 years.

What might have been!

Over the years I have often wondered what would have happened if it were not for my stand over the Car Park situation.

As I mentioned earlier, diesel locomotives held no real attraction for me and my enthusiasm had waned considerably.

Towards the end of my railway career, the boredom was often only relieved by watching the East Coast expresses, still predominantly steam hauled by Gresley Pacifics, hammering up Holloway Bank and settling into their stride as they thundered through Hornsey.

But steam was disappearing fast, with only a matter of months to go before it was all gone. I believe Hornsey shed itself closed to steam before the end of 1961 and what was left was transferred for the remaining period to Top Shed. I had no inkling of this at the time.

235

Above. Hertford East station *c.* 1960.
Below. A London-bound train hauled by a Class L1 2-6-4 approaches 'Hoppo's' Crossing at the bottom end of Mead Lane in the 1950s. Driver Ron Hopkins' mother tended the crossing gates and the family lived in the timber-built cottage beside the line that can just be seen on the left in the photograph.

Above. The sad end of Hertford East Engine Shed early in 1961.
Below. The '24 miles to London' marker that stood for over a century against the station end of the Engine Shed wall – beside the Up line at Hertford East MPD - is cast aside during demolition. Was it preserved or simply dumped along with the rest of the rubble?

237

N7 69621 - minus it's coupling rods – in the yard at Colchester on 6/9/73. The engine is en-route to the East Anglian Railway Museum at Chappel & Wakes Colne in Essex, where she has been completely restored to full working order.

In hindsight I can only speculate what may have happened had I stayed until the end of steam at Kings Cross. Who knows, I may have (albeit briefly) achieved a burning ambition – to fire to Gresley Pacifics on the East Coast expresses!

Within 2 years of my departure, steam working finished altogether at Kings Cross Top Shed.

By that time I would probably have been a driver in one of the lower Links, or I may have obtained a transfer to Stratford, or even back to Hertford East.

Would I have left the railway then? No, I don't believe I ever would.

The 'Romance' of Steam

Several years ago I went on a 'Railway Weekend' which included a trip on the lovely Severn Valley Railway.

In chatting with some fellow enthusiasts in a little pub outside Bridgenorth Station, one member of the group sighed and said "*It must have been a wonderful job in the days of steam*".

Unfortunately, his perception of what the job must have been like was drawn from his experiences from visiting the sites of various preserved steam railways.

Whilst I for one am eternally grateful for the existence of these hardworking, dedicated preservationists, what one sees today is a far cry from what it was really like back then.   Compare just some of the differences:

We had to work under filthy conditions compared with today's neatly maintained Sheds.

We didn't have sparkling clean locomotives and equipment (unless we did it ourselves) and the crew had to carry out all the preparation and disposal.

In today's environment there is invariably a small army of volunteers who are more than willing to carry out the 'unpleasant ' jobs.

Today's engines are usually maintained in perfect running order whereas we worked with machines that were just a short step away from the knacker's yard.

On today's mainline trips, it seems usual to use at least 2 firemen to carry out the fireman's duties and maybe also have some further assistance in raking coal forward in the tender.

Now don't get me wrong, I'm not knocking the energies of modern-day locomotive crews.   The physical demands of their normal employment may fall a long way short of that demanded of a steam locomotive, so they cannot be expected to match the achievements of old-time enginemen.

My main point is that the job then was a great deal more demanding – and less glamorous - than it appears today, and can hardly have been termed 'romantic' from that point.

Having said all that, what was it then that compelled men to devote a lifetime to the steam locomotive?

 What made a man leave his warm bed at say, 1.30 on a winter's morning, cycle or walk however many miles in the icy rain to arrive at work soaked to the skin?   He then had to check over and prepare his grimy engine, which could include oiling the underneath, standing in a pit ankle-deep in slushy ash and clinker.

Out on the open road it may be thick fog, in which case both crew members would be leaning out of the cab of the engine straining their eyes to ensure the line ahead was clear and to check the position of the next signal.

On days like that, in the confines of a small cab, you could be roasting the lower half of your body in the heat coming from the firehole door whilst the top half of you is freezing!

Then there were the occasions when your engine may refuse to steam, turning what would normally be a comfortable trip into something of a nightmare. Then there would be much raking of the firebed and anxious looks at the boiler water level bobbing in and out of sight at the bottom of the gauge-glass.

 Having arrived at your destination late, you then suffered the muttered complaints and withering looks from passengers as they trudged by, then you would be busy taking on water and preparing to go through the whole thing again on the return trip.

At the end of the day you may go home tired out and with red-rimmed eyes, with the hope that tomorrow things would be better – but often they were not!

But I have to say these bad times were more than compensated for by the days when everything went like a dream.   There was great comradeship amongst the footplate crews and, one suspects, a feeling of quiet confidence in the knowledge that they were masters of those massive machines.

Those wonderfully preserved locomotives in the National Railway Museum at York no doubt gives great pleasure to thousands of visitors each year, and rightly so, but to me they are just a shadow of their real selves.

The power of a steam locomotive is pretty awesome - they are capable of unbelievable Herculean effort.

In steam days it was not unusual to see a steam locomotive at the head of an express train hauling up to seventeen heavy corridor coaches, containing hundreds of passenger, together with all their luggage. In addition the train would contain restaurant cars and maybe even sleeping facilities. During the War Years even longer trains, as many as 24 coaches, could be seen on Britain's railways.

I wonder how many of those passengers ever gave thought to the pair of men 'up front' who were on constant vigil to ensure that their speeding carriages arrived at their destination safely and on time?

The same effort and vigil was required of the crew of any train, even down to the humble freight train. The terrible consequences of a moment's inattention are well documented and emphatically highlight the great responsibility which enginemen, particularly the driver, must constantly bear.

This touches on another aspect of the addiction to the steam locomotive.

By the time the exalted status of driver is reached, he will have acquired skills that enable him to identify, by sight sound and smell, any defect in his locomotive. He will also be able to identify by sound alone, exactly where his train is on the route, purely by the change of sound when running over a bridge, through a cutting or junction, or even a recently re-laid section of track.

All of this gives the driver complete confidence in his abilities and immense pride in his job.

The rapport that existed between driver, fireman and their locomotive usually ensured that, even on a bad day, they had that great sense of job satisfaction, a special feeling unique to the men of steam.

Considering the shameful way those locomotives were allowed to deteriorate toward the end, enormous credit is due to the men who continued to get the best out of them and still maintain a standard of timekeeping that would be the envy of today's *modern* railway.

On today's railway, the blowing of a single fuse can bring a mighty diesel or electric locomotive to a grinding halt, and this expensive piece of ultra-modern technology will not move again until the fault is identified and rectified.

A steam locomotive could be literally falling to pieces, with parts actually missing, but it would continue with its train until a convenient point of relief is reached. Indeed, at the end, most of them were quite capable of travelling to meet their Maker under their own steam.

In their final, neglected years, one could compare them with a scruffy old mongrel dog – they wouldn't win any beauty contests but they were faithful to the bitter end.

Efficient and cleaner they may be, but I don't believe a diesel or electric locomotive has yet been built that could outpull a steam engine.

In the ensuing years since leaving the railway I have frequently experienced enormous job satisfaction from my work, but I have to say that it is not the same feeling that I enjoyed on the footplate.

Just to add some weight to what I have said, for a long time afterwards I continued to meet my old railway pals in the Great Eastern Tavern and we often chatted over old times. At the time the new Electric Service was having a lot of teething problems and we unanimously agreed that if steam ever returned to Hertford East, we would all be back like a shot!

The job was dirty, the hours unsociable and the pay poor. My colleagues and I frequently used to curse the steam locomotive and working conditions – but there was some unexplainable magnetism that kept us there!

I know of at least two of my fireman pals, Tony Parrott and Tiddler Deards, who could not stay away from the railway for long and joined the Permanent Way Department - maintaining the tracks. As far as I know, they are there still.

For me, it is only when I look back on those railway years that I realise that they were some of the most rewarding times of my entire working life.

Now it is all just a distant memory – even the structural evidence is fading fast.

Never again will it be a schoolboy's dream to be an Engine Driver when he grows up, I believe such dreams died with the passing of the steam locomotive.

At the end of this final Chapter, Appendices 1,2 and 3 list most of the engines that I worked on from the beginning of 1957 to July 1961.

Of course, within these lists, I would have worked on the same engine on maybe dozens of occasions. As I kept no records before January 1957, the lists are not quite complete.

Very little left

A recent drive down Mead Lane at Hertford yielded only the old Signalbox – in desperate need of some paint – but still surviving and in use. Embedded in the road surface of Mead Lane are the tracks that led from the old Great Northern line across to the Tar Works and, as mentioned earlier, the old Mead Lane Café was still there.

At the station end, one of the Dicker Mill Lane Level Crossing gates was incorporated in the fence where the GN line crossed the road.

On the opposite side of the tracks, in Railway Place, the Great Eastern Tavern still does a steady trade and retains much of its old character.

Apart from that, everything from the steam age has been obliterated and the entire site of the MPD is overgrown. I found it impossible even to pinpoint exactly where the engine shed and offices used to be.

Even the carriage washing plant that was installed after the Shed was demolished has long since disappeared.

As I stood staring across at that cold, desolate patch of land, I closed my eyes for a few moments and conjured up a picture of how I remembered it all those years ago.

There was the old Great Eastern Engine Shed, the Turntable and, close by, the huge iron water column beside a pile of smouldering clinker. I could see, at the far end of the Shed, the Locomotive Depot itself with half a dozen simmering N7s awaiting their next turn of duty – now alas, nothing but memories.

A final steam scene at Hertford East as it's original Station Pilot – Class J69 no. 68500 – parks empty coaches into the sidings parallel to Railway Street, on the West side of the station. The date is somewhere around late 1957.

Appendix One

The following 3 pages list locomotives worked on by the author between 1957-1961.
In many instances, the same locomotive was allocated on several occasions.

TANK LOCOMOTIVES

Class N7 0-6-2T

69614	69623	69624	69625	69633	69634	69635	69636
69641	69642	69645	69652	69653	69656	69657	69673
69674	69675	69676	69677	69678	69680	69681	69682
69683	69684	69685	69686	69687	69688	69691	69693
69697	69699	69700	69701	69702	69704	69705	69706
69707	69710	69711	69713	69715	69716	69717	69718
69720	69721	69722	69723	69724	69725	69726	69727
69728	69729	69730	69731	69732	69733		

Total 62

Class L1 2-6-4T

67701	67702	67703	67704	67705	67706	67708	67709
67711	67712	67714	67715	67716	67718	67720	67721
67723	67724	67725	67726	67727	67728	67729	67730
67731	67732	67734	67735	67736	67737	67739	67778
67779							

Total 33

Class J50 0-6-0T

68917	68926	68928	68936	68950	68966	68971	68972
68975	68976	68981	68982	68983	68986	68989	68990

Total 16

Class J69 0-6-0T

68500 68600 68619   **Total 3**

Class N2 0-6-2T

69498 69504 69520 69543 69579 69581   **Total 6**

LMS Class 4 2-6-4T

42255

Departmental Class Y4 0-4-0T

33 (68129)

243

Appendix Two

TENDER LOCOMOTIVES

Class J15 0-6-0

65440	65442	65443	65444	65445	65446	65448	65449
65450	65452	65454	65456	65461	65463	65464	65466
65473	65476					Total 18	

Class J17 0-6-0

65504	65505	65506	65511	65514	65520	65523	65525
65528	65536	65539	65541	65548	65555	65556	65582
						Total 16	

Class J19 0-6-0

| 64648 | 64650 | 64653 | 64655 | 64656 | 64657 | 64662 | 64663 |
| 64664 | 64665 | 64667 | 64670 | | | Total 12 | |

Class J20 0-6-0

| 64676 | 64677 | 64679 | 64680 | | | Total 4 |

Class J39 0-6-0

| 64708 | 64749 | 64722 | 64781 | 64784 | 64805 | 64807 | 64874 |
| | | | | | | Total 8 | |

LMS Class 4 2-6-0

| 43037 | 43084 | 43105 | 43144 | 43148 | 43150 | 43151 | 43153 |
| | | | | | | Total 8 | |

Austerity WD Class 4 2-8-0

| 90096 | 90129 | 90156 | 90508 | 90613 | | Total 5 |

Class B1 4-6-0   *Class B17 4-6-0*   *Class K1 2-6-0*

| 61179 | 61287 | 61360 | | 61608 | 61613 | | 62019 | 62053 |
| | Total 3 | | | Total 2 | | | Total 2 | |

Class 9F 2-10-0   *Class 4MT 2-6-0*   *Class K3 2-6-0*

| 92147 | 92145 | | 76030 | 76031 | 76033 | | 61977 |
| Total 2 | | | Total 3 | | | Total 1 |

Appendix Three

DIESEL/ELECTRIC LOCOMOTIVES

Class A1A-A1A Type "2" Brush Diesel Electric

D5591	D5593	D5594	D5595	D5596	D5599	D5601	D5605
D5606	D5610	D5612	D5615	D5639	D5640	D5641	D5642
D5644	D5645	D5646	D5647	D5649	D5650	D5651	D5652
D5653	D5672	D5673	D5674	D5675	D5676	D5677	D5678

Total 32

Class Bo-Bo Type "2" Sultzer Diesel Electric

D5050	D5052	D5053	D5055	D5056	D5057	D5058	D5060	D5062
D5063	D5064	D5065	D5066	D5067	D5068	D5069	D5070	D5072
D5094	D5095

Total 20

Class D3/5 0-6-0 "Shunter" Blackstone Diesel Electric 370hp

D3693   D3706   D3710   D3711   D3712   **Total 6**

Class Bo-Bo Type "1" Paxman Diesel Electric

D8238   D8239   D8242   **Total 3**

Class D3/2 0-6-0 "Shunter" English Electric 400hp

D13331

Class D1/2 0-4-0 "Shunter" Barclay Diesel 153hp

D2956 – this was the Ware-based locomotive, formerly numbered 11506

HERTFORD (EAST), BROXBOURNE AND LIVERPOOL STREET

Weekdays

Miles		Station		a.m	a.m	a.m	a.m U	a.m	a.m	a.m	a.m	a.m	a.m	a.m	a.m
-	-	Hertford (East)	dep	4 24	5 24	5 54	6 17	6 39	6 49	7 15	7 28	7 58	8 25	8 39	9 25
2	2	Ware		4 29	5 29	5 59	6 22	6 44	6 54	7 20	7 33	8 3	8 30	8 44	9 30
4	4	St. Margaret's	arr	4 33	5 33	6 3	6 26	6 48	6 58	7 24	7 37	8 7	8 34	8 48	9 35
-	-	Buntingford	dep					6 10			7 2			8 12	8 59
-	-	St. Margaret's	dep	4 34	5 34	6 4	6 27	6 49	6 59	7 25	7 38	8 8	8 35	8 52	9 39
5	5	Rye House		4 39	5 39	6 9	6 32	6 54	7 4	7 30	7 43	8 13	8 40	8 57	9 44
7	7	Broxbourne and	arr	4 43	5 43	6 13	6 36	6 58	7 8	7 34	7 47	8 17	8 44	9 1	9 48
-	-	Hoddesdon	dep	4 44	5 44	6 14	6 37	6 59	7 9	7 35	7 48	8 18		9 2	9 50
10	10	Cheshunt		4 50	5 50	6 20	6 43	7 5	7 15	7 41	7 54	8 24			9 56
11	11	Waltham Cross and Abbey		4 54	5 54	6 24	6 47	7 9	7 19	7 45	7 58	8 32		9 10	10 0
12	12	Enfield Lock		4 58	5 58	6 28	6 51	7 13	7 23	7 49	8 2	8 36			10 4
13	13	Brimsdown		5 2	6 2	6 32	6 55	7 17	7 27	7 53	8 6				10 8
14	14	Ponder's End		5 5	6 5	6 35	6 58	7 20	7 30	7 56	8 9				10 11
16	16	Angel Road		5 10	6 10	6 40	7 3	7 25	7 35	8 1	8 14				10 16
17	17	Northumberland Park		5 13	6 13	6 43	7 6		7 38	8 4	8 17				10 19
18	18	**Tottenham**		5 17	6 17	6 47	7 10		7 42	8 8	8 21				10 24
-	20	Lea Bridge		5 22	6 22	6 52	7 15		7 47						
-	22	**Stratford**	arr	5T27	6T27	6T57	7L14		7 52						
-	-		dep	5T28	6T29	6T58									
20	-	Clapton													
21	-	**Hackney Downs**					7 36		8 16	8 29	8 50				10 32
23	25	Bethnal Green													
24	26	**Liverpool Street**	arr	5 37	6 38	7 7	7 43		8 23	8 38	8 58			9 33	10 39

U = Through train to North Woolwich arr. 7 42 a.m.

LIVERPOOL STREET, BROXBOURNE AND HERTFORD (EAST)

Weekdays

		p.m	p.m		p.m	p.m	p.m	p.m	p.m	p.m	p.m	p.m	p.m
Liverpool Street	dep	6 3			6 16	6 46		7 28	8 2		9 36	1028	1133
Bethnal Green													
Hackney Downs	arr					6 54					9 44	1036	1141
Clapton					6 26				8 13		9 48	1040	1145
Stratford	arr			From									
	dep		6L10				6 56						
Lea Bridge			6 19	North			7 2						
Tottenham			6 24		6 32	7 2	7 7	7 42	8 20		9 54	1046	1151
Northumberland Park				Woolwich	6 35		7 10		8 23		9 57	1049	1154
Angel Road					6 38		7 13		8 26		10 0	1052	1157
Ponder's End			6 32		6 43		7 18		8 31		10 5	1057	12 2
Brimsdown			6 35	dep.	6 46		7 21	7 51	8 34		10 8	11 0	12 5
Enfield Lock			6 39	5.49	6 50		7 25	7 55	8 38		1012	11 4	12 9
Waltham Cross and Abbey			6 43	p.m.	6 54	7 14	7 29	7 59	8 42		1016	11 8	1213
Cheshunt			6 47		6 58	7 18	7 33	8 3	8 46		1020	1112	1217
Broxbourne and	arr	6 32	6 52		7 3	7 23	7 38	8 8	8 52		1025	1118	1222
Hoddesdon	dep	6 33	6 53		7 4	7 24	7 39	8 9		9 0	1026	1119	1223
Rye House		6 38	6 58		7 9	7 29	7 44	8 14		9 5	1031	1124	1228
St. Margaret's		6 41	7 1		7 12	7 32	7 47	8 17		9 8	1034	1127	1231
Buntingford	arr	7 23											
St. Margaret's	dep	6 44	7 2		7 13	7 33	7 48	8 18		9 9	1035	1128	1232
Ware		6 49	7 7		7 18	7 38	7 53	8 23		9 14	1040	1133	1237
Hertford (East)	arr	6 54	7 12		7 23	7 43	7 58	8 28		9 19	1045	1138	1242

Extract from a 1960 Weekday Timetable showing the early and late passenger trains including the morning service from Buntingford. Some of these services were operated by London men.

246

Applying for a job	9	Buntingford – A Cleaner's nightmare!	61
The Interview	9	Finding time to sleep	62
Not so important	9	Tiddler's 'lost' day	63
Success!	10	Buntingford drivers and engines	63
Introduction to Hertford East	10	Hadham Bank	63
Connection from North to East	10	A fright at Westmill	64
Cowbridge Station	11	Sheep at Widford	65
Latter-day traffic	11	Poaching tales	65
Hertford East MPD	12	VIP treatment	66
The Goods Yard	17	A very lucky dog	66
The locomotives	17	An Oasis at Buntingford	67
The Cleaner's job	17	Days of fame	67
The Shed Staff	19	The Temple Mills turn	101
Engine cleaning	24	Heavy burden for a 'little old lady'	103
Bill Bright's engine	24	The 6.03 p.m. Down 'fast'	103
Keeping myself clean	26	Money thrown away?	106
Learning about the locomotive	27	Don't take the bait!	107
The art of firing	29	No time to waste at Liverpool Street	108
Other Cleaner's duties	30	Enginemen's pride	109
Loading ash wagons	30	A brush with the law!	109
'Fly' shunting	32	The oil-drum accident	110
Acid, oil and sand	33	Shiftwork – the effect at home	110
The 'lean-to' buildings	33	My parent's sacrifice	111
Lunchbreaks	34	The Annual Holiday rota	111
Mead Lane Café	34	The Engineman's Holdall	112
Man with a motorbike	34	Food arrangements and the all-important tea!	112
Learning some tricks	35	An unwelcome additive in the tea!	114
My first footplate trip	35	Cooking on the shovel	114
Wormley Level Crossing	36	Hot food	115
Two lovely ladies	37	Night-shift feasts and cards	115
A Stratford Courier	37	An errant locomotive	115
Stratford Works	38	The night an L1 'shrunk'	117
Lost property!	40	First in line for overtime	117
Further education	41	Bank Holiday working	118
The Injector	42	A very sick L1	119
The Turntable	42	Loco Inspector George Mason	119
Moving up the ladder	47	16 Tons of overtime!	120
The Firing Examination	47	Stranded in London – by flood?	120
My week on Departmental No33	47	Off-duty trips to the Isle of Wight	121
On the footplate of a B1	48	Free Travel concessions	121
A Passed Cleaner	50	A very eventful week	122
The Payment System	50	Ice-cold milk	122
Nightshift duties	51	A Fireman at last!	123
Engine Preparation duties	52	My first 'Sandringham'	123
Late once too often!	52	Another Firing Examination	123
Locomotive Disposal duties	54	An attack of the 'Flu'	124
Night-life on the Shed	55	The Churchbury Loop	125
One frightened Coalman	56	My first (car) Driving Test	126
Gentleman Charlie	57	Into 1958	126
A near-fatal error	57	Snow and more snow	127
A Nutcracker in the Guards Van	58		
Broxbourne Goods Yard	59		

A visit to Wembley	127
The Bus Strike	128
National Service	128
The BSA 'Winged Wheel'	128
The Ware Shunter	129
Another Driving Test failure	129
A change of Driver	129
There goes my cap!	130
A beautiful black B1	130
'Off the road' at Hertford	130
How it happened	131
Avoiding further catastrophe	131
A near-miss at Broxbourne	132
Broxbourne with a 'museum piece'	133
Hertford's Station Pilot engine	133
Driver Arthur Tilcock	134
Into the Passenger Link	135
Route variations up the line	135
The Channelsea Loop	136
Temple Mills Avoiding Curve	136
Charlie Lee	138
Charlie's improvisation	138
69682 – My own regular engine	138
The job of keeping her shining	138
Jealousy?	139
Some driving experience	140
Waking the babies	141
Smart stopping	142
Important judgement	142
Who lost their garden shed?	143
An emergency stop	144
Staying alert	145
Finchy's lemon squeezer	145
North Woolwich	146
'Hair of the dog'	147
14 Hours at Premium rates	147
Heavier trains	147
Steam and water	147
Steam pressure/Vacuum brake	148
The dreaded 'blow-up'	149
Platforms too short	149
A High-flying City gent	150
An unusual passenger!	150
Lineside fire	150
Introduction to Welsh coal	151
'Lazy' firing	152
She wouldn't steam on anthracite!	152
Goodbye to 69682	154
Trying to polish an L1	154
Monday morning grime	154
The L1's rocking firegrate	156
Speedometers	156
Back with Ted Champ	157
Electrification looms closer	157
The long road to the Driver's seat	157
A few of Hertford's Drivers	158
George (Ernie) Castle	158
Frank Tarry	161
John Tarry	161
Charlie Lee	162
George Dawson	162
John (Jack) Black	164
Bill Bright	164
Ted Govier	164
Roy (Buck) Storey	165
Eric & Charlie Wrangles	166
Ron Hopkins	166
Arthur Tilcock	166
Jimmy Pratt	167
Bob Smith	168
Vic Finch	169
Fireman Herbie Howard	170
A local Railway Historian?	172
The Great Eastern Tavern	175
A crafty pair of Bills!	176
Gerry Wade and the 'Albion'	177
Characteristics of the L1	178
Mechanical Coaling at Hertford	179
The Greenham shovel driver	181
Nearly out in the road!	182
A 'foreigner' from the LMS	182
Off the road in the shed	182
An 'Austerity' WD 2-8-0	182
The effect of Driver Training	183
Bang goes the regular engine policy	183
We pass up some 'Hot Tips'	183
In comes 1960	185
The Electrics are coming	185
A tragedy at Hertford East	186
Never too careful	187
The Liverpool Street Pilots	187
The West Side Pilot	188
Another Test – 3rd time lucky	189
My first car	190
Water problems	190
The steam-driven dynamo	191
A burst water-gauge	191
Looking out for dad	191
Enginemen's outings	192
69614 – not as good as she looks	192
Were they happy to have her back	193
Water leaks – a suggested cure!	193
Good days – bad days	194
A very good morning	194

A bad afternoon	197
A nightmare!	198
A typical run to London	200
Views along the route	203
Ancient Lights?	204
Foggy memories	205
A close call at Hertford	205
Almost the end of Hertford steam	208
Derailment at Picketts Lock	208
A turn on the Ware Shunter	208
A medical at Marylebone	208
Redundancy Notices	209
Hornsey it has to be	210
The final day on 67735	210
Stratford and 68619	210
First day at Hornsey	210
South London freight trains	211
The Lewisham Flyover	211
Battersea Power Station	211
Nearly always in the dark	211
Some Destinations	212
The 'Widened Lines'	212
The Snow Hill Banker	212
Across Blackfriars Bridge	213
The 'U Boats'	213
A scary experience	214
Watch out for the Third Rail	214
Pity the lineside residents	215
Excessive hours	215
My first taste of Diesel	216
The impressive, 1,000 hp Brush	217
On the Snow Hill Banker	217
A rat's tale	218
Fact or Fiction?	219
1961 – I move up the Links	219
A variety of places	219
Working the 'Mainliners'!	220
Steam-heating boilers	220
Waiting at Kings Cross	220
A week on the 'dustbins'	220
Clouds on the horizon	222
Unpaid overtime	222
Expensive motoring	224
No help from the Union	224
The stigma of an ASLEF man	224
My first trip beyond Welwyn	224
Trips to Top Shed	225
Firing on a 'Spaceship'	226
Too thin a fire	227
A lucky break	227
Driving a Diesel	228
A hard 'bump' at Kings Cross	228

Only seeing is believing!	229
Off the road at Hitchin	230
An opportunity missed	230
A precarious position	230
Old enough to become a Driver	231
Losing the Magic	231
Single Manning	231
No light at the end of the tunnel	232
Those boring Diesels	233
Back to the Car Park	234
One Notice too many	234
Up before the Gaffer	234
Enough is enough	235
The final days	235
What might have been	235
The 'romance' of Steam	238
Very little left	241
Appendix One	
– Tank Locomotives	243
Appendix Two	
– Tender Locomotives	244
Appendix Three	
– Diesel/Electric Locomotives	245
Appendix Four – Timetables	246